Protecting Your Company's Intellectual Property

A Practical Guide to Trademarks, Copyrights, Patents & Trade Secrets

Deborah E. Bouchoux

AMACOM

American Management Association

New York • Atlanta • Boston • Chicago • Kansas City • San Francisco • Washington, D.C.
Brussels • Mexico City • Tokyo • Toronto

This publication is designed to provide accurate and authoritative information in regard to the subject matter covered. It is sold with the understanding that the publisher is not engaged in rendering legal, accounting, or other professional service. If legal advice or other expert assistance is required, the services of a competent professional person should be sought.

For my husband,
Donald,
and our children,
Meaghan, Elizabeth, Patrick, and **Robert**

Library of Congress Cataloging-in-Publication Data

Bouchoux, Deborah E., 1950–
    Protecting your company's intellectual property : a practical guide to trademarks, copyrights, patents & trade secrets / Deborah E. Bouchoux.
        p.   cm.
    Includes index.
    ISBN 0-8144-7381-4
    1. Intellectual property—United States—Popular works.   I. Title.

KF2980 .B38 2001
346.7304'8—dc21   00-052582

Printing number

10   9   8   7   6   5   4   3   2   1

Contents

Figures

Preface

The field of intellectual property is rapidly growing as companies begin to realize the value of the intellectual capital portfolios. At least one expert has predicted that the intangible assets of a typical company (namely, its trademarks, copyrights, patents, and trade secrets) will soon represent 80 percent of its value. For example, the trademarks of the Coca-Cola Company have been valued at more than $30 billion and are the most recognized commercial symbols in the world. Achieving and maintaining the value of intellectual property requires an understanding of what assets can be protected, how they can be protected, and how they can be used to generate revenue through licensing and other arrangements.

More and more businesses produce only intellectual property, meaning the products of human thought and creative effort, such as software, business methods, and information. As the economy continues to shift from the manufacture of durable goods to information services and technology, business professionals need guidance on how to protect that information. Over the past five years, the U.S. Patent and Trademark Office has witnessed a 50 percent growth rate in trademark and patent applications, testament to the increasing value of intellectual property and the critical need for companies to understand and protect their assets.

Because of the increasing mobility of employees in today's information-based economy, business professionals need to devote special attention to owning the products created by employees and to ensuring that employees do not compete unfairly after their term of employment ends by soliciting other employees or providing trade secrets to a competitor. This book thus provides both substantive and practical information on ensuring that business professionals own the work created by their employees and methods to prevent unfair competition by former employees.

The explosion of Internet use and commerce also contributes to intellectual property issues, requiring business professionals to understand how to acquire and protect domain names, the intersection of domain names with trademarks, how to prevent infringement of Web sites, and how to ensure that valuable trade secrets and copyrighted information are not lost through dissemination over the Internet.

In most instances, intellectual property assets are lost if they are not actively monitored and protected. Therefore, business professionals need a clear understanding of the types of assets that can be protected and the best way to protect those assets so that they can be used to increase revenue for a company.

This book is designed to provide a thorough explanation of the four key types of intellectual property (trademarks, copyrights, patents, and trade secrets) coupled with practical information, forms, and guides. For example, the following forms are included: trademark compliance policy; trademark license agreement; forms for assigning trademarks, copyrights, and patents; Internet usage policy; clauses to ensure that businesses own the work created by their employees and independent contractors; sample noncompete clauses; a nondisclosure agreement; a form business professionals can use to conduct audits of their intellectual property assets; and an action plan to help business professionals protect their intellectual property.

Throughout the book, references to useful Web sites are provided, and the Appendix lists the Web sites together with descriptions of what is available at the sites. Identifying and describing Web sites is not intended to represent endorsement of those sites.

It is hoped that this book gives business professionals the tools they need to understand what assets can be protected, how to achieve the widest possible scope of protection of those assets, how to maintain and enhance the value of those assets, and how to use those assets to create revenue.

Acknowledgments

No book is entirely the product of its author, and this book is no exception. I would like to express my appreciation to the following individuals at AMACOM for their assistance during the writing, revising, editing, and publishing of this book: Adrienne Hickey, executive editor; Andy Ambraziejus, managing editor; Lydia Lewis, production manager; and Jim Bessent, associate editor. Thanks also to Cathleen Oudenkirk for the cover design.

1

Recognizing and Protecting Your Company's Intellectual Property

Companies often fail to protect their valuable intellectual capital because they do not understand that even noncomplex items such as customer lists, names of products, and anticipated marketing plans are protectable. The first step in protecting intellectual property is to identify protectable assets. Once those intellectual capital assets are identified, they can be protected and used to generate income.

The Value of Intellectual Property

Until the 1990s, nearly all business owners could readily point to their company's valuable assets. Those assets usually consisted of real estate, referred to as real property, or durable goods, such as trucks, manufacturing facilities, or equipment, referred to as personal property. The past several years have seen tremendous growth in another type of property that is very different from real or personal property: intellectual property. It is called intellectual property because it is the product of human creativity, thought, and inventiveness. Although much of intellectual property is intangible, it can be more valuable than real or personal property.

1

Because the U.S. economy is witnessing a dramatic surge in the growth of technology-related services and products, the field of intellectual property is undergoing explosive growth. In fact, some companies own few assets other than intellectual property. Whereas it is easy to understand the value of real estate or tangible assets, such as inventory, it is more difficult to understand the value of intangible assets, such as a method of doing business, one's Internet domain name, a list of potential acquisition targets, the know-how of key employees, or the marketing materials used in a business. All these assets provide a competitive edge to their owner, and the loss of such assets can be just as devastating to a company as the loss of its equipment, inventory, or other physical goods.

Moreover, because of the ease of global communications today, such valuable information can be disseminated to millions of people with a simple keystroke. According to one expert, the estimated economic loss caused by misappropriation of intellectual property, including copyright piracy, theft of valuable trade secrets, and employee raiding, is $50 billion each year.[1] For example, a disgruntled employee may post a company's list of customers on the Internet, irreparably damaging the company's business. Thus, just as intellectual property is becoming more valuable, protecting it has become more challenging.

Intellectual property is legally fragile, meaning that once an owner's rights are lost or compromised, it is extremely difficult, if not impossible, to recover those rights. Thus, a license granted to another to use a trademark that does not allow the trademark owner to verify the quality of the goods produced under the trademark may well result in a complete loss of the mark. Similarly, marketing an important invention without seeking a patent for it may preclude one from later seeking patent protection. Employees who take valuable company information to a competitor without any restrictions imposed by the first, or original, employer on the use of the information may cause the information to lose its protected status.

Intellectual property can also be used to generate revenue. Trademarks and patents can be licensed to others for periodic license or royalty fees. Software can be sold to third parties. Companies can market and sell unneeded logos, trademarks, inventions, and processes. These assets cannot be mined for their revenue-generating possibilities if a company does not understand what assets it owns, however. Once a company identifies what it owns, it can protect the assets to ensure that it maintains its

---

1. Michael A. Epstein, *Modern Intellectual Property*, 3d ed. (New York: Aspen Publishers, Inc., 1995), p. xiii.

competitiveness and increases revenue through the strategic licensing and sale of its intellectual property capital.

The Four Key Types of Intellectual Property

Before discussing the specific types of intellectual property that are likely to be developed and used by various business departments, a brief introduction to the key types of intellectual property is useful. Intellectual property generally is viewed as comprising four separate but often overlapping types of property rights: trademarks, copyrights, patents, and trade secrets.

Trademarks

The names, designs, slogans, or other devices by which a company identifies its products and services can be among the most valuable assets a company owns. Most American consumers can readily fill in the blank in the following slogan: "Just Do ____." Nearly all consumers can easily hum the tune that accompanies the words "You Deserve a Break Today." Just a glimpse of aqua and orange at the edge of a highway lets consumers know there is a Howard Johnson's nearby. How did these businesses achieve such national and even international recognition for their goods and services? By selecting and then vigorously protecting their trademarks. In fact, the Coca-Cola Company estimates the value of its portfolio of trademarks at more than $30 billion.

The Term Defined

A trademark is a name, symbol, device, or combination thereof that identifies and distinguishes one's goods and services from those of another. Technically, a trademark is used to identify a good or product, such as WINDOWS® or CAMRY®, whereas a service mark is used to identify services, such as H & R BLOCK® or FLY THE FRIENDLY SKIES OF UNITED®. In practice, however, most people use the term *trademark* to refer to both goods and services.

How Trademark Rights Arise

Trademark rights arise through use of a mark. Thus, the owner of a small car repair service in Kansas City operating as TENDER, LOVING

CAR has rights in and to this mark against any later users who use a confusingly similar mark in Kansas City and a reasonable area of expansion beyond, even if the owner has not registered the mark with any federal or state agency. Rights to trademarks are not contingent on registration, but registration does afford the trademark owner certain advantages. For example, a federal registration of TENDER, LOVING CAR would protect the mark nationwide against later confusingly similar uses.

What Marks Are Protectable

Not all names or slogans qualify for protection. A mark cannot be generic, such as *SODA* for a beverage or *TV* for a television. Furthermore, marks that merely describe the goods or services offered under the marks generally are not protectable. For example, the name *Tax Preparation Software* for a software program that enables its users to prepare their tax returns probably would not be protectable.

Trademark Registration

If a mark is used in interstate commerce, its owner should seek a federal registration for it to achieve the greatest protection for the mark. An application for registration is filed with the U.S. Patent and Trademark Office (PTO), located in Washington, D.C. The filing fee is $325, and it generally takes about a year for the registration to issue. Thereafter, the PTO requires periodic filings to ensure that the mark is in use. Marks not in use become available to others. Once the mark is registered with the PTO, its owner can use the federal registration symbol ® to identify that fact, although use of the registration symbol is not required, and alternative forms of registration notice may be used.

Trademarks are powerful tools for achieving consumer recognition and market share. It has been estimated that most American consumers encounter more than 1,000 trademarks during a day. The marks are found on the clothes they wear, on the packaging for the foods they eat, on the cars they drive, and in the ads they encounter in magazines and on the radio and television. If properly protected, trademarks can last forever and can provide a business with a unique and immediately visible identification to its customers and the world beyond.

Copyrights

Copyright is a form of protection available to a wide variety of works, including literary, musical, dramatic, graphic, sculptural, and architectural works, motion pictures, and sound recordings. The majority of copyrighted works are literary works, meaning works that can be expressed in words or numbers. The use of the term *literary* does not imply that only critically acclaimed works are protectable. Even advertising brochures and copy are protectable as literary works. Similarly, because computer programs are expressed in words and numbers, they are protectable as literary works.

How Copyright Rights Arise

Copyright protection exists from the moment a work is created. No registration with the U.S. Copyright Office, the government agency charged with copyright registration and searching, is required, although registration affords the copyright owner certain advantages. Copyrights can be registered only at the federal level; there is no state protection for copyrights.

What Is Protectable

Copyright protects works of original authorship, and a wide variety of works are protectable, including books, magazines, promotional materials, music, posters, movies, slide presentations, dance routines, and Web site content. Not every work of authorship is protectable. Copyright protection does not extend to ideas, procedures, processes, systems, or concepts, and mere slogans, titles, and blank forms cannot be protected under copyright law. Copyright gives the owner the right to reproduce, distribute, perform, and display the work, and the right to create derivative works based on the original work, such as preparing a sequel to a book or movie or an upgrade of a software program.

Copyright Registration

Copyrights can be registered with the U.S. Copyright Office, a division of the Library of Congress, located in Washington, D.C. Registration is inexpensive and easy. At present, the filing fee is $30. Moreover, the process is fairly rapid, with the U.S. Copyright Office generally reviewing the application and issuing the registration within four to eight months. Once registered, the copyright need not be renewed, and the registration lasts for the author's life plus 70 years (or in the case of works created by employees for their employers, for 95 years from publication of the work or 120 years from its creation, whichever is shorter).

Patents

A patent is a grant from the U.S. government allowing its owner to exclude another from making, using, or selling his or her invention. There are three types of patents: utility patents, which protect new and useful inventions and processes; design patents, which protect new and ornamental designs for articles; and plant patents, which protect new and distinctive plant varieties that are asexually reproduced. Utility patents are the most common type of patent, accounting for more than 90 percent of all patents granted in 1999.

What Is Protectable

Utility patents are available to anyone who invents or discovers any new, useful, and nonobvious process, machine, or invention. The category is broad enough to cover the cotton gin, the Wright brothers' airplane, King Gillette's safety razor, pharmaceuticals, genetically altered mice, and the one-click system patented by Amazon.com allowing its online users to place orders without having to reenter mailing and credit card information.

Registration of Patents

Unlike trademarks, rights to which arise upon use of the mark, and copyrights, rights to which arise upon creation of a work, patent rights arise only upon issuance of a patent registration by the PTO. There are no state laws relating to patents, and patents are governed exclusively by federal law. Utility patents are valid for twenty years from the date the inventor files an application. After this period the invention falls into the public domain, and anyone is free to make, use, or sell the invention. The inventor is given the twenty-year monopoly to market and sell the invention in return for giving up all rights after the twenty-year period of protection. Patent registration is expensive and complex. The application filing fee is $710 ($355 for small entities), and the process generally takes about eighteen months.

Trade Secrets

Trade secrets consist of any valuable information that gives its owner a competitive advantage. Nearly any kind of information is protectable, including customer lists, recipes, formulas, marketing plans, employee rosters, financial information and forecasts, and methods of conducting business. Trade secret protection arises as soon as the information comes into being and lasts as long as the owner makes reasonable efforts to keep the information secret. No registration with any government authority, whether federal or state, is required. If properly safeguarded, trade secrets can last forever.

Types of Intellectual Property Owned by Business Professionals

Intellectual property is not the exclusive province of the dot.com companies. Nearly all business enterprises have valuable intellectual property assets. The names of planned products or goods, anticipated advertising slogans, valuable forms and checklists, and training materials should all be protected. Each division or department within a company probably is using valuable intellectual property assets, and each should conduct a thorough audit of its assets. Although Chapter 20 provides information on conducting an intellectual property audit, a brief introduction to the types of intellectual property used by various business groups is helpful.

Sales and Marketing Departments

A company's sales and marketing department may possess a wide variety of intellectual property assets, including names, slogans, marketing materials, advertisements, and similar materials. A name by which the department refers to a product or service may be protectable. For example, if the sales and marketing group is informally referring to a planned financial service the company will offer as "Capital Ideas," the name should be considered for trademark protection. Slogans such as "We Bring Your Savings Home" can be similarly protected. Sales and marketing professionals should be encouraged to review the company's letterhead, marketing brochures, and any other literature to determine whether the company is already using trademarks, designs, logos, and slogans.

Brochures, ad copy, anticipated radio and television promotions, and other materials that are in the planning stage should be identified to ensure that they are protected against inadvertent disclosure or leaking to competitors. Such materials should not be released to focus groups or others without a nondisclosure agreement by which the reviewer agrees not to disclose the information. Similarly, new products, such as snack foods or computer programs, should not be test-marketed unless nondisclosure agreements have been signed. Those who assist the sales and marketing group in developing materials, such as independent contractors developing a new company logo, should be required to assign any rights in the work product to the company and to agree to protect the product from disclosure. During the planning stage, these materials are protectable as trade secrets. Once created in a fixed form, they are subject to copyright protection.

Power Point® presentations and other slides, movies, and audiovisual materials used by a company are protectable as copyrightable works. Although live sales pitches and presentations are not protectable under copyright law, written materials that accompany those presentations are.

Human Resources Departments

A company's human resources group may have a wide variety of forms and materials that can be protected through copyright. The company's employee handbook is subject to copyright protection, as are any forms the company uses, as long as those forms are more than blank template forms. If a company uses written materials explaining its mentoring program or termination procedures, they can also be protected. Similarly, forms and checklists used by recruiters in qualifying and hiring candidates and the forms the company uses for exit interviews can be protected.

Contracts and Administrative Departments

The contractual forms a company uses are protectable under copyright law. Although contracts can be drafted easily and many companies use composite forms drawn from forms they have seen others use, care should be taken to ensure that the forms are released only to those who need to use them. For example, a company may want to avoid sending its form contracts and templates by e-mail because such forms can then be disseminated to thousands of others. Some companies insist on a mail-only policy for their key contract documents.

If the company has a formalized written methodology explaining the way it conducts its business, these materials are protectable as trade secrets and should not be released to anyone except those who have a demonstrated need to know the information and have signed agreements promising to protect the information. Logs should be kept identifying the employees who have been given the methodology materials, and the materials should be collected from employees who leave the company.

Training materials and handbooks prepared for managers also are protectable. The company's contracts and administrative groups should assess the written materials they use to identify valuable intellectual property resources.

Graphics, Production, and Information Services Departments

A company's graphics department may be creating valuable logos, designs, and artwork that can be protected. Similarly, care should be taken to ensure that all material posted on the company's Web site is original and is not taken from any other source or site and that only nonconfidential information is displayed on the site. For example, case studies that specifically identify one's clients give competitors a chance to review what a company has done and then target the client with a different or cheaper approach. Moreover, agreements with clients may prohibit identifying them in such a public manner. Identifying the company's employees on a Web site invites soliciting and poaching of these valuable human assets. The Web site content itself is copyrightable, and terms and conditions for use of the site should be included on the site as well as a copyright notice stating that the site is subject to copyright protection.

Research and Development Departments

A company's research and development group may be sitting on a gold mine of valuable intellectual property assets. Because patent law covers new and useful inventions and processes and improvements to existing inventions and processes, all work conducted by the research and development team should be considered trade secrets during the formative stage and should then be considered for patent protection as it nears completion. Because patent law protects only new inventions, once an invention is in public use, is offered for sale in the United States, or is described in a printed publication anywhere in the world, the inventor has only one year within which to file a patent application. Failure to file within this one-year grace period precludes the inventor from obtaining patent protection, and the invention enters the public domain.

Employees in the company's research and development group should maintain accurate laboratory notebooks describing their work and progress. These notebooks can be used to demonstrate the originality of the work and the date of its completion for the purpose of obtaining a patent.

Other Departments

Other groups or departments within a company may use and develop intellectual property. Group leaders and managers should be urged to carefully consider the names and designs they use for company products and services, the written materials and forms they use in their work, any new inventions or business methods they have implemented, and any improvements to existing inventions or business methods. Once the company has identified its intellectual capital, it can protect it and use it to increase revenue.

Complementary Strategies to Protect Intellectual Property

There are four primary types of intellectual property, but rights to intellectual property often intersect and overlap. Protecting intellectual assets often is a challenge, and effort must be made to determine the best way to achieve that protection. For example, many people believe that the recipe for Coca-Cola is the best example of the value of trade secret protection. Legend has it that the recipe or formula for Coca-Cola is locked in a vault with no one person having access. Although the formula for Coca-Cola would be protectable under patent law, because patents have limited duration, the formula would be available for anyone to use after the period of patent protection expired. However, trade secrets can last forever if the company takes reasonable measures to ensure their secrecy. Thus, protecting the formula for Coca-Cola as a trade secret rather than as a patented composition gives the company vastly superior protection. On the other hand, if someone independently discovers the recipe for Coca-Cola, the original owner has lost valuable trade secret rights. If the recipe is protected by patent, the patent owner has the right to exclude others from making, using, or selling the invention during the term of the patent, whether or not they discovered the recipe innocently.

Similarly, the distinctive curvy shape of Coca-Cola's glass bottle is subject to trademark protection. The shape could have been protected as a design patent, but the term of protection for a design patent is fourteen years from the date of grant, whereas trademark protection can last forever, as long as appropriate documents are filed with the PTO.

Some items of jewelry can be protected under both copyright and patent law. Obtaining a copyright registration is inexpensive and easy; obtaining a patent registration is far more expensive and complex. Because many items of jewelry go out of style within a few years, it may be more economical for a company to protect the item under copyright law rather than go to the time and expense to obtain a patent. Additionally, the term of copyright protection generally is the life of the author plus seventy years, whereas the term of design patent protection is fourteen years from the date of the grant, after which time the invention is free for all to copy and use.

Similarly, if a company intends to use a trademark for a key product it is launching, obtaining a trademark registration is prudent. However, if the name or slogan is intended only for a single promotion of limited duration, it may not be worth the time, effort, and money to secure a federal registration for the mark. Once a search has been conducted to verify that the mark is available, the mark can simply be used without any registration and then rights to it are abandoned upon nonuse.

Thus, business professionals need to consider that although a number of business assets may be protectable and registrable, a variety of strategies and complementary approaches should be considered to obtain the broadest possible protection for the company's intellectual assets.

Using Intellectual Property Assets to Increase Revenue

Intellectual property can be bought, sold, and licensed just as any other asset can. Rather than develop a software program, a company may choose to buy it from another. In fact, companies have been known to purchase certain assets or business divisions to make themselves less attractive to aggressors, who may then encounter antitrust objections if they attempt to acquire the first company.

Companies that no longer use certain assets should consider selling them outright. The sale of a company or of most or all of its assets is accompanied by a thorough review by the buyer, called the due diligence review. The buyer will want to know what trademarks, copyrights, patents, and trade secrets the company owns, which it has licensed to or from others, and whether any claims have been made regarding such assets.

Companies can license their intellectual capital assets to others to use. Agreements for such licenses should be drafted carefully to ensure that the user's rights are limited and that the owner has the right to control the use of the assets and recover the assets in the event of a default. Such licensing arrangements can be used to produce a continuing source of revenue. License fees can be lump sums or royalty arrangements, in which case fees generally are a percentage of sales of the licensed products or services. In some cases companies obtain additional revenue from their trademarks by licensing the marks for use in connection with related products. For example, Kodak licenses the use of its trademark to a contact lens manufacturer, and the MELITTA® mark, used to identify coffee filters, has been licensed to a coffeepot maker. In each case the trademark owner receives royalties arising out of the licensing arrangements.

Intellectual property can also be used as security for the performance of obligations or repayment of loans. Just as real property often is pledged by a borrower to ensure that the lender will have an asset to seize if the borrower defaults in repaying the loan, intellectual property assets, including trademarks, copyrights, and patents, are increasingly being pledged as collateral. In the event of a default, the secured party then has the right to take possession and ownership of the trademarks, copyrights, or patents. In a novel financing arrangement in the mid-1990s, pop star David Bowie sold bonds to raise money to finance a future concert tour. The bonds were collateralized by projected revenue from the tour, which depended on and used Bowie's copyrighted music. Thus, intellectual capital can be sold, licensed, or used as security to increase income for its owner.

Finally, some companies have begun donating patents and other intellectual property to universities and research institutions. For example, Ford Motor Company donated $40 million of patents in 1999. In most cases, the patents donated are no longer central to the donor's core business but are valuable to the donee. The donation generally is tax deductible and promotes the donor's image and reputation.

A number of Web sites operate as intellectual property bazaars or virtual marketplaces where companies can value, sell, or license their intellectual property. These sites include www.yet2.com, www.pl-x.com, http://valuationcorp.com, and www.Ipnetwork.com. A company's competitors and customers may also serve as potential buyers or licensees of the company's valuable intellectual capital.

When to Obtain Legal Counsel

The decision to engage legal counsel is a bit like Justice Potter Stewart's famous quote about obscenity. Justice Stewart remarked that he could not provide a precise definition of obscenity but that he would know it when he saw it. Similarly, knowing when to obtain the assistance of experienced legal counsel is a judgment call. For example, the temporary use of a trademark may not require registration with the PTO. Similarly, even a company's application for trademark registration for a key mark may be handled in house, although if the PTO makes objections to the registration, outside counsel may be needed. Most copyright applications can be handled in house. On the other hand, companies that have portfolios of software and other computer-related information should seek outside legal counsel because the issues surrounding software protection continue to shift and evolve. In nearly all cases, patent applications should be handled by experienced patent attorneys. Additionally, any allegation that a company is infringing the intellectual property rights of another should be referred to legal counsel to ensure that the company's rights are adequately and promptly asserted and protected. Because companies may be liable for punitive damages for infringing activities after receiving notice of an infringement, obtaining advice of counsel after receiving such a notice is critical.

It is important to obtain experienced legal advice. The field of intellectual property law, which was for many years a backwater in the legal profession, has achieved a certain cachet. Thus, a number of law firms and practitioners announce that they are specialists in the intellectual property field, although their experience may consist of having attended a few lectures. Do not be afraid to ask about experience and qualifications. Competent legal professionals are ready and often pleased to explain their experience and credentials. Because the issues surrounding intellectual property can be highly technical, requiring a thorough understanding of software development, mechanical engineering, and the Internet, not all lawyers are equally familiar with the issues. Moreover, a practical understanding of the workings of the PTO and the U.S. Copyright Office is essential. Knowing the ins and outs of the offices, filing fees, and document submission procedures is critical inside information. Companies should retain experienced attorneys who are thoroughly conversant in intellectual property protection, rights, prosecution, and infringement. Attempting to save money by retaining counsel who may be unfamiliar with intellectual property will only result in additional costs in the long run and may lead to the loss of critical rights and defenses. Money expended to protect intellectual property is nearly always worthwhile.

Affirmative Strategies to Protect Intellectual Property Assets

Although strategies to protect intellectual capital are discussed throughout this book, a brief overview of some strategies is useful. For thorough protection, companies should

- Conduct periodic intellectual property audits to identify intellectual property assets and improvements thereto
- Appoint committees made up of sales, marketing, and research and development team members to periodically discuss the company's products and services to ensure that the company recognizes its intellectual capital
- Determine the appropriate means to protect such assets from infringement and to use such assets to generate revenue
- Control access to and mark trade secret information as protected or confidential
- Review periodicals and trade journals to monitor competitors' activities and to ensure that competitors do not infringe the company's intellectual property assets
- Initiate intellectual property compliance policies to provide information and training to employees and others on the proper use of the company's intellectual assets
- Institute routine review of their own and competitors' Web sites to ensure that materials posted on such sites are not infringing
- Retain experienced legal counsel as soon as an intellectual property infringement claim may arise, whether on behalf of or against the company
- Investigate the possibility of obtaining insurance coverage for claims made against the company for intellectual property infringement

2

Trademark Basics

At the core of every successful business are the trademarks the business uses to identify its products and services. Trademarks not only identify the offeror of a product or service but also provide assurances of quality and consistency to consumers. For instance, consumers know that the BIG MAC® they buy in Poughkeepsie is the same as one purchased in Boston.

Careful mark selection is critical to achieving consumer recognition of the company's products and services. For example, when one sees a print ad of a celebrity with a milk mustache, one immediately knows that the caption "Got Milk?" will be displayed. Just a few bars of music is enough for consumers to understand that McDonald's products are being advertised. Some consumers can retain jingles for years after they have been discontinued. For many, the slogan "See the USA in your Chevrolet" is instantly linked with certain images, tunes, and products, although the slogan has not been used for years. Thus, companies should exercise great care to select the strongest marks they can to achieve the widest possible market penetration. Because the mark will be displayed on products, in advertising materials, on the company Web site, and on its contracts, letterhead, and stationery, a variety of people should play a part in selecting the company's marks and slogans. Those participating in this selection should include employees in the sales, marketing, and legal departments.

The Four Types of Trademarks

There are four different types of trademarks:

1. *Trademark.* A trademark includes any word, name, symbol, or device (or combination of such) used to identify and distinguish one's goods or products from those of another and to indicate the source of such goods or products. Thus, trademarks are used in the advertising and marketing of tangible goods, such as WHEAT-IES® for cereal, WINDOWS® for software, or ACURA® for cars.

2. *Service mark.* A service mark includes any word, name, symbol, or device (or a combination of such) used to identify the services or intangible activities performed by one person for another, identify and distinguish one's services from those of another, and indicate the source of such services, such as BURGER KING® for restaurant services, UNITED AIRLINES® for transportation services, or SPRINT® for communication services.

3. *Collective marks.* A collective mark is a trademark or service mark used by the members of a cooperative, association, or other collective group or organization, including marks indicating membership in a union or other organization, such as AMERICAN BAR ASSOC-ATION®, LIONS CLUB®, or FRATERNAL ORDER OF POLICE®; these marks indicate membership in the organization identified.

4. *Certification marks.* A certification mark is a word, name, symbol, or device (or combination of such) used by a person other than its owner to certify quality, accuracy, or some other characteristics of goods or services, such as the famous UL (& Design)® mark used by Underwriters' Laboratories, Inc., to certify that products conform to certain safety standards established by Underwriters' Laboratories. The UL (& Design)® mark is not used by the trademark owner, Underwriters' Laboratories, but by the manufacturer of an appliance to indicate to consumers that the item meets the safety standards established by Underwriters' Laboratories. Other examples of certification marks are 100% PURE FLORIDA'S SEAL OF APPROVAL (& DESIGN)® (used to certify that orange juice products meet the U.S. Department of Agriculture's standards for Grade A orange juice products) and OCCUPATIONAL THERA-PIST REGISTERED OTR® (used to certify that occupational therapists meet certain standards of competency, skill, and knowledge).

The most common marks are trademarks and service marks; collective marks and certification marks are far less common. Moreover, although technically the term *trademark* is used in connection with goods and the term *service mark* is used in connection with services, in common parlance the two terms are used interchangeably; thus, the term *trademark* often is used to refer to goods or services. Similarly, the term *mark* generally is used to refer to either trademarks or service marks. Accordingly, in this book, the terms *trademark* and *mark* are used to refer to both trademarks and service marks.

In sum, trademarks are used to identify the source of a product or service and provide assurances of quality and consistency to consumers, who, upon encountering a trademark, are then able to make informed purchasing decisions.

Business Names

Merely identifying a business by a certain name does not result in trademark rights. Trademarks refer to goods or services, whereas a business name or trade name merely identifies the proprietor of a certain commercial enterprise. For example, when Nabisco places its name on its business cards and stationery, such is a nontrademark use; however, when the NABISCO® mark is placed on boxes for snack products, the word is being used as a trademark and can be federally registered.

Many business owners have incorporated their companies or filed partnership documents with their secretary of state. Obtaining permission from a secretary of state to use a name is not permission to use that name as a trademark. The secretary of state merely checks to ensure that no other businesses are operated within the state with a confusingly similar name. There is no assurance or guarantee that the name does not infringe a trademark registered with the U.S. Patent and Trademark Office (PTO). Therefore, a thorough trademark search should be conducted to determine that the business name can be used as a mark. Trademark searches are discussed in Chapter 3.

How Rights in Marks Are Acquired: Federal Registration, State Registration, and Common Law Rights

In most countries, rights to trademarks arise through registration of the mark with some government agency. The law in the United States is very different in that rights to marks arise through use of the mark. There is no requirement that a person secure any government approval or registration for a mark to have rights to the mark and prevent the use of a confusingly similar mark. There is one exception to the rule that rights in marks stem from use: the intent-to-use trademark application. Since 1989, individuals and companies have been able to apply for federal registration of a mark based on their bona fide intent to use the mark in interstate commerce. Although the application can be filed based on this intent to use, actual use of the mark is required before the PTO will issue a registration. Intent-to-use applications are discussed in Chapter 4.

Federal Registration

Although registration of a mark with the PTO is not required for one to establish trademark rights, it is recommended because it confers several advantages on a trademark owner, chief among them nationwide priority for use of the mark; the right to bring an action in federal court for infringement; the right to use the trademark registration symbol (®), which provides actual notice of a trademark owner's registration (thus allowing the owner to recover damages in an infringement action and eliminating a party's ability to claim that it used a mark innocently); and the right to block the importation of infringing goods into the United States. Consequently, federal registration should be pursued whenever one plans to use a mark in interstate commerce for more than a short period. However, the PTO's registers reflect only a small portion of the trademarks now in use in the United States.

Federal trademark registration is governed by the U.S. Trademark Act, also called the Lanham Act after its chief sponsor. The Lanham Act is found at 15 U.S.C. §§ 1051 et seq. The federal statutes governing trademarks can be located by accessing the Web site www4.law.cornell.edu/uscode.

The key requirement for obtaining a federal registration is actual use of the mark in interstate commerce. Interstate commerce is commerce between persons in different states. Thus, if one makes a coffeepot called *The Grinder* in Massachusetts and sells it in Massachusetts and New York, the product is in interstate commerce and the owner is entitled to apply for federal registration of the mark. The use must be more than token use. Sham sales to friends and neighbors or sales only within a company are insufficient to support an application for federal registration of a mark.

State Registration

Each of the fifty states (but not the District of Columbia) allows registration of a trademark at the state level. Generally, one applies for a state registration when a mark is not eligible for federal registration (usually because the mark is used only in intrastate commerce rather than interstate commerce). Applying for a state registration is easy and inexpensive. The process is accomplished by completing an application form and filing it, together with a modest fee, with the secretary of state of your state. Most states offer the application forms on the Internet. Access the Web site www.nass.org for a complete list and direct links to the secretaries of state of all fifty states. Look for references to trademarks and then download and print the appropriate form and instructions. Trademark protection in the various states usually lasts for either five or ten years.

If a mark is eligible for federal registration, such registration should be secured because it affords a wider scope of protection than a state registration. Moreover, once a federal registration is secured from the PTO, there is no advantage to securing additional state registrations because a federal registration affords nationwide protection against later uses of confusingly similar marks.

Common Law Rights

The use of a mark without federal or state registration is called common law use. Although the benefits of securing a registration are significant, because the United States follows the rule that rights to trademarks arise from use rather than registration, one who uses a mark without a registration has the right to prevent later users from adopting and using a confusingly similar mark in any geographic area in which the common law mark is used and in a reasonable area of expansion beyond. Thus, the owner of a bookstore operated in St. Paul, Minnesota, under the mark *The Bookworm* can preclude a later user from using a confusingly similar mark in connection with similar goods or services in St. Paul and a reasonable geographic area beyond, even if the later user has a federal registration for its mark. The owner cannot prevent a later user from using the same or a confusingly similar mark in San Francisco, however. On the other hand, if the owner had secured a federal registration for the mark with the PTO, he or she could prevent any later confusingly similar use anywhere in the United States.

What Can Be Protected under Trademark Law

The definition of a trademark is any word, name, symbol, device, or combination of such used to identify and distinguish one's goods. The word *device* is construed broadly enough to include more than conventional words or designs, so trademark law has evolved to keep pace with new technologies. The following are protectable under trademark law and are eligible for federal registration:

▾ *Words.* Either single words or multiple words and slogans are eligible for federal registration. Thus, the marks FORD® and HAVE YOU DRIVEN A FORD LATELY® are protectable. The style or particular lettering in which the words are presented also is protectable.

▾ *Numbers and letters.* Numbers and letters are eligible for registration as long as they do not describe the mark. Thus, CNN® is registered, as are several radio station call letters and car models, such as Q45®, but a mark such as VCR10 would not be registrable if the mark referred to the tenth series model of a videocassette recorder. Even an alphanumeric mark such as 1-800-PIN-DROP® is registrable.

▾ *Designs.* A mark consisting solely of a design, such as Nike's famous "swoosh" mark or the picture of the smiling Quaker on a box of Quaker oatmeal is registrable. Moreover, a mark may consist of a word or words together with a design element, as in the RICE-A-RONI® mark that appears with a design of a San Francisco streetcar. Such marks are called composite marks. To be protected, a design must be distinctive. A common shape, such as a rectangle, or purely ornamental background is not registrable.

▾ *Fragrances.* A fragrance of a product may be registrable as long as the product is not known for the fragrance or the fragrance does not enhance use of the product. Thus, a floral fragrance was held registrable for yarn and thread, but such a fragrance would not be registrable for perfumes or room deodorizers.

▾ *Sounds.* In 1950, NBC received the first sound registration, for its famous three-note chime. Similarly, the sound of a roaring lion heard at the beginning of Metro-Goldwyn-Mayer movies and Tarzan's famous yell are registered.

▾ *Shapes.* The shape of a product may be registered as a trademark as long as the shape is not functional. A shape is functional if it affects the product's use or performance. Thus, the Coca-Cola Company has registered its famous curved bottle shape. The shape of the Coke bottle does nothing to promote or enhance use of the beverage and therefore is not functional. Competitors have a wide variety of other shapes to use for beverages, so the marketplace is not harmed by Coke's exclusive appropriation of one particular shape for a beverage container.

• *Color.* A trademark may consist of color as long as the color is not functional. For example, Owens-Corning was allowed to register the color pink for its insulation because there is no need for competitors to use the color pink for their insulation materials, and the color pink is not naturally associated with insulation, nor does it enhance the product's use. If a color is natural to a product or is useful in connection with a product, it cannot be registered. Thus, the colors yellow and orange were held functional and not registrable for public telephones because they are more visible in an emergency, and there is a competitive need for the colors to remain available to others. If there is a competitive need for a color in an industry, one company cannot appropriate exclusive rights to the color and thereby deprive others of its use. The registration of color is a new and still developing field.

• *Moving images.* An emerging field in trademark law is the registration of moving images, such as Microsoft's spinning globe or the image of light rays shining on the robed lady holding a torch used by Columbia Pictures Industries, Inc. Many trademark experts predict increasing registrations for moving images displayed on company Web sites and perhaps holograms as well.

• *Trade dress.* The overall packaging, design, and configuration of a product is protectable as its trade dress. In a famous case, *Two Pesos, Inc. v. Taco Cabana International, Inc.*, 505 U.S. 763 (1992), the U.S. Supreme Court protected the overall design, colors, and configuration of a chain of Mexican restaurants from a competitor using similar decor and design. Legislation is pending in Congress to allow trade dress to be registered as a mark with the PTO. Thus, the total image of a product or service can be protected even if it does not qualify as a trademark. In many cases, parties without trademark registrations have relied on the theory of trade dress to seek protection for their products and services, leading some experts to remark that when plaintiffs cannot determine what to sue for, they simply sue for infringement of trade dress. Recent decisions confirm that not every image or design is protectable as trade dress; rather, the product must have acquired distinctiveness such that the product is so well known that consumers have learned to link the product with its source.

In sum, nearly any word, symbol, or device can serve as a trademark as long as it is not functional or descriptive of a product or service. Moreover, many trademark owners use a variety and combination of marks. For example, the rounded container for Morton's salt bears the following three marks: the word mark MORTON'S®, the design of the young girl holding an umbrella, and the slogan WHEN IT RAINS IT POURS®.

Exclusions from Trademark Protection

A vast array of words, symbols, designs, and devices can function as trademarks, but there are several exclusions to trademark protection set forth in the U.S. Trademark Act, including the following:

▾ *Immoral or scandalous matter.* The Trademark Act prohibits the registration of immoral or scandalous matter, including profane words. Thus, a mark consisting of a photo of a nude man and woman embracing and kissing in a graphic manner for a social club service newsletter was held to be scandalous and not registrable.

▾ *Deceptive matter.* Marks comprising deceptive matter cannot be registered. For example, LOVEE LAMB was held to be deceptive for seat covers not made of lambskin, and ORGANIK was held to be deceptive for clothing made from cotton that was neither organically grown nor free from chemical treatment.

▾ *Disparaging matter.* Marks that consist of matter that disparages or falsely suggests a connection with persons, institutions, or national symbols or brings them into contempt or disrepute are excluded from registration. Thus, a group of Native Americans recently succeeded in canceling several registrations owned by Pro-Football, Inc., for various marks including the term *Redskins* on the basis that the marks disparage Native Americans. The team is appealing the 1999 decision, and although the registrations may be canceled, the team would not be prevented from using the marks on a common law basis but rather prevented from owning registrations for the marks. Similarly, falsely suggesting an association with a person or institution is prohibited. Thus, the mark WESTPOINT for guns was held to falsely suggest an association with the U.S. Military Academy and was not registrable.

▾ *Government insignia.* Marks that consist of the flag or coat of arms or other insignia of the United States or another country cannot be registered.

▾ *Names, portraits, and signatures.* Names, portraits, or signatures of living persons cannot be registered without their consent. Additionally, the name, portrait, or signature of a deceased president cannot be used without the widow's written consent.

▾ *Merely descriptive marks.* Marks that are merely descriptive of the products or services offered under the mark cannot be registered. For example, the mark MOUNTAIN CAMPER used in connection with mail order services relating to outdoor equipment and apparel was refused registration as merely descriptive of the services offered under the mark. If a descriptive mark achieves secondary meaning, however, it may be registered. Secondary meaning (sometimes called acquired distinctiveness) is the link consumers make between a mark and its source. Thus, if the owner of MOUNTAIN CAMPER can prove that consumers have come to recognize the mark as indicating the owner's products, the mark may be registered. Trademark owners usually try to show that a mark has acquired secondary meaning by showing extensive advertising of the mark and submitting affidavits by consumers indicating that they have linked the mark with its owner. Alternatively, five years of consecutive use of a mark results in a presumption that it has achieved secondary meaning. Refusal of registration on the basis of descriptiveness is discussed further in Chapter 4.

▾ *Geographic terms.* Marks consisting of geographic terms present special problems. A mark including a geographic term cannot be registered if it is primarily geographically descriptive (meaning it describes its place of origin) unless it has acquired secondary meaning or widespread consumer renown. Thus, DENVER WESTERNS for western-style shirts originating in Denver was refused registration. Moreover, a mark cannot be registered if it is geographically deceptively misdescriptive, meaning that the goods do not originate in the place identified in the mark and the misrepresentation would be material to a purchasing decision. For example, the mark MAID IN PARIS for perfume originating in the United States was held to be geographically deceptive because Paris is renowned for perfume products; upon encountering the mark, consumers would believe that the perfume originated in Paris and would therefore perceive the perfume as being superior. Conversely, NANTUCKET was allowed for men's shirts not originating in Nantucket because consumers do not associate Nantucket with clothing and would not be favorably influenced by clothing made in that location. Finally, under the General Agreement on Tariffs and Trade (GATT), after January 1996 the use of a geographic name for wines and spirits is not permissible unless the goods originate from that place. Thus, a wine bearing the term *Sonoma* must originate in the Sonoma region of California.

▾ *Surnames.* A mark consisting primarily of a surname, such as Kimball or Davis, cannot be registered unless it has acquired distinctiveness. On the other hand, a surname such as Hunter has a primary significance or meaning other than as a surname and is thus registrable. Similarly, combining a surname with other wording may make the mark registrable. Thus, KIMBALL CRUNCHIES for snack products would be registrable.

▾ *Functional marks.* A design or device that is functional cannot be registered. A feature is functional if it affects the purpose, performance, or use of a product. Thus, if a certain shape of a guitar is ornamental rather than functional, and serves no useful purpose, it may be registered; however, if the shape aids in the sound and use of the guitar, it cannot be registered because registration would deprive others in the marketplace of a critical function needed to make the product a commercial success.

▾ *Confusingly similar marks.* To prevent consumer confusion and deception, marks that are confusingly similar to another's mark cannot be registered. Refusals on the basis of confusing similarity are discussed in Chapter 4.

▾ *Statutorily protected marks.* By law, some marks have received special protection. Thus, marks associated with the Olympics, the American Red Cross, Smokey the Bear, and certain veterans' organizations are reserved to their owners and cannot be appropriated by others.

In sum, a broad range of designs, slogans, words, shapes, sounds, colors, and images are available to companies to use as trademarks. Moreover, trademark law has been sufficiently flexible to accommodate changes in technology, such as moving images displayed on Web pages, demonstrating that there are no limits to what may be registered as long as the matter is not expressly excluded by statute.

3

Trademark Selection and Searching

Because a company's trademarks are among its most visible assets, great care should be taken in selecting a mark. Some marks, such as coined or fanciful marks, are stronger and more protectable than others, such as merely descriptive marks. Once a mark has been selected it should be cleared for availability. Because trademark infringement can lead to both compensatory damages (intended to compensate the wronged party for harm suffered) and punitive damages (intended to punish the wrong-doer), it is critical to conduct a trademark search before launching a new mark.

Trademark Selection: Picking the Strongest Mark

Selecting a trademark presents unique challenges. The natural tendency is to select a mark that has some connection with the product or service that will be associated with the mark. However, the U.S. Patent and Trademark Office (PTO) will reject a mark that is merely descriptive unless the mark has acquired secondary meaning, generally requiring five consecutive years of use of the mark or such significant advertising and marketing that consumers immediately link the mark with its owner or source. A mark that is wholly coined or made up, such as PEPSI® or XEROX®, is meaningless to consumers upon its initial use, and the company must expend time and money to teach consumers to link the mark with the company's products or services. Thus, there is a dynamic tension between selecting a mark that conveys something about the company (but might be descriptive) and one that is unique (but conveys no information to consumers).

Not all trademarks are equal. Some are stronger than others. Following are the four categories of trademarks, from weakest to strongest:

▾ *Descriptive marks.* Descriptive marks are the weakest of all trademarks. These marks describe something about the quality, purpose, or characteristics of the product or service offered under the mark. If one owner is allowed to select a mark that merely describes the goods and services offered under the mark, competition is inhibited. Examples of merely descriptive marks include BED & BREAKFAST REGISTRY for lodging reservations services, SHOOTING, HUNTING, OUTDOOR TRADE SHOW & CONFERENCE for conducting trade shows in the hunting and outdoor sports field, and SCREENWIPE for cloths used to clean computer and television screens. Moreover, using a foreign equivalent or a slight misspelling does not turn a descriptive mark into a nondescriptive one. Thus, OPTIQUE was refused for eyeglass frames and C-THRU was held to be descriptive of transparent rulers. Furthermore, laudatory terms such as *best* or *superior* are descriptive. For example, SUPER BUY was held to be merely descriptive of tobacco products. A mark that is merely descriptive cannot be registered on the Principal Register of the PTO (the PTO list or roll providing the most protection to a mark) unless it has achieved secondary meaning, also known as *acquired distinctiveness.* Secondary meaning is achieved either through five years' consecutive use of a mark or when consumers have learned to link a mark with its owner or the source of the goods or services offered under the mark.

▾ *Suggestive marks.* Marks that merely suggest something about the quality, nature, or characteristics of goods and services are registrable without proof of secondary meaning. Suggestive marks are those that demand imagination or thought to reach a conclusion about the nature of the goods or services rather than immediately telling something about the goods. Examples of suggestive marks include SUNKIST® for fruit products, GREYHOUND® for transportation services, COPPERTONE® for tanning oil, and ICE BREAKERS® for chewing gum. Those marks suggest something about the goods and services offered under the marks but do not immediately describe them.

▾ *Arbitrary marks.* An arbitrary mark is a dictionary term or word used for a product or service totally unrelated to the word, such as APPLE® for computers, CAMEL® for cigarettes, or OLD CROW® for whiskey. Arbitrary marks are registrable without proof of secondary meaning.

▾ *Fanciful marks.* A fanciful or coined mark is one that is invented for the sole purpose of functioning as a trademark, such as KODAK®, PEPSI®, or EXXON®. Such marks are the strongest of all, and it is nearly impossible for another user to claim that he or she innocently created the same or a similar mark. Thus, they are readily protected against infringing uses.

A generic mark is not a protectable mark at all but merely an actual name for goods and services. Generic terms cannot function as trademarks. Thus, the term *crackers* could not be registered for crackers and the word *battery* could not be registered for batteries. In several instances, words that once functioned as trademarks have become victims of their own success. For example, *aspirin, thermos, escalator*, and *cellophane* were once registered trademarks. Through misuse by consumers, the words became so associated with products that they lost their significance as trademarks. Thus, many companies embark on extensive advertising campaigns to prevent this "genericide" of marks, as is seen in references to "VASELINE® *brand* petroleum jelly," meant to remind consumers that VASELINE® is a registered trademark, not the common descriptive word for petroleum jelly. Xerox Corporation aggressively protects its XEROX® mark against genericide, spending significant sums on ad messages such as "When you use Xerox the way you use aspirin, we get a headache." Users are reminded not to say, "Make a xerox of this document." Use of a mark as a common noun can result in such genericide and loss of rights.

Methods of Selecting a Mark

Companies use a variety of methods to select a trademark. Some retain consulting or advertising firms. Others rely on their internal sales and marketing departments. Still others conduct internal promotions, asking all employees to submit possible marks. The danger of relying on employees who are not trademark experts is that an employee may unknowingly suggest an infringing mark. Moreover, employees often do not understand that the standard for trademark infringement is not identicality but confusing similarity, so they often believe that by changing a few words or a spelling, they have created a new mark. Professional firms conduct searches to prevent selection of an infringing mark.

Companies should give careful consideration to words in common use in their field. For example, the current glut of marks preceded by *e-* to signify electronic commerce results in marks that lack creativity and strength. It may be easy to obtain a registration for such a weak mark, but such a mark is very difficult to protect from later users. Similarly, thousands of marks include the elements *tech* or *compu*. Such a mark is protectable only against nearly identical uses. Courts have consistently held that when numerous similar marks exist for related goods or services, consumers become adept at distinguishing the marks, so only nearly identical marks used for highly related goods infringe.

Determining Trademark Availability

The best way to determine whether a mark is protectable and does not infringe another is to conduct a trademark availability search. There are several methods of checking availability, from self-help searches to engaging the services of firms that specialize in trademark clearance checks.

For marks that will be in use for only a very limited time, such as during a one-month local advertising campaign, a more limited search of the PTO database may be acceptable. Access the PTO Web site at www. uspto.gov and select "Trademark Electronic Search System" (TESS). A form is provided allowing one to check the PTO's database of 2.7 million registered, abandoned, canceled, and expired marks and pending applications. The searching is somewhat primitive, the PTO records may be up to two months old, and an inexperienced searcher probably will obtain incomplete or inconclusive results. Moreover, the records reflect only marks applied for or registered with the PTO; marks in use on a common law basis or registered only with a state agency or foreign country cannot be found through this method. Searching for marks with design elements takes significant expertise. Other methods include searching on the Internet, accessing yellow and white page directories available through most search engines. The site www.hoovers.com lists hundreds of companies in its directory, allowing one to determine whether an existing company has adopted a similar or identical business name. Similarly, some states allow searching of corporate names and marks on their Web sites. Access www. nass.org and select "States." Then select the state you are interested in and look under "Name Availability" or "Trademarks." These methods of searching are advisable only to eliminate marks from consideration.

Trademark searching can also be done at the PTO offices at 2900 Crystal Drive, Second Floor, Arlington, Virginia 22202. Additionally, the PTO has designated more than eighty libraries in cities throughout the United States as Patent and Trademark Depository Libraries. These libraries have CD-ROMs containing the database of registered and pending marks (although the CD-ROMs do not contain images of design marks). A list of the Trademark Depository Libraries is located on the PTO Web site at www.uspto.gov.

The next level of searching involves retaining the services of a professional trademark search firm. These firms charge fixed fees and conduct searches tailored to a company's needs, searching PTO records, individual state trademark records, domain names, Internet uses, and international uses and registrations. Their databases include thousands of telephone directories, journals, and periodicals that can be searched to determine whether a mark is in use. Searches can be conducted for a few hundred dollars and the results obtained within a matter of days or hours. A written report is issued, disclosing not only identical marks but marks that are similar in pronunciation or connotation. Images and designs can also be searched. The following companies specialize in conducting trademark searches:

CCH Corsearch, Inc.   Thomson & Thomson
28 West 23rd Street.   500 Victory Blvd.
7th Floor   North Quincy, MA 02171-3145
New York, NY 10010   (800) 692-8833
(800) SEARCH-1   www.thomson-thomson.com
www.corsearch.com

Although these companies conduct searches and issue written reports, they do not provide an opinion as to whether a mark is available for use. The report merely identifies identical or similar marks. Thus, the services of a skilled trademark attorney are needed to review and interpret the report and provide a written opinion as to whether the mark is available for use. Moreover, if the report discloses that an identical mark is registered, most law firms will conduct some investigation to determine whether the mark is in actual use. Because marks are presumed to be abandoned after three years of nonuse, such investigation may give a company the ammunition it needs to petition the PTO to cancel a registration for nonuse. Alternatively, a company may enter into negotiations to license the use of a mark or buy it outright from a party identified in the written report. Attorneys can also advise whether the marks are used in different trade channels or for such different customers that both may be used.

Adopting a mark for a product or service without conducting an availability search poses significant risk. If the mark is later challenged as an infringement and the company must destroy all its goods that bear the mark and any advertising collateral and then select a new mark and reestablish consumer recognition, the company will lose a great deal of time, effort, money, and credibility. Moreover, it may be required to disclose to its lenders, insurers, and strategic business partners that it has been sued for trademark infringement, causing a host of other problems. Finally, because two recent cases have suggested that failure to conduct a trademark search before commencing use of a mark may subject a user to a finding of willful infringement, leading to the imposition of punitive damages, obtaining a written opinion from counsel about availability of a mark is well worth the cost. See *International Star Class Yacht Racing Ass'n v. Tommy Hilfiger U.S.A., Inc.*, 146 F.3d 66 (2d Cir. 1998) and *Securacomm Consulting Inc. v. Securacom Inc.*, 166 F.3d 182 (3d Cir. 1999).

In sum, selecting a mark for a company's goods or services is a critically important business decision with far-reaching implications. The strongest mark possible should be selected and then searched to determine its availability. Particularly if the company intends to launch a product or service on a nationwide basis, a comprehensive search must be conducted and then evaluated by legal counsel to ensure that the mark is available in all jurisdictions. As in many instances, companies should err on the side of caution: When in doubt, select another mark.

Trademark Search Tips

The following guidelines summarize the importance of a comprehensive trademark search before adoption and use of a mark:

▾ Because liability for infringement is determined by whether two marks are confusingly similar, a search will disclose potentially conflicting marks and thereby help a company avoid liability for trademark infringement.

▾ A preliminary or knockout search of PTO records may suffice for a mark intended for short-term use.

▾ A thorough search (including PTO records, state records, common law, and Internet uses) should always be conducted before launching a mark intended for long-term or nationwide use or before incurring costs related to marketing materials displaying the mark.

▾ The best searches are conducted by trademark search experts with access to databases of thousands of marks. The search results should then be interpreted by an experienced trademark attorney.

4

The Trademark Application Process

If a trademark search discloses that a mark is available and is eligible for federal registration, an application should be filed promptly with the U.S. Patent and Trademark Office (PTO). Delay may allow another to select the mark, and search results can quickly become stale. After examining the application, the PTO issues a registration for the mark. The process generally takes about twelve to eighteen months.

Types of Applications

Two types of applications may be filed with the PTO by a U.S. applicant: an application based on actual use of the mark in interstate commerce and an application based on the applicant's bona fide intent to use the mark in interstate commerce. The intent-to-use application process affords companies significant advantages. Until the late 1980s, companies were required to use a mark before applying for its registration with the PTO. If the PTO determined that the mark was merely descriptive or was confusingly similar to that of another, the application was rejected and the company was forced to select another mark, spend money advertising and using it, and then take another gamble that the PTO would approve the mark for registration. The intent-to-use application solves this problem by allowing individuals and companies to file an application based on their intent to use a mark in the future. If the PTO rejects the application, the applicant has lost only the filing fees and perhaps some attorneys' fees. If the application is approved, the applicant then begins use of the mark, verifies such use to the PTO, and then receives a registration. The intent to use the mark must be a bona fide one, and a party cannot file a trademark application with the PTO merely to warehouse a mark.

In addition to the actual use application and the intent-to-use application, foreign applicants may file for trademark registration in the United States, based on an application filed in or registration issued by their home country.

The U.S. Patent and Trademark Office

The PTO is a noncommercial federal entity and is one of fourteen bureaus within the U.S. Department of Commerce. The PTO occupies a combined total of more than 1,400,000 square feet in numerous buildings in Arlington, Virginia. Since 1991, the PTO has operated in much the same way as a private business, providing products and services to its customers in exchange for fees that fully fund its operations. More than 5,000 people are employed by the PTO, and in 1999 the PTO issued approximately 104,000 trademark registrations, an increase of 27 percent from the previous year, making it one of the busiest of government agencies. Useful PTO telephone numbers are found in Figure 4-1.

Figure 4-1. Useful PTO telephone numbers.

General trademark or patent information	(703) 308-HELP
Automated (recorded) general trademark or patent information	(703) 557-INFO
Automated line for checking status of trademark applications and registrations	(703) 305-8747
Assignment and certificate branch	(703) 308-9723
Trademark assistance center	(703) 308-9000 or (800) 786-9199
Information about renewals and other postregistration matters	(703) 308-9500
Trademark Trial and Appeal Board	(703) 308-9300
Assistant Commissioner for Trademarks	(703) 308-8900

The Benefits of Federal Registration

As discussed in Chapters 1 and 2, one need not secure a registration from the PTO to have rights to a trademark; however, federal registration affords significant benefits. The PTO maintains two rolls or registers of marks: the Principal Register and the Supplemental Register. Registration on the Principal Register is preferred because it affords the following advantages:

- Presumption that the mark has been used nationwide since the filing date of the application, thus allowing its owner to preclude later confusingly similar uses anywhere in the United States
- Nationwide notice of the trademark owner's claim of ownership of the mark so that a later user cannot claim that it used the mark in good faith
- Right to initiate an action in federal court for infringement with the right to recover lost profits, damages, costs, and, in some cases, triple damages
- Right to bar importation of infringing foreign goods
- Right to use the U.S. registration as a basis to obtain a registration in various foreign countries
- Right to obtain incontestable status of the mark after five years of continuous use so as to narrow later challenges to the mark
- Right to use the federal registration symbol (®) with the mark
- Prima facie (literally, "on its face") evidence of the owner's exclusive right to use the mark

Registration on the PTO's Supplemental Register does not afford all these advantages. For example, although a mark registered on the Supplemental Register is eligible to use the federal registration symbol (®) and can be protected against infringement through action in federal court, a Supplemental Registration can never achieve incontestable status and cannot be used to stop importation of infringing foreign goods. However, the registration will be on file with the PTO, and the PTO will refuse a later application for a confusingly similar mark.

Generally, marks that are not eligible for protection on the Principal Register are registered on the Supplemental Register. For example, a mark that is merely descriptive, such as STRUDEL POCKETS for strudel-filled pastries, cannot be registered on the Principal Register unless it has acquired secondary meaning. However, it may be registered on the Supplemental Register; once it acquires secondary meaning (either through five consecutive years of use or through extensive renown), the registration can then be moved to the Principal Register. A supplemental registration indicates that the matter does not yet but eventually could function as a trademark.

The Trademark Application

Trademark applications can be made only by the owner of a mark, and the applicant's name should be set out in its correct legal form. Municipalities and government agencies can also own marks, as is the case with PATRIOT®, owned by the Department of the Army for its air defense missile system. Generally, applications are made by one party. The PTO is reluctant to accept applications by joint applicants because ownership of a mark by two people is contrary to the notion that a trademark identifies a single source of goods or services. An application for a mark owned by a partnership is thus made by the partnership itself rather than in the names of the individual partners. Applications must be in English, and although the PTO provides forms for applications, one may use another format as long as it complies with all PTO requirements.

Contents of Trademark Application

A use-based application includes several elements:

▾ The owner's domicile and citizenship must be given. If the owner is an individual, it is sufficient to indicate "United States citizen." If the owner is a corporation or partnership, it is acceptable to state "a New York corporation" or "a California limited partnership."

▾ The date the mark was first used and the date it was first used in interstate commerce must be provided (either at the time of filing the application or later).

▾ The applicant must describe the goods or services used in connection with the mark. For example, it is acceptable to state "the mark is used in connection with hotel services," or "the mark is used in connection with engineering, design, research, testing, and consulting services in the area of computer chips," or "the mark is used in connection with cookies, crackers, snack cakes, and cereal bars." The PTO uses a classification scheme to identify goods and services and designates forty-two separate classes of goods and services. For example, International Class 3 covers cosmetics and cleaning preparations, and International Class 39 covers transportation services. The applicant should identify the class for which the application is sought; however, such a designation is not absolutely required, and if an error is made in selecting the class, the PTO will correct it. The identification must clearly and concisely list each item covered by the application. The use of indefinite terms such as "accessories," "components," or "systems" is acceptable only if the applicant follows such words with the word "namely" and lists the specific items. Thus, a description of goods such as "computer programs, including programs for calculating social security deductions" will be rejected as indefinite, whereas the description "computer programs, namely, programs for calculating social security deductions" is permissible. The important thing to note is that a trademark registration covers only the goods or services designated in the application. Thus, if an application states that it is for "men's clothing," only that item will be covered. Although the applicant may later clarify the identification by stating "men's clothing, namely pants, shirts, ties, and socks," the application could not be amended to add "pens." A new application would be required for the new goods. Moreover, each class of goods and services requires a separate $325 filing fee. Thus, if an application covers soap in International Class (or I.C.) 3, mail order catalogs in I.C. 16, and yogurt in I.C. 29, a filing fee of $975 is required. The applicant may identify all the desired goods and services in one application or may file three separate applications for the three different types of goods. Some experts prefer to file separate applications; then if the PTO objects to one of the applications, the remaining ones will not be delayed and can proceed to registration. A list of the International Classes is provided in Figure 4-2, and they are also available at the PTO Web site at www.uspto.gov.

▾ A drawing of the mark is required. A drawing is a single page that identifies the applicant's complete name, address, goods and services specified in the application, the date of first use of the mark, and the date of first use of the mark in interstate commerce. A drawing or rendition of the mark as it is actually used should appear at the center of the page. If the mark is a word or phrase, such as MICROSOFT® or CHIPS AHOY!®, it is typed on the page in capital letters. This type of drawing is called a typed form drawing. If the mark includes a design element, such as the image of a duck in Disney Enterprises' THE MIGHTY DUCKS OF

Figure 4-2. International trademark classes for goods and services.

Class 1	Chemicals
Class 2	Paints
Class 3	Cosmetics and cleaning preparations
Class 4	Lubricants and oils
Class 5	Pharmaceuticals
Class 6	Metal goods
Class 7	Machinery
Class 8	Hand tools
Class 9	Electrical and scientific apparatus (including data-processing machines and computers)
Class 10	Medical apparatus
Class 11	Environmental control apparatus
Class 12	Vehicles
Class 13	Firearms
Class 14	Jewelry
Class 15	Musical instruments
Class 16	Paper goods and printed matter
Class 17	Rubber goods
Class 18	Leather goods
Class 19	Nonmetallic building materials
Class 20	Furniture and articles not otherwise classified
Class 21	Housewares and glass
Class 22	Cordage and fibers
Class 23	Yarn and threads
Class 24	Fabrics
Class 25	Clothing
Class 26	Fancy goods (including lace and ribbons)
Class 27	Floor coverings
Class 28	Toys and sporting goods
Class 29	Meats and processed foods
Class 30	Staple foods
Class 31	Natural agricultural products (including fruits, vegetables, and seeds)
Class 32	Light beverages
Class 33	Wines and spirits
Class 34	Smokers' articles
Class 35	Advertising and business services

Class 36   Insurance and financial services

Class 37   Building construction and repair services

Class 38   Telecommunications services

Class 39   Transportation and storage services

Class 40   Treatment of materials services

Class 41   Education and entertainment services

Class 42   Miscellaneous services (including providing food and drink, temporary accommodations, legal services, and computer programming services)

ANAHEIM®, the drawing is called a special-form drawing and should clearly reproduce the desired image. If a special typeface or script is desired, it should be shown. Most applicants photocopy their special-form drawings onto the drawing page. If the image will not reproduce satisfactorily, the applicant may need to retain a graphic artist to draw the image. The drawing may not be larger than 4 inches by 4 inches. Thus, many applicants repeatedly reduce the size of their photocopied image to meet these requirements. The size requirements are necessary because the PTO eventually will publish the mark in its publication called the *Official Gazette* (*OG*), and uniformity of size assists in preparing the *OG*. If an applicant claims color as part of the mark, a statement to this effect should be included. Most drawings do not indicate specific colors, allowing the trademark owner to display the mark in any color. Generally, color is claimed only when an owner intends to display a mark exclusively in a certain color, such as the distinctive red used on cans of DR PEPPER®.

    ▾ The applicant must include a verification of the application, stating that he believes himself to be the owner of the mark, to the best of his knowledge and belief the facts recited in the application are accurate, and no other person has the right to use the mark applied for.

    ▾ A filing fee must be included. At present the filing fee for an application is $325 per class of goods or services. Changes to filing fees are indicated on the PTO's Web site. Applicants may submit a check or money order. Companies or law firms that file large numbers of applications usually establish a deposit account with the PTO, and application fees are charged against the account, which is replenished periodically.

    ▾ The application must be signed by the trademark owner/applicant or one acting on his or her behalf, such as an attorney, and contact information (address and phone number) must be given.

    Applications based on a bona fide intent to use a mark include the preceding components, except that dates of use are not given because the mark is not yet in use. The application states that the applicant has a bona fide intention to use the mark in commerce.

Until late 1999, applicants filing use-based applications were also required to submit three specimens with their applications and to identify the method of use of the mark. Although these items now can be provided to the PTO after the filing of the application, most applicants continue to include a specimen with the application.

Specimens are real-world samples showing how the mark is being used in commerce. The PTO currently requires only one specimen per class of goods or services. If the mark is used on goods, acceptable specimens are tags or labels that are attached to the goods, containers for the goods, or photographs of the goods showing the mark affixed to the goods, if it is impractical to send an actual specimen because of its size. Thus, for clothing, an acceptable specimen would be a hangtag affixed to the item of clothing. For a computer program, the plastic container in which the disk is sold, together with its label, would be acceptable. Invoices, brochures, letterhead, stationery, and business cards are not acceptable specimens for goods.

If the mark is used in connection with services, examples of acceptable specimens include signs, brochures about the services, advertisements for the services, or photographs showing the mark as it is used with the services. For example, for restaurant services, a menu would be an acceptable specimen. For airline transportation services, a newspaper ad showing the mark would be acceptable. The PTO rejects bulky specimens.

Applicants filing intent-to-use applications will not have a specimen to submit at the time of filing. A specimen is required before the PTO will issue a registration for the mark, however.

Applicants generally indicate the method of use of the mark by stating, "The mark is used on labels affixed to the goods" or "The mark is used in advertisements and promotional materials for the services." Intent-to-use applications can also indicate the method of use by stating, "The mark will be used on containers for the goods." If this method of use is not set forth in the original application, the PTO will require it later.

Filing and Other Formalities

The completed application should be filed with the PTO by U.S. mail or hand delivery. The PTO prefers original applications but will accept copies. Applicants may also use the Trademark Electronic Application System (TEAS). TEAS allows an applicant to fill out an application form and check it for completeness over the Internet. Using e-TEAS, the applicant submits the application directly to the PTO over the Internet, paying by credit card or an existing deposit account. A specimen can be submitted later.

TEAS offers extensive online help and can be accessed twenty-four hours a day, seven days a week. Because of increased international business, TEAS offers foreign applicants and distant clients the ability to review and sign the application electronically. The TEAS system is gaining widespread acceptance in big companies such as Mattel, Inc., the number-one filer of trademark applications in the United States. The PTO anticipates that by the end of 2001, electronic filings will make up or exceed 20 to 30 percent of the total number of trademark applications filed with the PTO. Additional information can be obtained at the TEAS Web site at www.uspto.gov/teas/index.html.

The application and all other correspondence should be addressed to The Assistant Commissioner for Trademarks, 2900 Crystal Drive, Arlington, Virginia 22202-3513. The initial application should be directed to Box NEW APP/FEE. The PTO advises submitting a stamped, self-addressed postcard with the application specifically identifying the mark, the applicant, the goods, and the International Class. The PTO will stamp the filing date and serial number of the application on the postcard to acknowledge receipt. The applicant can use this serial number to monitor the progress of the application by calling the PTO's status line at (703) 305-8747 or accessing the PTO's Trademark Applications and Registrations Retrieval (TARR) database on the PTO's Web site at http://tarr.uspto.gov.

When the application is received, the PTO reviews it to determine whether it meets the minimum requirements for receiving a filing date. If it does, the PTO assigns the application a serial number and then sends the applicant an official filing receipt about two months after filing. The official filing receipt includes all the application details. Errors in the official filing receipt should be brought to the attention of the PTO; otherwise, the registration certificate will include errors from the filing receipt. The serial number assigned to the application remains with the application during the entire examination process and is the means by which the PTO tracks the application. The file maintained by the PTO for the application is called the file wrapper, and the process of moving an application through the PTO to achieve a registration is called prosecution.

Examination of the Application

About four months after the application is filed, it is assigned to an examining attorney who reviews it and determines whether the mark should proceed to registration.

Common Grounds for Refusal of Registration

Following are the most common grounds for refusing registration:

▾ The proposed mark consists of or comprises immoral, deceptive, or scandalous matter.

▾ The proposed mark disparages or falsely suggests a connection with persons (living or dead), institutions, beliefs, or national symbols or brings them into contempt or disrepute.

▾ The proposed mark consists of or comprises the flag or coat of arms of the United States or a state or foreign nation.

▾ The proposed mark consists of or comprises a name, portrait, or signature identifying a particular living person who has not consented in writing to such use, or the mark comprises the name, signature, or portrait of a deceased president of the United States without his widow's written consent.

▾ The proposed mark is primarily merely a surname.

▾ The proposed mark, as a whole, is functional.

▾ The proposed mark is deceptive in that it misdescribes the goods, such as using CEDAR RIDGE for hardboard siding not made of cedar.

▾ The proposed mark is primarily geographically descriptive (using DENVER WESTERNS for western clothing originating in Denver) or deceptively geographically misdescriptive of the goods and services (using CALIFORNIA MIX for fruits and nuts not originating in California, because consumers know that California is a major producer of fruits and nuts).

▾ The proposed mark is merely descriptive.

▾ The proposed mark so resembles a mark already registered or applied for with the PTO that use of the mark by the applicant is likely to cause confusion, mistake, or deception.

▾ The specimen does not match the drawing of the mark or is incorrectly sized.

The examining attorney sets forth the objections in a written communication called an office action, listing the grounds for refusal of registration and any corrections required in the application. Alternatively, for minor corrections, the examining attorney may contact the applicant by telephone. The applicant must respond to any objections within six months of the office action, or the application will be deemed abandoned unless the failure to respond was unintentional.

Some office actions are easily responded to by submitting a written consent, providing a new specimen, or correcting the size of the drawing. The more difficult office actions are those that refuse registration on the basis that the mark is merely descriptive or is confusingly similar to another mark.

Refusals on the Basis of Descriptiveness

If a proposed mark is rejected on the basis that it is merely descriptive, the applicant may be able to overcome the objection by showing that the mark has acquired secondary meaning. Secondary meaning can be shown through five consecutive years of use of a mark or through such extensive use, advertising, and renown that consumers have come to link the mark with its source. If secondary meaning cannot be shown, the applicant may argue that the mark is not merely descriptive but is rather suggestive and should thus be allowed to register without proof of secondary meaning. To show such suggestiveness, the applicant can provide evidence of similar marks that were allowed to register, comparing and contrasting these to his or her mark.

If the mark includes descriptive elements in addition to nondescriptive elements, the applicant may disclaim the descriptive portion of the mark so it can proceed to registration. Thus, the applicant for GOLDEN GRIDDLE PANCAKE HOUSE disclaimed the descriptive words *pancake house.* A disclaimer is an acknowledgement by the applicant that it does not claim exclusive rights to use of the descriptive portion of the mark. An entire mark may not be disclaimed. The proper wording for a disclaimer is as follows: "No claim is made to the exclusive right to use _____ apart from the mark as shown." A disclaimer does not affect the display of the mark or its validity; it is merely an acknowledgement that the mark's owner does not claim exclusive rights to certain matter, such as descriptive words or a surname.

Refusals on the Basis of Confusing Similarity

If a mark is refused registration on the basis that it is confusingly similar to another registered or applied-for mark, the applicant can argue in the response to office action that the mark is not confusingly similar to the other mark. Although each case is decided on its own facts and there is no litmus test to determine confusing similarity, the following factors are considered:

   ▾ The similarity of the marks in their entireties as to appearance, sound, connotation, and commercial impression
   ▾ The similarity and nature of the goods and services used in connection with the marks
   ▾ The channels of trade in which the marks are used
   ▾ The conditions under which and the buyers to whom sales are made, namely, whether the items are impulse purchases or whether they are the result of careful and sophisticated purchasing
   ▾ The fame of the prior mark, judged by sales, advertising, and length of use
   ▾ The number and nature of similar marks in use on similar goods
   ▾ Whether actual confusion exists
   ▾ The length of time that the marks have coexisted without actual confusion

   The goods or services need not be identical for confusion to be likely. It is sufficient that the goods or services of the applicant and the prior user are related in some matter. Thus, LAREDO for land vehicles was held likely to be confused with LAREDO for tires, and MARTIN'S for bread was held likely to be confused with MARTIN'S for cheese.
   Marks may be confusingly similar even though letters or words are added, deleted, or substituted. For example, COMMCASH was held likely to be confused with COMMUNICASH when both were used for banking services, and PERRY'S was held likely to be confused with PERRY'S PIZZA when both were used for restaurant services. Similarly, GAS CITY

was held likely to be confused with GAS TOWN, both for gasoline, because of the similarity in meaning.

If a mark includes both wording and a design element, greater weight often is accorded to the wording because it is used by purchasers in requesting the goods or services. Strong marks may be infringed or confused more easily than weak marks. For example, MUCKY DUCK® for restaurant services is so unique that the use of the terms MUCKY DUCK in another mark likely will cause consumers to believe the marks are the product of the same source. Similarly, consumers become adept at distinguishing even minor differences between marks when numerous similar marks exist for similar products. Thus, MICROSOFT® can coexist with MICRON® and MICRO STRATEGY®. If a mark is weak in that it uses descriptive wording, similar marks may be able to coexist with it. Finally, it is well established that the relevant test is likelihood of confusion, not actual confusion. It is not necessary to show that consumers have experienced actual confusion. The PTO position is that if there is any doubt as to whether there is a likelihood of confusion, that doubt must be resolved against the newcomer.

If the examining attorney refuses registration on the basis that the applied-for mark is confusingly similar to another, the applicant can submit evidence of other registrations and applications to demonstrate that a mark or a portion thereof is suggestive or descriptive and is thus entitled to registration. The existence of other registrations is not conclusive, however, and previous decisions by the PTO in approving other marks are not binding on the agency.

If the PTO continues to refuse the applicant's argument that the marks are not confusingly similar, the applicant may attempt to obtain the consent of the prior user to use and registration of the applicant's mark. A consent agreement between the parties is given great weight by the PTO because parties in the marketplace are believed to be in the best position to judge potential confusion. If they agree that confusion is unlikely and consent to each other's use and registration of the mark, the PTO generally accepts such a consent agreement.

Another possibility is that the parties can agree to concurrent use of their marks. Concurrent use is acceptable only if the parties use their marks in different geographic areas. If so, they can essentially carve up the United States and agree as to which party will use its mark in which regions, states, or areas. The parties will enter into a concurrent use agreement, and the later party's application will be amended to state that concurrent use is being sought. The registration will then identify the particular areas or states in which the registration is valid. The PTO will allow concurrent use only when confusion is not likely to result from the parties' uses of their marks. Concurrent use proceedings are somewhat rare.

The process of office action by the examining attorney and responses to office action by the applicant continue until registration is allowed or the examining attorney issues a final refusal. The applicant may appeal a final refusal to the Trademark Trial and Appeal Board (TTAB), an administrative tribunal within the PTO. A party who is dissatisfied with a TTAB ruling may file an appeal in the Court of Appeals for the Federal Circuit located in Washington, D.C., but the Court of Appeals generally sets aside PTO findings only when there has been an abuse of discretion or an arbitrary holding.

Publication for Opposition

If the PTO has no objections to the application or the applicant successfully overcomes all objections, the examining attorney will approve the mark for publication in the *OG*, a weekly publication of the PTO. The PTO sends a notice informing the applicant of the date of publication. Publication in the *OG* is intended to provide notice to the world so that anyone who believes he or she may be damaged by registration of the mark can oppose its registration. Many large companies subscribe to watch services provided by the trademark search professionals identified in Chapter 3. Those search companies review newly filed applications and the *OG* and then notify companies of potentially conflicting marks.

Oppositions must be filed within 30 days after publication in the *OG*. If additional time in which to oppose is desired, a written request for the extension must be filed before expiration of the 30 days. There is no fee for requesting an extension. Extensions often are sought to give a party time to evaluate whether the mark applied for is a threat or to allow the parties to negotiate their differences. A first extension of time for 30 days is granted upon request without any showing of good cause. The TTAB may grant further extensions of time for good cause up to a total of 120 days from the date of publication. The requirement of good cause typically is satisfied by a statement by the potential opposer that it needs the additional time to evaluate whether registration of the mark will cause damage. Additional extensions beyond the 120-day total are granted only if the applicant consents.

Anyone who believes he or she would be damaged by the registration of a mark on the Principal Register may oppose registration by filing a notice of opposition with the TTAB. The filing fee is $300 per class of goods or services. The notice of opposition looks much like a complaint that initiates a lawsuit. The applicant then responds to the notice of opposition. Discovery may commence and briefs are submitted to the TTAB, which renders a decision based solely on the written briefs and other documents. Personal testimony is not given. Like most lawsuits, the vast majority of oppositions are resolved by voluntary agreement.

Issuance of Certificate of Registration or Notice of Allowance

If no opposition is filed, or once the opposition is resolved, the application enters the next stage of the registration process. If the application was based on actual use of the mark in commerce, the PTO registers the mark and issues a registration certificate about twelve weeks after publication in the *OG*.

However, if the application was based on the applicant's intent to use the mark in commerce, the PTO issues a Notice of Allowance about twelve weeks after publication of the mark in the *OG*. The applicant then has six months from the date of the Notice of Allowance to either use the mark in commerce and verify such to the PTO by submitting a Statement of Use (together with a specimen and a filing fee of $100 per class) or request a six-month extension of time to file a Statement of Use. The applicant may obtain additional six-month extensions of time upon a showing of good cause (typically satisfied by stating that the applicant needs additional time to formulate its marketing plans and to begin use of the mark). Extensions of time are available for up to three years from the date of the Notice of Allowance, upon payment of a $150 filing fee per class.

If an intent-to-use applicant has commenced use of the mark between the application filing date and the date the examining attorney approves the mark for publication in the *OG*, he or she may file an Amendment to Allege Use (with a filing fee of $100 per class) to convert the intent-to-use application to a use-based one.

See Figure 4-3 for a flowchart showing the process of prosecution of

Figure 4-3. Flowchart showing prosecution of trademark applications.

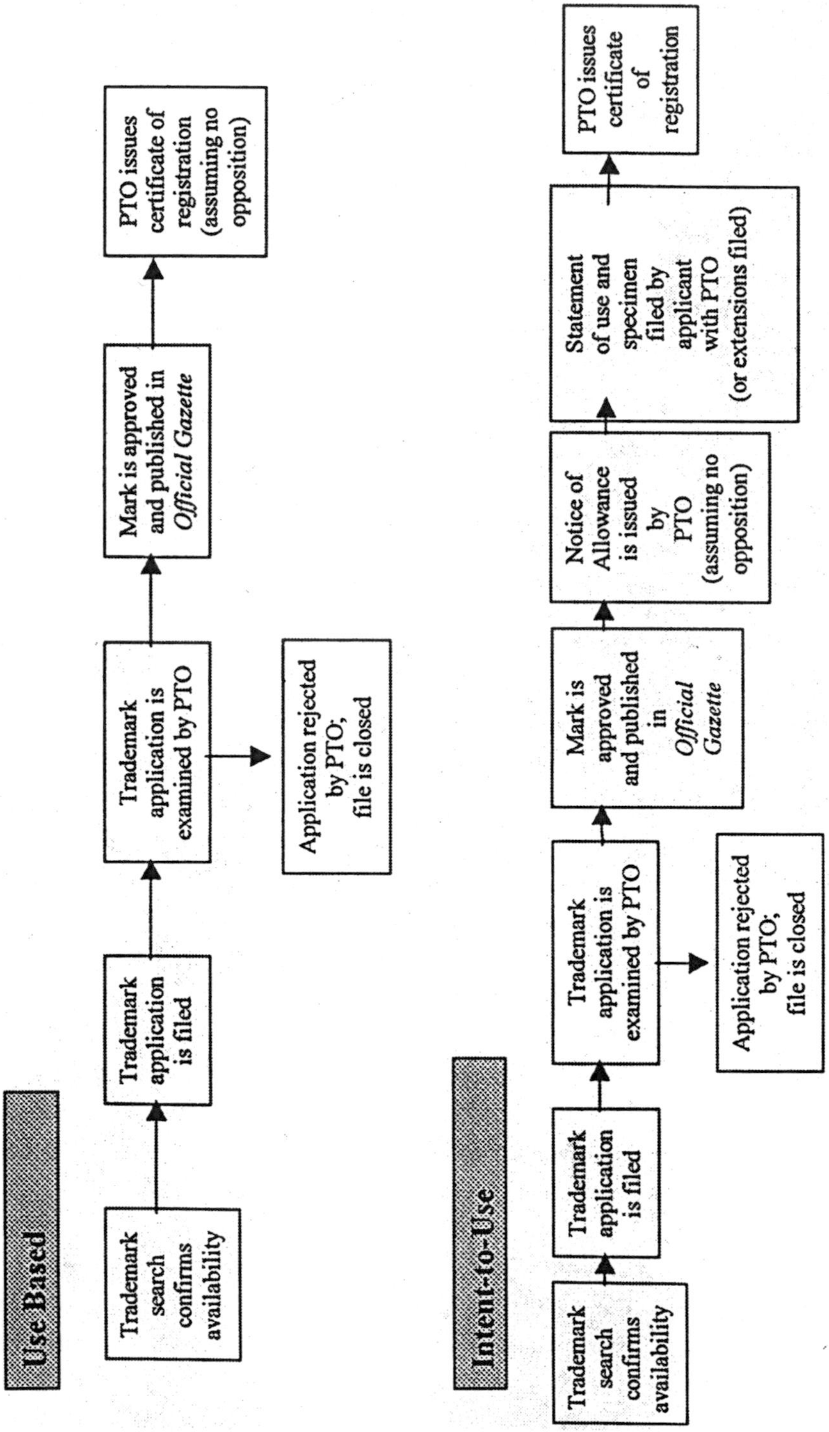

Use-Based

Trademark search confirms availability → Trademark application is filed → Trademark application is examined by PTO → Mark is approved and published in *Official Gazette* → PTO issues certificate of registration (assuming no opposition)

Trademark application is examined by PTO → Application rejected by PTO; file is closed

Intent-to-Use

Trademark search confirms availability → Trademark application is filed → Trademark application is examined by PTO → Mark is approved and published in *Official Gazette* → Notice of Allowance is issued by PTO (assuming no opposition) → Statement of use and specimen filed by applicant with PTO (or extensions filed) → PTO issues certificate of registration

Trademark application is examined by PTO → Application rejected by PTO; file is closed actual use and intent-to-use applications and Figure 4-4 for trademark filing and processing fees.

Once the Statement of Use is filed and approved, the PTO issues the registration certificate, and the owner of the mark has nationwide priority reverting to the date it filed its application.

Effect of Registration

The Certificate of Registration issued by the PTO should be checked for errors. Errors can be corrected upon request. Once a mark is registered, the owner, who is now called the registrant, may use any of the following notices:

- Registered in the U.S. Patent and Trademark Office
- Reg. U.S. Pat. & Tm. Off.
- ® (the most commonly used form of notice)

Registrants are not required to use a notice; however, use of the notice informs the public that the registrant claims ownership rights in the mark. The notice usually is placed to the right of and slightly above the mark, as in CHEERIOS®. Use of the notice before registration is unlawful. Before registration, trademark owners generally use the notice ™ for trademarks and ˢᴹ for service marks. See Figure 4-5 for a sample trademark application.

Figure 4-4. Trademark filing and processing fees.

Application for registration, per class	$325
Filing an Amendment to Allege Use, per class	$100
Filing a Statement of Use, per class	$100
Filing a Request for a Six-Month Extension of Time for Filing a Statement of Use, per class	$150
Application for Renewal, per class	$400
Filing Affidavit of Incontestability, per class	$200
Notice of Opposition, per class	$300
Petition for Cancellation, per class	$300
Recording Trademark Assignment (for first mark) for second and subsequent marks in same document	$40 $25 per mark
Issuing a New Certificate of Registration	$100

Figure 4-5. Trademark application.

IN THE UNITED STATES PATENT AND TRADEMARK OFFICE

Trademark: DYNACCESS
International Class: 9
Applicant: Dynamic Decisions
                      Consulting, Inc.

Box NEW APP/FEE
Assistant Commissioner for Trademarks
2900 Crystal Drive
Arlington, Virginia 22202-3513

Dynamic Decisions Consulting, Inc.
A Delaware Corporation
4220 West Fairfax Road
Suite 401
Wilmington, Delaware 43099

Applicant requests registration of the trademark shown in the accompanying drawing in the United States Patent and Trademark Office on the Principal Register established by the Act of July 5, 1946 (15 U.S.C. 1051 et seq., as amended) for the following goods in International Class 9:

Computer software and instruction and user manuals sold as a unit therewith for use in security systems.

Applicant is using the mark in commerce on labels placed on the above-identified goods. Applicant first used the mark on February 1, 1999, and first used the mark in interstate commerce on February 1, 1999. One specimen showing the mark as used in commerce is submitted with this application.

DECLARATION

The undersigned being hereby warned that willful false statements and the like so made are punishable by fine or imprisonment, or both, under 18 U.S.C. 1001, and that such willful false statements may jeopardize the validity of the application or any resulting registration, declares that he is properly authorized to execute this application on behalf of the applicant; he believes the applicant to be the owner of the trademark sought to be registered; to the best of his knowledge and belief no other person, firm, corporation or association has the right to use the above-identified mark in commerce, either in the identical form thereof or in such near resemblance thereto as to be likely, when used on or in connection with the goods/services of such other person, to cause confusion, or to cause mistake, or to deceive; and that all statements made of his own knowledge are true and that all statements made on information and belief are believed to be true.

DYNAMIC DECISIONS CONSULTING, INC.

By: _____

      Teresa Anderson, President

Date: March ___, 2000

Telephone Number: (301) 445-9009

APPLICANT'S NAME: Dynamic Decisions Consulting, Inc.

APPLICANT'S ADDRESS: 4220 West Fairfax Road
Suite 401
Wilmington, Delaware 43099

FIRST USE: At least as early as February 1, 1999

FIRST USE IN COMMERCE: At least as early as February 1, 1999

GOODS: Computer software and instruction and user manuals
sold as a unit therewith for use in security systems

DYNACCESS

International Protection

Obtaining Protection for Your Mark Outside the United States

Trademarks issued by the PTO have no effect outside the United States and its territories. Companies desiring protection for their marks in other countries must register their marks in those countries. In most instances, owners of U.S. registrations rely on the protections of the Paris Convention of 1883, adhered to by more than 130 countries, including those in Europe and most of South America, Canada, Mexico, and many African and Asian nations. The Paris Convention is based on the principle that countries will provide the same patent and trademark protection to citizens of other member nations as they do their own citizens.

The most significant feature of the Paris Convention is that it offers priority to member nations. If a citizen of a member nation files an application for a trademark registration in any Paris Convention nation within six months after filing in his or her home country, the foreign application is given the filing priority date of the earlier home application.

Other significant rights arise from the 1996 European Community Trademark System (the CTM System) adhered to by the fifteen member nations of the European Union (Austria, Belgium, Denmark, Finland, France, Germany, Greece, Ireland, Italy, Luxembourg, Netherlands, Portugal, Spain, Sweden, and the United Kingdom). Rather than filing separate trademark applications in each foreign country, a trademark applicant can file one CTM application; when the registration is issued, protection is afforded in all fifteen member nations. The European Union is considering allowing Bulgaria, Romania, Slovakia, Latvia, Lithuania, Malta, and Turkey to join.

Because the searching systems and databases in foreign countries vary from nation to nation and because each country has its own trademark laws, most trademark applicants need the assistance of experienced foreign counsel to prosecute applications in other countries. Many U.S. law firms have relationships with these foreign attorneys, called associates, and rely extensively on them to advise U.S. trademark owners wanting international protection.

Companies wanting to do business internationally should give immediate and careful consideration to protecting their marks in other countries. Many countries follow a first-to-file principle, meaning that the first party to file a trademark application owns the rights to the mark, even if the mark has not yet been used. This has encouraged stockpiling of marks in some foreign countries with later attempts to "ransom back" marks to their true owners. Although the United States works carefully with many countries to encourage them to strengthen their intellectual property laws, trademark piracy is still common in many foreign countries. Thus, early filing is strongly encouraged for companies wanting to go global.

Rights of Foreign Nationals to U.S. Trademark Protection

Just as U.S. trademark owners can file applications in other countries, one need not be a U.S. citizen to obtain a trademark registration from the PTO. Foreign nationals can file applications with the PTO, and those applications are prosecuted nearly identically to their U.S. counterparts. If a foreign owner is a citizen of a Paris Convention member, he or she can file in the home country and then, if the application is filed in the United States within six months, can obtain the benefits of the earlier filing date. The foreign applicant must designate someone in the United States who will receive communications and documents relating to the mark.

Additionally, because of various treaty commitments, the United States allows owners of marks registered in most foreign countries to file an application and secure a U.S. registration even if the mark has not been used anywhere in the world. This is because many foreign countries grant registrations even if the mark has not been used in that country. This foreign registration can then be used as a basis to obtain a U.S. registration. Ultimately, the mark must be used in the United States, or the U.S. registration will be canceled. In sum, whereas U.S. citizens must always use a mark before the PTO will issue a registration, owners of foreign registrations are able to obtain a registration from the PTO without a showing of such use.

5

Maintaining, Monitoring, and Transferring Your Trademark

Trademark rights exist only as long as the owner uses and protects the mark. Moreover, once a registration is issued by the U.S. Patent and Trademark Office (PTO), the registrant must file renewal and other documents with the PTO to verify continued use of the mark. Failure to file the appropriate documents results in cancellation of the registration. Many companies institute formal trademark compliance policies to ensure that rights are not lost by improper use of their marks. Marks can be sold to others or licensed to others as long as the trademark owner retains the right to control the quality of the goods or services offered under the licensed mark.

Maintaining Your Registration

Because trademark rights stem from use, the PTO wants to ensure that registered marks are actually in use. Marks not being used are cleared from the PTO registers and are then available to others. The PTO requires that trademark owners take the following actions to maintain a registration:

▾ Between years five and six after registration, and every ten years after registration, the owner must file an affidavit of use (called the Section 8 Affidavit) with the PTO verifying that he or she continues to use the mark. The current filing fee is $100 per class of goods or services offered under the mark.

▾ A renewal application (called a Section 9 Application) for the registration must be filed every ten years. The affidavit of use required under Section 8 every ten years can be combined with the renewal application. The current renewal filing fee is $400 per class of goods or services offered under the mark.

These documents can be filed within one year before the due date. The PTO allows a grace period of six months for late filings (a fee of $100 per class of goods and services is assessed for filing during the grace period) and requires that a specimen be submitted with the Section 8 and renewal filings, showing how the mark is used. If the specimen differs from that shown in the original registration in a material manner, the PTO probably will determine that the mark as originally registered is no longer in use and will cancel the registration, and the owner will be required to file a new trademark application for the new mark. Mere changes in style of lettering or changing the mark from uppercase to lowercase are acceptable. Until late 1989, the term of a trademark was twenty years; trademark registrations issued after late 1989 have a term of ten years and renewal periods of ten years.

The PTO allows nonuse of a mark only for exceptional circumstances, such as labor strikes or destruction of the registrant's facilities, forcing a halt in production of the trademarked goods. Failing to use the mark merely because the product is unprofitable or for other economic reasons is not excusable, and the registration will be canceled.

Although the PTO may cancel a registration, the owner may continue to use the mark. Because trademark rights in the United States arise from use, not registration, cancellation of a registration does not preclude the owner from using the mark. In many instances, registrations are canceled only because registrants forget to file the requisite documents. Thus, when checking PTO records, do not assume that because a mark is canceled that you have the right to use it. The owner may still be using the mark, relying on common law rights.

Making Your Mark Incontestable

After a mark registered on the Principal Register has been in continuous use for five years, and assuming there is no final decision adverse to or pending proceeding involving the owner's rights to the mark, the registrant may file an Affidavit of Incontestability (called a Section 15 Affidavit) with the PTO. Although a registrant is not required to file the Affidavit of Incontestability, it provides significant advantages to a trademark owner in that his or her rights to use the trademark become incontestable, meaning that the registration can be challenged only on the basis that the mark has been abandoned, it is functional, it has become generic, or the registration was procured through fraud. Thus, once a mark has achieved incontestability, it cannot be attacked as being confusingly similar to or infringing another's mark, and the grounds on which it can be challenged are very narrow. The filing fee for the Section 15 Affidavit of Incontestability is $200 per class.

Using the PTO's Trademark Electronic Application System (TEAS), registrants can file all postregistration documents electronically. TEAS is available 24 hours each day, seven days a week at the PTO's Web site at www.uspto.gov/teas/index.html.

Docketing Maintenance Dates

The process of filing required documents with the PTO to continue a registration in force is called maintenance. Trademark owners should establish a calendar or docketing system to remind them of the various maintenance filing dates. Alternatively, the trademark search companies identified in Chapter 3 will provide reminders for a fee. If properly maintained, trademarks can last forever; thus, investing some time and money in a docketing system, particularly for companies with significant inventories of marks, is critical. To check the status of a registered mark, call the PTO's status line at (703) 305-8747 or access the PTO's Trademark Applications and Registration Retrieval (TARR) database through the PTO's Web site at http://tarr.uspto.gov.

Abandonment of Trademarks

In the world of trademarks, the common saying is "Use it or lose it," referring to the fact that trademark rights can be lost or abandoned through nonuse. In fact, nonuse of a mark for three years creates a presumption that a mark has been abandoned. Although the owner can rebut this presumption, usually clear and convincing evidence is required to show that one has not abandoned a mark. Abandonment can occur even earlier than three years if an intent to abandon is shown. For example, if a company announces publicly that it is changing the name of its financial reporting software from REPORT RIGHT to MONEY TRACK, a court may well hold that the owner showed a clear intent to abandon REPORT RIGHT, thus making the mark available for use by another. Once a mark is lost, its owner cannot revive it. The owner must begin using the mark again, and its right of priority stems from the date use was resumed, not the date of original use.

Trademark owners cannot defeat the presumption of abandonment by a showing of some token use, such as for using the mark on a catalog that is distributed only within the company. On the other hand, if the product is expensive, such as an airplane, the fact that the owner sold only two planes in three years may well be sufficient use if such is standard in the industry.

Companies that believe another has abandoned its mark often petition to cancel the registration for the abandoned mark. Petitions to cancel are discussed in Chapter 6.

Genericide of Trademarks

Rights to marks can also be lost if the mark ceases to become an identifier of the source of goods and instead becomes a common name for goods, as is the case with *aspirin, yo-yo,* and *cellophane,* all of which were once valid trademarks and have lost their trademark significance through misuse by consumers. This genericide typically occurs when marks are used as nouns, as in "I need an aspirin for my headache." Thus, companies whose marks are well known guard against genericide by educating consumers as to the use of marks and often inserting the word "brand" after the mark. Thus, proper use is "I need adhesive tape" or "I need SCOTCH® brand tape" rather than "I need scotch tape."

Protecting Your Marks

Because lost marks cannot be revived, companies must be vigilant to protect against misuse of their marks that can lead to loss of rights. Following are some tips to promote proper use of marks:

▾ Marks should be used as adjectives, not as nouns. Marks used as nouns run the risk of becoming generic. Thus, it is acceptable to say

"DRAMAMINE® pills prevent motion sickness" and risky to say "Drama-mine is a motion sickness remedy." Famous marks are allowed some latitude, so the well-known jingle "Have you driven a Ford lately?" is permissible because of the long-standing fame of the FORD® trademark.

▾ Marks should not be used in the possessive or plural form. Thus, saying "Give me some dramamines" may convert the mark into a generic word.

▾ Marks should be displayed prominently in text. Many users capitalize the entire mark or display it in different font size or style from the surrounding text to draw attention to the fact that the word or matter is being used as a trademark.

▾ Marks should be displayed with the appropriate notice (® for registered marks and ™ or ℠ for unregistered marks). The notices show that the word or symbol is being used as a trademark. Because advertising material and brochures can appear cluttered if the registration notice is repeated numerous times, it is acceptable to use the notice the first time the mark is used and then omit it in subsequent uses in the copy.

▾ A notice should appear on the product or material that "XXX® is a registered trademark of ABC, Inc." The notice can be placed unobtrusively at the end of advertising copy in fine print.

▾ Marks should be used consistently. Continually changing typeface, script, or presentation creates consumer confusion and may lead to abandonment of a mark. Perhaps the most famous mark in the world, COKE®, has been consistently displayed in a stylized script fashion for years, and consumers the world over have come to instantly recognize the script style. Companies should endeavor to create a unified image for their goods and services. Constant revisions to trademarks undermine this goal.

Many companies with significant trademark inventories implement trademark compliance policies to educate their employees and those the company does business with about proper use of the company's marks. In some instances, a trademark compliance officer is appointed, and all advertising copy or other materials that display the mark must be approved by this officer before being released or disseminated. Companies also provide samples of their marks to others to ensure that they use the proper version of marks and not some modified version. See Figure 5-1 for a sample trademark compliance policy.

To ensure that others are not infringing on the company's marks, employees should be urged to monitor relevant trade journals, other publica-

Figure 5-1. Trademark compliance policy.

At the core of our business at Star Enterprises, Inc., are the trademarks we have developed over the years. We have expended a great deal of time, money, and effort in developing consumer recognition of our marks, and the marks are important company assets. Trademarks can be protected only if they are used properly. Therefore, this compliance policy provides guidelines to ensure that our marks are used properly by our employees, customers, and those with whom we do business, whether in internal or external communications, documents, packaging, or electronic messages. If you need additional assistance, please contact the Trademark Compliance Officer in the Legal Department.

1. *Identification of Marks.* Following are the registered trademarks ("marks") of Star Enterprises, Inc:

    STAR® (for high-quality watches)
    PARAGON® (for watchbands)
    POINTVISION® (for sports watches)

2. *Display of Marks.* Always display marks in capital letters or in distinctive typeface and with the trademark registration symbol ® slightly above and to the right of any mark, as is shown above. The registration symbol ® must be used the first time a mark appears in the copy of any printed or electronic media material. At the end of printed matter, use the following type of notice: "STAR® is a registered trademark of Star Enterprises, Inc."

3. *Use of Marks.* There are five rules relating to use of the company's marks:

    ▾ Always use any mark as an adjective, as in the following: "STAR® brand watches are the finest timepieces available" or "PARAGON® watchbands use the best leather in the marketplace."
    ▾ Do not use any mark as a noun. It is improper to say, "Buy a Star," "You'll never regret your purchase of a Paragon," or "A Pointvision is the top-selling sports watch today."
    ▾ Do not use marks in the plural or possessive form. It is improper to say, "Buy two Stars" or "Paragon's workmanship will astound you."
    ▾ Do not abbreviate or modify the marks in any way.
    ▾ Do not use the marks for goods for which they are not registered. Thus, STAR® may be used only in connection with high-quality watches, not in connection with watchbands.

---

tions, and trade shows to determine whether the company's marks are being infringed or misused. Many companies subscribe to a clipping service to locate uses of their marks. Similarly, competitors' Web sites should be visited periodically to check for infringing uses. Customers and business partners who are allowed to use the mark should be provided with usage guidelines, and their advertisements and Web sites should be checked to make sure they are displaying the company's marks properly.

Sale of Trademarks

Because trademarks are items of property, they can be sold to another. The sale of a trademark, whether of a registered mark or one subject to a pending use-based application, is called an assignment and must be in writing. The written document must state that the goodwill symbolized by the mark is being assigned with the mark. An assignment that fails to assign the goodwill of the mark with the mark is ineffective to transfer trademark rights. The new "owner" does not capture the seller's or assignor's prior use date and begins his or her own date of use of the mark. The assignment document need not be in any special form and is usually less than one page. See Figure 5-2 for a sample trademark assignment.

An owner need not assign all its marks. For example, a company could assign a mark relating to its wireless communication device and retain other marks it owns relating to computer software for accounting purposes. If an entire business is sold, however, it is presumed that all of the marks and their goodwill are sold or assigned with the business.

Although common law rights to a mark, registered marks, and applications based on actual use of a mark are all assignable, intent-to-use applications generally are not assignable. If the mark is the subject of an intent-to-use application, it has not been used. If it has not been used, there is no goodwill attached to the mark. Thus, there is really nothing to be assigned, and the PTO wants to ensure that parties do not apply for marks merely for the purpose of stockpiling them and then selling them to others. An exception exists when the mark is being assigned to a successor of the business of the applicant to which the mark pertains if that business is ongoing and existing. In such a case, an intent-to-use application can be assigned.

Although there is no requirement to notify the PTO of the assignment, it is prudent to file or record the assignment document with the PTO. Fees are minimal ($40 for the first mark being assigned in a document and $25 for each mark thereafter) and a form (Form 1681A) is available for downloading from the PTO Web site at www.uspto.gov. Recording the assignment provides public notice of the ownership of the mark so that later purchasers are bound by the sale. Recording also allows the PTO to correspond with the correct owner and provides a chain of title of the mark so that when a renewal application or Section 8 Affidavit of Use is filed by the new owner, the PTO will accept it. For example, if an original registration issues to

Figure 5-2. Trademark assignment.

WHEREAS Sanders & Hill, Inc., a New York corporation, with its address at 567 Tenth Avenue, Buffalo, New York ("Assignor"), is the owner of U.S. Registration No. 1,897,884 for the trademark OAK RIDGE CELLARS for wine issued May 15, 1994 (the "Mark") by the U.S. Patent and Trademark Office.

WHEREAS Bailey, Anders, and Franklin, LLC, a California limited liability company with its address at 1490 Ashford Place, St. Helena, California 98002 ("Assignee"), desires to acquire all of Assignor's right, title, and interest in and to the Mark, the registration therefor, and the goodwill symbolized thereby.

NOW, THEREFORE, for good and valuable consideration, the receipt and sufficiency of which are hereby acknowledged, Assignor hereby sells, transfers, and conveys all of its interest in and to the Mark together with the goodwill of the business associated with the Mark and the registration therefor.

Assignor represents and warrants that it owns the Mark, that no other party has any right, interest, or title in or to the Mark, that it has the legal right to assign the Mark to Assignee, and that such assignment does not infringe the rights of any other party. Assignor further represents and warrants that there are no pending claims or actions relating to the Mark.

Assignee shall have the right to file appropriate documents with the U.S. Patent and Trademark Office to ensure that title to and ownership of the Mark is registered in Assignee's name, and Assignor shall cooperate with Assignee with regard thereto and execute any documents reasonably required to effect the purposes of this Assignment. Assignee shall have the right to sue for and retain all damages for any past, present, or future infringements of the Mark.

This Assignment shall be binding on and inure to the benefit of the parties hereto and their respective successors and assigns.

Executed this 18th day of August 2000 at Buffalo, New York.

Sanders & Hill, Inc.   Bailey, Anders, and Franklin, LLC

By: _____   By: _____

Its: _____   Its: _____

Gap Company and then Gap assigns the mark to Eddie Bauer Limited without recording the assignment with the PTO, Eddie Bauer Limited's renewal documents will be rejected because the PTO records will reflect that Gap is the owner of the mark.

Licensing of Trademarks

Rather than selling a mark outright to another, a trademark owner can license the right to use a mark to another and continue to retain ownership of the mark. Trademark licensing arrangements are routinely seen in franchise agreements in which a franchisor, such as Burger King, allows its franchisees to use Burger King's marks. The licensor may grant an exclusive license, in which case the mark can be used only by the licensee, or a nonexclusive license, as is the case with franchise agreements, by which several parties have the right to use the licensor's marks. The licensor may retain rights to use the mark or may agree not to use the mark while the license is in effect. The licensor is paid a one-time lump sum license fee or receives periodic payments, called royalty payments, based on sales of the licensed product or service. In this way, trademarks provide a revenue stream for their owners.

A critical component of a license agreement is that the licensor must retain quality control of the mark, meaning that the licensor must retain the right to ensure that the goods and services offered by the licensee meet the licensor's standards. For example, Burger King must retain the right to monitor its franchisees to determine that the food products, cups, bags, and other items that bear the Burger King marks are of the quality and consistency used by Burger King itself. Failure to include quality control provisions results in what is called a naked license, and the licensor loses all rights to the mark. Thus, license agreements not only state that the licensee's use must be consistent with the licensor's quality control standards but generally allow the licensor to inspect use of the mark, review advertising materials that will display the mark, and be provided samples on a routine basis of the goods or materials that will bear the mark.

Although license agreements can be recorded with the PTO, there is no requirement to do so, and most parties do not record their license agreements on the basis that the agreement is a private one between parties and there is no need for it to become a public record. Foreign practice is quite different, however, and many foreign countries require that license agreements, called registered user agreements, be placed on file with the foreign trademark office in which the mark was originally registered. See Figure 5-3 for a sample trademark license agreement.

Using Trademarks as Collateral

Trademark owners may need to borrow money from lenders. Lenders typically require security for loans so that in the event of a default the lender can seize the property pledged as collateral or security for the loan. Trademarks can also be used as security or collateral. The parties usually enter

Figure 5-3. Trademark license agreement.

This Trademark License Agreement ("Agreement") is entered into February 15, 2001, by and between Jamison, Inc., a Washington corporation with its principal address at 4545 First Avenue, Seattle, Washington 89909 ("Licensor"), and McKnight Enterprises Co., a California corporation with its principal address at 1010 Van Ness Avenue, San Francisco, California 96601 ("Licensee").

WHEREAS Licensor is the owner of the trademark JAMISON (the "Mark") and U.S. Registration No. 1,980,990 therefor registered for men's clothing, namely shirts in I.C. 25 (the "Goods") and has the right to license the right to use the Mark to others;

WHEREAS Licensee desires to acquire an exclusive right to use the Mark subject to the terms of this Agreement and Licensor desires to grant a license therefor to Licensee;

NOW, THEREFORE, for good and valuable consideration, the receipt and sufficiency of which are hereby acknowledged, the parties agree as follows:

1. *Grant of License.* Subject to the terms of this Agreement Licensor grants to Licensee an exclusive, nontransferable right and license to use the Mark throughout the State of California (the "Territory") in connection with the Goods.
2. *Term.* Unless sooner terminated pursuant to Paragraph 6 below, this license is granted for a term of five (5) years.
3. *Ownership of Mark.* Licensee acknowledges that Licensor is the owner of the Mark and all rights thereto. Licensee further acknowledges that it has the right only to use the Mark pursuant to the terms of this Agreement and will not challenge or contest Licensor's ownership of the Mark or take any actions inconsistent with Licensor's sole and exclusive ownership of the Mark. Any use by Licensee of the Mark will inure to the benefit of Licensor, and Licensee acknowledges that this Agreement does not confer any rights to the Mark or any goodwill therein to Licensee except the right to use the Mark in accordance with the terms of this Agreement.
4. *Quality Control.* Licensee understands and acknowledges that the nature and quality of the Goods offered under the Mark shall be consistent with the Goods offered by Licensor under the Mark and shall be of the highest quality. At any time during the term of this Agreement, Licensor shall have the right to inspect the Goods offered by Licensee under the Mark. Licensor shall further have the right to inspect all uses by Licensee of the Mark to ensure that such uses are in compliance with Licensor's quality control standards. In the event of a breach by Licensee of any of such quality control standards, which breach remains uncured for fifteen (15) days after written notice thereof by Licensor, Licensor shall have the right to terminate this Agreement, and Licensee shall thereafter have no right to use the Mark in any manner or form.
5. *Infringement.* Licensee shall notify Licensor in writing of any unauthorized use of the Mark by any third parties.
6. *Default.* Licensee shall be in default of this Agreement and this Agreement shall automatically terminate upon the occurrence of any of the following events:
   a. Licensee ceases to conduct business for more than five (5) days.

      b. Licensee purports to transfer any rights to the Mark or any rights under this Agreement without Licensor's prior written consent.

      c. Licensee fails to maintain any of Licensor's quality control standards prescribed by Licensor for use of the Mark after fifteen (15) days written notice of such failure by Licensor.

      d. Licensee uses any mark confusingly similar to the Mark.

7. *General.* This Agreement shall be construed under the laws of the State of Washington. This Agreement contains the entire agreement of the parties with respect to the subject matter hereof and supersedes any prior understandings or agreements, whether oral or written. This Agreement may not be amended except by a writing signed by both parties. Licensee shall not transfer or assign any of its rights under this Agreement without the prior written consent of Licensor. Any notice required under this Agreement shall be made by registered mail, postage prepaid, to the addresses set forth in this Agreement and shall be effective when placed in the U.S. mail. This Agreement shall be binding on and shall inure to the benefit of the parties to this Agreement and their successors and assigns, if any.

Jamison, Inc.   McKnight Enterprises Co.

By: _____   By: _____

Its: _____   Its: _____

into a security agreement that specifies the particular marks being used as collateral. The security agreement is recorded with the PTO (using Form 1618A, the same form used to record assignments). When the debt is paid, Form 1618A is again filed or recorded with the PTO to release the marks from the security interest held by the bank or lender. While the security agreement exists, the trademark owner has all rights of ownership of the mark. The secured party's rights to the mark arise only upon a default by the trademark owner.

6

Trademark Infringement, Cancellations, and Dilution

Trademarks can be infringed by others. If a mark is registered with the U.S. Patent and Trademark Office (PTO), an infringement action can be initiated in federal court, and a variety of remedies can be imposed, from compensatory monetary damages, to destruction of offending goods, to punitive damages, to attorney's fees and costs. Trademark registrations can be cancelled if a petitioner proves that the registration should not have issued or that the mark has been abandoned. Finally, trademarks can also lose their distinctive quality by dilution, a whittling away of a trademark's strength or tarnishment of its reputation.

The Test for Determining Trademark Infringement

The test used to determine whether one party's mark infringes that of another is whether the use is likely to cause confusion, mistake, or deception among the relevant consuming public. Actual confusion is not necessary; it is likelihood of confusion that is measured. The factors discussed in Chapter 4, used by the PTO in determining whether to allow a registration for a mark that is similar to another's, are the same as those used by courts in determining whether infringement has occurred. Furthermore, intent to infringe is not necessary. An innocent infringement is just as damaging to a trademark owner as an intentional one. Although the defendant's intent to infringe may play a role in assessing damages, there is no requirement that a defendant have intended to infringe another's mark.

Although different courts apply slightly different tests, and no one factor is determinative, in general the following factors are considered in determining trademark infringement:

▼ *Similarity of the marks as to their appearance, sound, connotation, and commercial impression.* Marks need not be identical to infringe. In evaluating the similarities in marks, the emphasis is on the recollection of the average purchaser, who normally retains a general rather than specific impression of trademarks. Thus, SEYCOS used for watches was held likely to be confused with SEIKO® for watches, AQUA-CARE was held likely to be confused with WATERCARE® when both marks were used for water conditioning products, and RESPONSE was held likely to be confused with RESPONSE CARD® (with "Card" disclaimed) when both marks were used for banking services.

▼ *Similarity and nature of the goods and services offered under the marks.* Goods and services need not be identical or even competitive for likelihood of confusion to exist. It is sufficient that the goods and services of the parties are related in some manner or that the circumstances surrounding their marketing are such that they are likely to be encountered by consumers who would have the mistaken belief that they originate from the same source. For example, CAREER IMAGES used for retail women's clothing store services and clothing was held likely to be confused with CREST CAREER IMAGES® for uniforms. On the other hand, LITTLE PLUMBER® for a liquid drain opener was held not confusingly similar to LITTLE PLUMBER® for advertising services because the goods and services were highly unrelated, although the marks were identical.

▼ *The similarity of the channels of trade for the goods or services.* If goods offered under one mark are distributed only through retail and goods offered under the other mark are sold only to distributors, confusion may be reduced. Similarly, if goods bearing the marks are sold to different groups or advertised in different media, confusion is less likely.

▼ *The nature of the buyers for the goods.* Marks for goods bought on impulse or marks used with inexpensive items generally are more readily confused than marks used for expensive goods. Consumers do not exercise great care when purchasing inexpensive items, so similar marks are more likely to infringe. On the other hand, when purchasing expensive items, consumers give a great deal of thought and consideration to their purchasing decisions, and confusion is less likely. In sum, marks for goods offered to sophisticated consumers who are knowledgeable about the products and services they purchase are less likely to be confused than marks used in connection with inexpensive items.

▾ *The relative strength and weakness of the marks.* Strong marks are more easily infringed than weak, descriptive marks. Thus, numerous marks with *tech* or *plus* coexist, and consumers become adept at distinguishing between these numerous similar marks. Conversely, a strong coined mark such as XEROX® that has achieved wide fame and notoriety probably will be infringed by nearly any similar mark, no matter what goods or services are offered under the mark. Similarly, McDonald's has developed such a strong family of "Mc" marks that marks such as McPRETZEL, McRIB, and McDONUT have all been held confusingly similar to various McDonald's marks. In sum, strong marks are given broader protection than weak marks.

▾ *The existence of actual confusion.* Actual confusion is not necessary to find infringement. The test is whether confusion is likely. Nevertheless, if actual confusion is shown, the junior mark is likely to be held to infringe the senior mark. If the marks have coexisted for a number of years and there has been no confusion, a court may well hold that no confusion is likely. Owners generally establish confusion by submitting testimony from consumers who state that they were confused (usually shown by complaint letters to the company) or by survey evidence. Consumers often are randomly selected and are presented with both marks. The survey results are then presented to court. Surveys often are challenged on the basis that they suffer from design or methodology flaws that compromise their results. Even if there is some actual confusion, infringement is not necessarily found. For example, in one case, a court found that there was no likelihood of confusion between SCOTT® for plastic and paper household goods and SCOTT'S LIQUID GOLD® for furniture polish because the products had coexisted for four years, and there were fewer than twenty instances of actual confusion, although fifty million cans of the furniture polish had been sold.[1]

▾ *The defendant's intent.* Although intent is not a necessary element in a trademark infringement case, if it can be shown that a defendant adopted a mark similar to the plaintiff's mark with the intention of deriving a benefit from the plaintiff's business reputation, this fact alone may be enough to justify the inference that there is confusing similarity.

---

1. *Scott Paper Co. v. Scott's Liquid Gold*, 589 F.2d 1225 (3d Cir. 1978).

Infringement Actions

Once it is determined that another mark may be confusingly similar, a trademark owner should take aggressive action. Failure to take steps to protect a mark can be held to constitute a waiver of any rights in the mark. If a mark is federally registered, the U.S. Trademark Act allows the registrant to initiate a civil action in federal court against any party who used the mark without the registrant's consent in a manner likely to cause confusion. Prospective plaintiffs generally send a notice or letter called a cease and desist letter to the party who uses the allegedly infringing mark. The letter usually describes the first party's mark, states that the second party's mark is junior in time to the first mark, and demands that the alleged infringer cease and desist any further use of its competing mark. The prospective plaintiff needs to conduct some investigation before sending such a letter; if the recipient of the letter has seniority over the sender, the sender is now in the unfortunate position of having stated in writing the belief that the two marks are confusingly similar and may have difficulty defending against an infringement action brought by the other. See Figure 6-1 for a sample cease and desist letter.

If the cease and desist letter is ignored or the parties cannot resolve their differences, the plaintiff may bring an action for trademark infringement in federal court. The action is initiated by the filing of a complaint that sets forth a short and plain statement of the plaintiff's allegations. The defendant normally files an answer to the complaint and usually denies the plaintiff's allegations and asserts several defenses. The defendant may assert that the mark was abandoned, that it was procured through fraud, that it is functional, that it has become generic, that the plaintiff has acquiesced in the defendant's use of the mark and has waived its rights such that it is now barred from asserting infringement, or that the plaintiff has so unreasonably delayed in enforcing his or her rights that the defendant is prejudiced thereby in that it has expended significant sums in advertising and promoting the mark (a defense called laches). Another defense that is often asserted is that the defendant's use of the plaintiff's mark is a fair use. For example, assume ABC Paper Co. has a registration for BLUE DENIM® for its stationery product. If a competitor merely describes the color of its paper as blue denim, such is probably a fair use. The term *blue denim* is used merely to describe the color of a product and is not used in a trademark sense. Finally, defendants usually assert that the marks are not confusingly similar and introduce evidence of other similar marks to show that numerous other similar marks are coexisting.

Figure 6-1. Cease and desist letter.

November 30, 2000

Mr. James K. Kenney
Intellisystems, Inc.
506 Park Avenue
New York, New York 10090

> Re: Trademark STRATEGICON
>   U.S. Registration No. 1,980,778

Dear Mr. Kenney:

Strategic E-Systems, Inc. ("SES"), is the owner of U.S. Trademark Registration No. 1,980,778, registered on December 16, 1998 for the mark STRATEGICON, used in connection with computer programs for accounting and financial purposes. SES has used the STRATEGICON mark since at least February 1994 and has expended a great deal of time and money in establishing goodwill in its mark, which is known to consumers both nationally and internationally.

It has come to our attention that Intellisystems, Inc., has recently begun using the mark STRATEGIC-ON in connection with computer programs for maintaining accounting records. Your use of STRATEGIC-ON in connection with such goods is likely to cause confusion, deception, and mistake in the marketplace in that consumers, upon encountering your mark, may believe that the goods offered under the mark are associated with or emanate from SES.

SES therefore hereby demands that Intellisystems, Inc., immediately cease and desist from any further use of the mark STRATEGIC-ON or any confusingly similar mark in connection with any goods or services and cease and desist from offering, marketing, or selling any goods or services under such mark.

If SES does not receive your response within ten days of the date of this letter confirming that Intellisystems, Inc., has ceased all use of STRATEGIC-ON or any confusingly similar mark, SES will initiate an action in federal court for trademark infringement and will pursue all appropriate legal remedies, including injunctive relief, damages, and attorney's fees and costs incurred in protecting its valuable mark.

We look forward to hearing from you.

Sincerely,

_____
Strategic E-Systems, Inc.

Discovery will commence and the parties will take depositions of each other's employees, officers, and others to determine how and when the marks were created, how they are used, quantities of sales under the marks, and any other relevant evidence that would tend to show or disprove that the marks are likely to be confused. Documents can be requested, and interrogatories (sets of written questions) will be propounded by each party. If the parties cannot resolve the matter amicably, it proceeds to trial. A jury may be requested by either party but is not required.

Remedies for Infringement

Courts have wide latitude in fashioning remedies to protect marks from infringement. They can enter injunctions to forbid the defendant from any further use of the infringing mark; they can order a recall or destruction of infringing articles; they can order the offending party to use a disclaimer when it offers its goods, stating "ABC Inc. is not affiliated with XYZ Co."; and they can impose actual damages to compensate the plaintiff for the harm he or she has suffered. Damages often take the form of lost profits and lost sales. The defendant may be ordered to disgorge profits it has made from sales of products that used the infringing mark. The plaintiff's costs in bringing the action are recoverable (assuming the plaintiff is the prevailing party). The actual damages ordered by the court can be tripled. Such tripled damages generally are assessed only when the defendant intentionally infringed the mark. Similarly, attorney's fees generally are awarded only when the defendant's conduct has been willful or in bad faith, or if a contract provides for them. Damage awards can be significant.

Although it is possible to obtain insurance to protect against intellectual property claims, such insurance often is expensive, especially for companies engaged in business on the Internet, those in high-tech industries, and those with significant inventories of trademarks, patents, and copyrights. Consult a broker to determine the costs and feasibility of such insurance. Even without an intellectual property rider to a policy, consider relying on your general liability insurance if a claim is made against you for intellectual property infringement. Immediately notify your carrier and request that the carrier assume your defense. It is possible that protection for general advertising injury or other matters may be broad enough to cover certain intellectual property claims.

Petitions to Cancel Registrations

As discussed in Chapter 4, one who believes that a mark applied for with the PTO will cause damage if it is allowed to proceed to registration may oppose registration of the mark. The notice of opposition must be filed within thirty days of publication of the mark in the *Official Gazette*. Because this time period is so limited, the Lanham Act also allows one to petition to cancel a registration issued by the PTO.

A petition to cancel is filed by one who believes that continued registration of a mark will cause harm to the petitioner. The grounds on which a registration may be canceled are those that would have prevented registration, including alleging that the mark is scandalous, it comprises a living person's name without consent, it is deceptive, and so forth. In general, however, the most common grounds alleged in petitions to cancel are that the mark is merely descriptive, it is confusingly similar to that of a prior user, or it has been abandoned. In many cases, petitions to cancel are filed by those wanting to eliminate a prior registration so that their applications may proceed to registration.

A petition to cancel a mark registered on the Supplemental Register may be filed at any time. A petition to cancel a mark registered on the Principal Register may be filed within five years after registration if the grounds are those that would have justified a denial of registration (such as that the mark is merely descriptive, is primarily merely a surname, and the like). After five years, a petition to cancel a mark registered on the Principal Register can be filed only on the grounds that the mark has become generic, the mark is functional, the registration was obtained through fraud, or the mark has been abandoned.

The cancellation proceeding is initiated by the filing of a petition to cancel, with the Trademark Trial and Appeal Board (TTAB) setting forth a short and plain statement of the petitioner's grounds for cancellation. The filing fee is $300 per class. The cancellation proceeds much like an opposition. The registrant responds to the petition, discovery is conducted, and written briefs are filed. The TTAB renders a decision. Most cancellation proceedings, like oppositions, are resolved by voluntary agreement between the parties.

Trademark Dilution

Because the standard for infringement of a trademark is whether the junior mark is confusingly similar to the senior mark, instances arose in which challenged marks were not confusingly similar but still harmed the first mark. For example, consider a use of the mark REEBOK® for orange juice. Because the products offered under the REEBOK® marks are so different, there is little or no likelihood that consumers will confuse the marks and purchase orange juice when they really want to purchase shoes. Nevertheless, the owner of REEBOK® for shoes is damaged because the strength of its mark is being whittled away, blurred, and diluted. Similarly, using another's marks in an unsavory or disparaging fashion, such as selling dog food under the mark TIFFANY®, could not be precluded using traditional infringement confusion principles. Thus, courts and various state legislatures developed the dilution doctrine to protect marks from blurring or tarnishment.

In 1996, legislation was passed by Congress to add the dilution doctrine to the U.S. Trademark Act. According to current federal law, the owner of a famous mark is entitled to an injunction against another person's later commercial use in commerce of a famous mark if such use causes dilution of the distinctive quality of the famous mark. Other remedies, including damages, are also available. In determining whether a mark is famous, a court may consider the following factors:

- The degree of inherent or acquired distinctiveness of the mark
- The duration and extent of use of the mark in connection with the goods and services offered under the mark
- The duration and extent of advertising and publicity of the mark
- The geographic extent of the trading area in which the mark is used
- The channels of trade for the goods or services in which the mark is used
- The degree of recognition of the mark in the trading areas and channels of trade of both parties
- The nature and extent of the use of same or similar marks by other parties
- Whether the mark is registered with the PTO

Only famous marks are protected under the new Dilution Act. Examples of dilution of famous marks by blurring would include using PEPSI® for jewelry, TOYOTA® for cosmetics, or BANANA REPUBLIC® for motor-scooters. Those marks have achieved wide renown and fame, and to allow another to use the marks, even for entirely unrelated goods or services, would cause the famous marks to lose the distinctive quality they have achieved through the hard work and advertising funds invested in them by their owners.

Famous marks can also be diluted through tarnishment, a use that brings the mark into disrepute or contempt or that occurs when the famous mark is used to promote inferior goods. One of the first examples of tarnishment was the use of Coca-Cola Company's famous mark on a poster promoting cocaine use that displayed the slogan ENJOY COCAINE in the same color and script as the Coca-Cola Company used in promoting its beverages. Such a use will not cause confusion of consumers but clearly harms Coca-Cola's interests in its internationally famous mark. Other examples of dilution by tarnishment have included "Genital Electric" and "Buttwiser" for t-shirts, which were found to tarnish the GENERAL ELECTRIC® and BUDWEISER® marks, respectively.

Under the new federal Dilution Act, three forms of uses of famous marks are permissible:

1. Use of a famous mark in comparative advertising (thus making it acceptable to advertise that "STARBUCKS® brand coffee is not as full-bodied as the MAXWELL HOUSE® brand," assuming such statement is true)
2. Noncommercial use of a famous mark (thus allowing use of a famous mark for educational or nonprofit purposes)
3. All forms of news reporting (thus enabling news commentary about lawsuits or other matters involving famous marks)

Until passage of the anti-cybersquatting law in late 1999 (discussed in Chapter 7), the dilution doctrine was often used to shut down Web sites that used famous marks for the purpose of luring traffic to the site. For example, in 1996 Hasbro Inc., the owner of the famous CANDYLAND® mark, successfully precluded another company from using the address *candyland.com* for a site promoting sexually explicit goods and services. Under the new anti-cybersquatting legislation, such uses can be prohibited directly without the need for reliance on the dilution doctrine.

Trademark Counterfeiting

Trademark counterfeiting is the use of a party's mark on "knockoff" goods, such as placing the ROLEX® mark on inferior watches, placing the GUCCI® mark on inferior quality handbags, and placing BEANIE BABY® tags on nonauthentic toys. The inferior goods often are sold at swap meets or on the street at vendors' stands. Universities, music groups, and athletic teams routinely encounter unauthorized uses of their names and logos in connection with inferior quality t-shirts or athletic gear. For example, before game four of the 2000 World Series, Major League Professional Base-ball Properties, Inc. seized 15,000 items of unauthorized merchandise that displayed the league's trademarks. Although statutes allow the immediate seizure and destruction of the counterfeit goods, long-term relief often is difficult to obtain, with the counterfeiters simply moving their wares to another street corner or flea market until the next detection.

Owners of federally registered marks can deposit their registrations with the U.S. Customs Office, which will then monitor incoming goods and block importation of infringing articles. This method of protection against counterfeiters is effective in stopping importation of counterfeit goods from foreign countries.

7

Trademarks and the Internet

The phenomenal growth in the use of the Internet and electronic commerce has led to a variety of new issues in trademark law. Trademarks can be easily infringed by others' domain names and on others' Web sites. To remedy abuse, Congress has outlawed the practice of cybersquatting, the bad faith registration of a domain name for the purpose of selling it to its rightful owner. Congress and the courts are struggling to keep pace with the impact of technology on trademarks.

Domain Names and Trademark Law: Cybersquatting

A domain name is one's address on the World Wide Web. Although individuals and companies throughout the United States can share more than one name or address (for example, DELTA AIR LINES® coexists with DELTA DENTAL®, and DOVE BAR® for ice cream coexists with DOVE® for soap), domain names are unique identifiers and cannot be shared by more than one entity. Most companies use part of their name as their domain name. For example, IBM's domain name or Web address is www. ibm.com. Such an address makes it easier for consumers to locate IBM on the Web because many will simply make an educated guess that a company's Web address is the same as its name plus the identifier *.com* used for commercial sites.

77

As many small companies register their names on the Web and establish Web sites, there are greater chances that companies with similar or identical names will bump into each other in cyberspace. Previously, the seller of gift baskets in a small suburb of Boston might never have known that another company was offering similar services under a similar or identical name in Idaho. When each offered its goods locally, there was little chance of confusion or infringement. However, the Internet has allowed these companies to discover each other, leading to numerous disputes over trademarks and domain names, and making even more compelling the need for a comprehensive trademark search before the launch of a mark for a product or service.

There are two parts to a domain name: the generic top-level domain (the portion to the right of a period, such as *com* or *gov*, sometimes called a suffix) and the secondary domain (the portion to the left of the period, such as *hoovers* in *www.hoovers.com*, sometimes called a prefix). The typical generic top-level domain indicators are *com* and *net*, representing commercial sites; *gov*, representing government sites; *edu*, indicating educational institutions' sites; *mil*, indicating military sites; and *org*, which originally indicated a nonprofit organization but may indicate a commercial enterprise as well. Domain names are valuable property and have been sold as assets by one company to another.

In the early 1990s the National Science Foundation granted exclusive rights to a company called Network Solutions, Inc. (NSI), located in northern Virginia, to register domain names. NSI registered only 7,000 domain names in 1993. By late 1999, NSI had registered 8.1 million domain name registrations, charging moderate registration fees.[1] Because many individuals challenged NSI's exclusive franchise on assigning domain names, a new nonprofit corporation, the Internet Corporation for Assigned Names and Numbers (ICANN), was created in the late 1990s to foster competition in the lucrative business of registering domain names and to oversee the domain name industry. In late 2000, ICANN approved seven new top-level domains, including *biz*, restricted to businesses; *pro*, for licensed professionals; and *name*, for personal name registrations.

In the early days of domain name registrations, unscrupulous individuals and companies often registered domain names including the names or marks of famous companies or individuals for the sole purpose of ransoming or selling the addresses to their rightful owners. For exam-

1. Mary Gravely, "Lord of the Domain," *TECHNOLOGY Virginia*, (March/April 2000): 30–32.

ple, one person alone registered nearly 250 domain names, including www.deltaairlines.com and www.neiman-marcus.com. To end this practice, Congress passed the Anticybersquatting Consumer Protection Act in 1999 to outlaw domain name piracy. The act added a new provision to the U.S. Trademark Act to allow injured parties to sue for bad faith registration of their names, trafficking in the use of domain names that infringe or dilute famous marks, and profiteering in registering the names of famous people as domain names. A court may award damages and may order the cancellation of the infringing domain name or its transfer to its rightful owner. The new law permits an award of $1,000 to $100,000 per domain name, in lieu of the owner having to prove actual damages.

In October 2000, a cybersquatter who registered five Internet domain names in bad faith was ordered to pay $500,000 in damages and more than $30,000 in attorney's fees.

Not all uses are prohibited. For example, in *Hasbro, Inc. v. Clue Computing, Inc.*, 66 F. Supp. 2d 117 (D. Mass. 1999), the court held that Clue Computing did not infringe or dilute Hasbro's famous CLUE® mark used for its board game because the computer company had its own rights in the name. However, it is clear that bad faith registrations of another's name or a confusingly similar name can be enjoined. Immediately after the act was passed, actor Brad Pitt used it to sue the registrants of www.bradpitt.net and www.bradpitt.com in federal court in California. In mid-2000, the International Olympic Committee and two related organizations filed a civil suit under the act to shut down more than 1,800 Web sites containing the words *Olympic*, *Olympics*, or *Olympiad*, most of which related to pornography and gambling.

Even a good faith use might be prohibited. In June 2000, the United States District Court for the Northern District of Iowa held that Ford Financial Services (a company named after its founder) could not use *Ford* in its trademark or domain name because it was likely to produce consumer confusion with Ford Motor Company, which held a variety of trademark registrations for related financial services including *Ford* and also used *Ford* in its domain name. The court held that the right to use a personal name is not unlimited, and because the automaker had prior, distinctive, and famous use, consumers were likely to be deceived by Ford Financial Service's domain name. On the other hand, the use of *Ford* for a service not offered by or related to one used by Ford Motor Company, such as catering services or health care services, should be permissible.

The Anticybersquatting Act shields domain name registrars such as

NSI from liability for registration of domain names unless there is a showing of bad faith intent to profit from such registration. ICANN has taken the position that it is the responsibility of the party wanting to register a domain name to determine whether the application infringes another's rights.

ICANN has also issued a Uniform Domain Name Dispute Resolution Policy to resolve disputes between parties over their domain names. In its first six months, ICANN's dispute policy resulted in 327 decisions. Disputes arising from abusive registrations, such as cybersquatting, are quickly and inexpensively handled, mainly online, and ICANN has the authority to cancel domain names or to order transfers of domain names to their rightful owners, leading many experts to believe that the new anticybersquatting legislation coupled with ICANN's dispute resolution policy will eventually eliminate the practice of cybersquatting. Some uncertainty remains, however, because in mid-2000 a federal judge in Illinois ruled that courts are not bound by the administrative proceedings of ICANN. Thus, although ICANN can cancel a domain name, its decision may not be the final word in the matter.

Domain names can be registered with the U.S. Patent and Trademark Office (PTO) as trademarks as long as they function as source identifiers and not mere addresses. In fact, as of mid-2000, the PTO had more than 15,000 pending applications including the term *.com.*

Hyperlinking, Jurisdiction, and Complaint Sites

A variety of new trademark issues have emerged as use of the Internet has expanded. Three of the thorniest issues involve linking to others' sites, the question of where a Web site owner can be sued, and whether complaint sites set up to disparage a company can be prohibited.

Linking

Many Web sites display links, allowing users to click on a word or symbol and be immediately transported to a new location, either within that Web site or on another site. Although the practice of linking to another's Web site is common, the legality of the practice of deeplinking, or transporting a user deep within another's site rather than to the first page of the site, is unclear. Some companies have argued that a link that takes users beyond their home pages and deep within the site allows users to bypass valuable advertising that traditionally appears on the home page. Courts are divided on the issue, with some holding that such linking is merely a form of protected free speech and others concentrating on whether the information linked to is a trade secret or libelous material, in which case the linking may be prohibited. Moreover, courts are examining whether providing links to a site featuring copyrighted material is a form of copyright infringement. Thus, linking to any portion of another's Web site is legally risky.

An issue similar to hyperlinking involves the use of metatags, which transport a user to an unintended site. Some plaintiffs have been successful in alleging that the use of such metatags is a form of trademark infringement because it is an improper and harmful use of another's valuable mark.

Jurisdiction

Generally, a person can be sued only in a jurisdiction in which the person is present, conducts systematic business, or has some minimum contacts. Thus, a person who sells goods only in Miami cannot be forced to defend himself or herself in Cleveland. Because the Internet knows no borders, questions have arisen as to whether Web site operators can be sued outside their home state or those in which they actively conduct business.

Although the courts are continuing to explore this issue, at present asserting jurisdiction over a party depends on the nature and extent of business being conducted on the Web. If a party merely posts information about itself on a Web site and describes its services, such a passive site will not subject the party to jurisdiction throughout the United States. At the other end of the spectrum, if users can purchase goods and services and enter into contracts with the Web site owner by using the Web site, the owner will be subject to jurisdiction in any forum in which the Web site is accessible and such business is conducted. The more difficult cases are those in the middle, in which users interact to some extent with the Web site owner, sharing and communicating information. In general, courts have required a fairly high level of interactivity between the site and the user before imposing jurisdiction on Web site owners, based on their virtual rather than physical presence in a state.

Complaint Sites

The ease of communicating over the Web has fostered the growth of consumer complaint sites in which consumers post messages and information
complaining about various companies. One of the more famous recent
cases involved a site called Bally Sucks, in which an individual posted
vitriolic messages about Bally Total Fitness Centers. The court held that
there was no infringement for the following reasons:

- The site was a noncommercial form of protected free speech.
- Consumers would not be confused because the addition of the word
  Sucks to *Bally* clearly distinguished the consumer site from Bally's
  own marks.

Thus, posting information about a company on a Web site is permissible as long as there is no confusing use of a trademark, the information
is noncommercial, and it is consumer commentary rather than false and
defamatory.

Tips for Trademark Use in the Internet Age

Because the issues involving the use of trademarks on the Internet continue to evolve, users of another's mark on the Web should err on the side
of caution. Follow these tips:

- Never use another party's trademark on your Web site without permission. Even companies with whom you have strategic alliances may require prior consent before their mark can be displayed on your site.
- Never use a mark that is confusingly similar to that of another on
your Web site. Infringement can occur just as readily in the cyberworld as
in the real world.
- Do not link to another party's Web site without permission. Most
companies readily grant permission, believing that the more people who
visit their site, the better it is for their business.
- Be extremely careful in posting information about another person
or company. Tarnishment of a mark is actionable under the new federal
Dilution Act, and defamation (false oral or written statements) is always

actionable, no matter what form it takes and through what media it is offered.

▾ Understand that operating an active Web site, taking orders, and allowing purchases through your site may subject you to jurisdiction in any location in which your site is accessible.

8

Copyright Basics

Businesses generally possess a wealth of copyrightable information. Literary works, meaning those expressed in letters and numbers, possessing a minimum of creativity, are eligible for copyright protection. Works need not have artistic merit to qualify for copyright protection. Thus, even advertising and marketing materials, POWER POINT® presentations, and other audiovisual works qualify for protection. Although ideas, systems, and methods are not protectable under copyright law, even forms used by businesses are copyrightable if they measure up to some minimum threshold of creativity. There are many advantages to securing a federal copyright registration, but copyright protection exists from the time a work is created in fixed form, and no advance permission is required from the U.S. Copyright Office to use a copyright notice. Because of the ease of dissemination of works using the Internet, companies must aggressively protect their works from infringement by others.

Introduction to Copyrights

Copyright is a form of intellectual property protection that protects original works of authorship that are fixed in a tangible form of expression, including literary, dramatic, musical, and artistic works such as poetry, novels, movies, songs, computer software, and architecture. Copyright registration is inexpensive and easily accomplished.

Before the 1976 Copyright Act was passed, a distinction was drawn between published and unpublished works. A published work is one that is distributed to the public for sale or otherwise transferred to another, such as by rental or lending. An example of an unpublished work is a diary or journal maintained by the author and not distributed to the public. Rights to an unpublished work lasted forever; once the work was published, however, it became subject to a term of protection for fifty-six years.

The 1976 Copyright Act eliminated the distinctions between published and unpublished works. Under current law, an original work is protected automatically from the moment of its creation in a fixed form, whether it is published or not. Fixation requires that the work be sufficiently stable or permanent that it can be perceived, reproduced, or otherwise communicated for a period of more than transitory duration. A song, for example, can be fixed in sheet music or in phonographic disks, or both, and a poem is fixed when it is written or typed. Thus, nearly anything that can be expressed in a tangible form can be protected, including computer software and videotapes. Live performances, such as street performances, campaign speeches, and standup comedy routines are not protectable unless the material is written down or the performance is simultaneously recorded.

Copyrights are governed exclusively by the U.S. Copyright Act, found at 17 U.S.C. §§ 101 et seq. The Copyright Act can be located on the Copyright Office Web site at www.loc.gov/copyright (or http://lcweb.loc.gov/copyright) or by accessing the Web site www4.law.cornell.edu/uscode. There is no such thing as a state copyright, and all rights relating to copyright are found in federal law. Another excellent Web site providing links to numerous copyright resources is Copyright Resources on the Internet at http://groton.k12.ct.us/mts/pt2a.htm.

The U.S. Copyright Office

The U.S. Copyright Office is a department of the Library of Congress, the world's largest library, and is located at 101 Independence Avenue SE, Washington, DC 20559-6000. The Copyright Office administers copyright law and handles the process of copyright registration. The Copyright Office generally registers about 600,000 copyrights each year; it is implementing a system by which applications and other copyright-related documents can be submitted electronically.

The Copyright Office offers a variety of useful publications and forms. These materials can be obtained by writing to the office (Publications Section, LM-455, Copyright Office, Library of Congress, Washington, DC 20559-6000), ordering through a forms hotline (202-707-9100), ordering through a fax-on-demand service (202-707-2600), or downloading the publications and forms from the Internet. The Copyright Public Information Office provides information specialists to answer questions by phone (202-707-3000).

What Can Be Protected under Copyright Law

Article I, Section 8 of the U.S. Constitution provides that Congress has the power to promote the progress of science and useful arts by securing to authors and inventors the exclusive right to their respective writings and discoveries. This provision is the foundation of our copyright law. The term *writings* has been construed broadly over the past two hundred years to protect musical works, architectural works, sculptures, videogames, and developing technologies. The nearly insatiable demand of consumers for books, movies, music, and computer software has resulted in copyright industries (any stores or entities that sell or offer copyrighted materials) accounting for nearly 6.5 percent of America's gross domestic product.

The first requirement for copyrightability is that a work must be original, meaning that it must arise from its author's creative intellectual effort, as distinguished from the copying of an existing work.[1] Although a work must be original, it need not be the only one of its kind. Thus, if two authors independently create the same song, both works are original and copyrightable, although they are not novel. As long as the work is not copied, it is original. Moreover, the level of creativity required is not high. Even a slight amount of creativity suffices.

The broad scope of copyright protection extends to all writings, and there is thus no inherent constitutional limitation as to what is protected under copyright law, but the following are the primary categories of copyrightable works:

▾ *Literary works.* Literary works are those expressed in words, numbers, or other verbal or numerical symbols and include a wide variety of works, such as fiction, nonfiction, poetry, textbooks, reference works, some directories, dissertations, speeches, catalogs, advertising copy, compila-

1. *Feist Publications, Inc. v. Rural Telephone Svc. Co.*, 499 U.S. 340 (1991).

tions of information, and computer programs. Characters found in literary works may be protectable if they possess a high degree of distinctiveness. Thus, the idea of a hero who saves innocent victims from peril is not protectable; however, an individual who changes from a meek character to a red-caped flying hero is protectable. Similarly, the concept of an athlete who triumphs against insurmountable odds is not copyrightable; however, a boxer with characteristics similar to those of Rocky Balboa would infringe the literary character in the *Rocky* movies. Finally, unlike trademark law, which forbids registration of scandalous and immoral matter, even immoral works merit copyright protection. Thus, even vile and racist matter is protectable under copyright law, primarily to protect First Amendment rights.

▾ *Musical works, including accompanying words.* A musical composition consists of music, including any accompanying words, and may be in the form of sheet music, a cassette tape, record, or CD. The author usually is the composer and possibly a lyricist. A musician who performs the work has an independent copyrightable interest in his or her arrangement of the work as a sound recording, separate and distinct from the composer's rights in the underlying musical work.

▾ *Dramatic works, including accompanying words.* A dramatic work is a play or theatrical performance. Scripts prepared for cinema, radio, and television are also protectable as dramatic works. Dramatic works usually include spoken text, plot, and directions for actions. If music accompanies a play or drama, the entire work is viewed as a dramatic work, and the music is not an independent musical work.

▾ *Pantomimes and choreographic works.* A pantomime is a performance that uses gestures and expressions rather than sound to communicate an idea or situation. Choreography is the composition and arrangement of dance movements and patterns (usually intended to be accompanied by music) but does not include simple and well-known dances such as the polka or foxtrot. However, if the steps in a polka are incorporated into an original dance, the entire work is protectable. Because of the fixation requirement, pantomimes cannot be protected unless they are recorded or filmed, and choreographic works must be notated on paper or filmed to be protectable.

▾ *Pictorial, graphic, and sculptural works.* This broad category of visual arts consists of two- and three-dimensional works of fine, graphic, and applied art, photographs, prints, art reproductions, cartoons, maps, globes, jewelry, fabrics, games, technical drawings, diagrams, posters, toys, sculptures, and charts.

▾ *Motion pictures and other audiovisual works.* Motion pictures are audiovisual works consisting of a series of related images that, when shown in succession, convey an impression of motion, together with accompanying sound, if any. They are typically embodied in film, videotape, or videodisk. Feature films, training videos, documentaries, and slide presentations are all protectable. Sounds accompanying motion pictures and audiovisual works are protectable with the motion picture or audiovisual work; they are not separately protectable as musical works or sound recordings.

▾ *Sound recordings.* A sound recording is different from a musical work. A sound recording may include musical sounds but often includes recordings of dramas or lectures. The author of a musical work is the composer and lyricist, if any. The author of a sound recording is the performer whose performance is fixed or the record producer who processes the sounds, or both. For example, the music and lyrics for the song "All I Wanna Do" were written by Sheryl Crow. If Toni Braxton wants to perform "All I Wanna Do," she must obtain permission from the songwriter, Sheryl Crow. Toni Braxton's rendition of "All I Wanna Do" is copyrightable as a sound recording. Toni Braxton and her record producer can claim copyright in the sound recording only to protect their particular arrangement of "All I Wanna Do" from misappropriation or duplication. If Garth Brooks later wants to perform "All I Wanna Do," he must obtain permission from Sheryl Crow; no permission need be obtained from Toni Braxton or her record producer because they are not the authors of the underlying musical work.

▾ *Architectural works.* An architectural work is the design of a building as embodied in some tangible medium of expression, including a building, architectural plans, or drawings. Individual standard features such as windows or doors are not protectable. Although copyright protection does not extend to useful articles, an exception has been made since late 1990 to protect buildings, whether used for human habitation or commercial purposes. Although the design of a building cannot be copied and reproduced, because the building is visible to the public, anyone can take pictures of it or display it in a movie or photograph. Thus, the image of the famous pyramid-shaped Transamerica Building in San Francisco routinely appears in movies.

Exclusions from Copyright Protection

According to federal law, copyright protection does not extend to the following:

▾ *Ideas, methods, or systems.* Copyright protection is not available for ideas or procedures for doing, making, or building things; scientific or technical methods or discoveries; business operations or procedures; mathematical principles, formulas, or algorithms; or any other concept, process, or method of operation (as distinguished from a description, explanation, or illustration of such). Thus, once an idea is described or expressed, it is protected by copyright. For example, assume you have a brilliant idea for a television game show in which people will answer questions posed by a television personality and can win a million dollars. If you mention the idea to a friend who then develops a written script for the television program, there has been no copyright violation. Your idea is not protectable. Your friend's expression of that idea is protectable. The legal principle describing this concept often is called the idea–expression dichotomy, referring to the fact that ideas are not copyrightable but the expression of those ideas is copyrightable.

▾ *Useful articles.* Designs for useful articles, such as vehicular bodies, wearing apparel, household appliances, and the like are not protected by copyright; however, the design of a useful article is subject to copyright protection to the extent that its pictorial, graphic, or sculptural features can be said to exist independently from the useful object itself. Thus, although clothing is itself not copyrightable (as is clear from the release of knockoff imitations and reproductions of dresses immediately after the Academy Awards presentations), the actual sketches of the clothing are protectable; moreover, if certain distinctive appliques and items are embroidered on the apparel, they may be protectable. Similarly, although a car is not copyrightable, the famous statuette that appears as a hood ornament on a Jaguar automobile is protectable. In both cases, the item attached to the useful article can exist independently of the useful article itself.

▾ *Titles, names, short phrases, slogans, familiar symbols or designs, and mere lists of ingredients.* Names, titles, and phrases are not subject to copyright protection. Thus, numerous textbooks share the title *Introduction to American History.* Even if a title or slogan is distinctive, it cannot be protected by copyright. A distinctive slogan may well qualify for trademark protection, however. Moreover, recipes, labels, and formulas are not protectable. When a recipe or formula is accompanied by substantial literary explanation or directions, however, such written matter may be copyrightable, but the recipe or formula itself, a mere list of items, remains unprotected by copyright.

▾ *Common property.* Works consisting entirely of information that is common property and contains no original authorship, such as standard calendars, height and weight charts, tape measures and rulers, and lists or tables taken from public documents or other common sources, are not copyrightable.

▾ *U.S. government works.* Copyright protection is not available for any work of the United States government, such as statutes, reports, or white papers. Although the government can own a copyright granted to it by another, its own works are available and free to all to copy and use. Works produced by state and local government entities are not covered by federal copyright law; state statutes may control ownership and use of the material.

▾ *Public domain works.* Works of the U.S. government often are said to be in the *public domain*, meaning they are available for all to use. Other public domain works include works whose copyright has expired. At all times, copyrights have been of limited duration. Although the period of protection has varied, once protection expires, the work is available for all to use. Thus, a novel written during the Civil War can be made into a movie without any permission. Once the movie is made, however, a new copyright exists in the movie, and during its term of copyright protection, no one can make a sequel to the movie or some other derivative work based on the movie without its author's consent.

▾ *Facts.* Facts are not protected by copyright. Thus, dates of birth and death, population statistics, and so forth cannot be protected under copyright law. Although an individual may arrange certain facts in a creative way, creating a copyright in that particular arrangement, as is seen in an almanac, the underlying facts themselves are available to others to use.

Compilations, Collections, and Derivative Works

Copyright extends not only to newly created works but also to preexisting works that have been compiled or collected in some unique fashion and to new versions of old works.

Compilations and Collective Works

Authors often select preexisting materials and then combine them in a unique manner. Thus, an author might create an almanac of information containing birth and death dates of famous people, lists of award-winning novels, and tables relating to employment statistics. Although these elements in themselves are not copyrightable because they are facts, the author's selection and arrangement of them into a unique product qualifies for copyright protection as a compilation. Likewise, although recipes themselves are not copyrightable, a unique arrangement of them into a recipe book may qualify as a protectable compilation.

Not every compilation of otherwise uncopyrightable facts or common material qualifies for protection. For example, in *Feist Publications, Inc. v. Rural Telephone Svc. Co.*, the Supreme Court stated that a directory of telephone white pages was not copyrightable. Its alphabetical arrangement of names and phone numbers did not reflect sufficient creativity because listing names, phone numbers, and towns in alphabetical order is a common practice.

Included in the definition of *compilation* is *collective works*. A collection is a work such as a periodical issue, anthology, or encyclopedia in which a number of contributions, each of which is a separate work, are assembled into a collective whole. Thus, if an author decides to create a book collecting the ten best American short stories of 2000 or a CD assembling Academy Award–winning movie theme songs, the resulting arrangement is protected under copyright law as a collection. The author or collector must obtain permission from the author of each short story or song to include it in the collection. The unique resulting arrangement of previously copyrighted works is itself copyrightable by the new author as a collection because original authorship is involved in deciding which items to include and the manner of their arrangement.

Derivative Works

A derivative work is one based on a preexisting work. Thus, sequels, fictionalizations, translations, or other works that recast or transform a preexisting work qualify for protection as derivative works. The authors of the underlying original work and the derivative work may be different. For example, an expert psychiatrist may add a foreword to a previously published book about Dr. Sigmund Freud. The original author of the book continues to own all rights in the underlying book, and the psychiatrist owns rights to the foreword created by her. In other instances, the authors may be the same, as is the case when a programmer creates a computer program and then later creates a new version of it. Both the original work and the later derivative work are the product of the same author, and each work is separately copyrightable.

To be copyrightable, the derivative work must be different enough from the original to be regarded as a new work and must contain a substantial amount of new material. Making minor changes or additions of little substance to a preexisting work does not qualify the work as a new version for copyright purposes.

Following are some examples of derivative works:

- Television movie of the week based on a novel
- The movie *Chorus Line,* based on the earlier play
- An English translation of a novel originally written in Swedish

The copyright in the derivative work covers only the additions, changes, or other new material appearing for the first time in the work. It does not extend to any preexisting material and does not imply a copyright in that material. Consequently, only the owner of a copyright in a work has the right to prepare, or authorize someone else to create, a new version of that work. Thus, after you see the movie *The Matrix,* you cannot create a sequel based on the movie. Only its author can create the sequel or give consent to another to do so.

Semiconductor Chip Protection

In 1984 Congress established a new form of intellectual property right for the protection of the masks used to create the semiconductor chips used in a variety of consumer and commercial products. This new form of protection was deemed necessary to compensate for the fact that copyright law did not protect useful articles such as semiconductor chips used in many appliances, and patent law provided inadequate protection for these chips, primarily because they were mere obvious innovations of prior art. The Semiconductor Chip Protection Act of 1984 thus created an entirely new form of intellectual property protection. Because many of the concepts for semiconductor chip protection are based on copyright law principles, protection of the masks used to create the chips often is discussed concurrently with other copyright law concepts.

Masks are the stencils used to etch or encode an electronic circuit on a semiconductor chip. A mask work must be registered within two years after the work is first commercially exploited anywhere in the world, or rights are lost. The work is registered with the Copyright Office using Form MW, and protection lasts for ten years from the date protection begins (ten years from registration or ten years from commercial exploitation, whichever occurs first). The filing fee is $75. A mask work cannot be reproduced, imported, or distributed without its owner's authorization. The mask work registration form and additional information about semiconductor chip protection can be obtained at the Copyright Office Web site at www.lcweb.gov/copyright.

9

The Rights of Copyright Owners

Copyright owners have a variety of exclusive rights under federal law, including the right to reproduce their works, prepare derivative works based on the copyrighted work, distribute copies of the work by sale or lease, perform the work, and display the work. Although there are a number of limitations and exceptions, in general a violation of any of these exclusive rights is copyright infringement.

The Five Basic Rights of Copyright Owners

Under federal law, copyright owners have the exclusive right to do and authorize others to do the following:

- ▾ To reproduce the work
- ▾ To prepare derivative works based on the work
- ▾ To distribute copies of the work to the public by sale or other transfer of ownership or by rental, lease, or lending
- ▾ To perform the work publicly (in the case of literary, musical, dramatic, choreographic works, pantomimes, and motion pictures and other audiovisual works)
- ▾ To display the work publicly (in the case of literary, musical, dra-

matic, and choreographic works, pantomimes, and pictorial, graphic, or sculptural works, including the individual images of a motion picture of other audiovisual work)
▾ In the case of sound recordings, to perform the work publicly by means of a digital audio transmission

It is illegal for anyone to violate any of these rights, often called a bundle of rights, provided by law to copyright owners (although there are some limitations on these rights).

The Right of Reproduction

Perhaps the most significant right of copyright owners is the sole right to reproduce their works. Only the owner has the right to reproduce the work (or allow another to do so). Thus, if you rent the video *American Beauty* and make a duplicate tape of it, you have violated the author's right of reproduction, even if your only intent is to view it privately rather than to exploit it for some commercial or profit-making purpose. Similarly, photocopying pages from a book is a violation of copyright law, whether the use is intended for your convenience so you can read the material later at home or whether the use is for profit. Similarly, secretly taping a concert is a violation of the exclusive right of copyright owners to reproduce their work. Only the copyright owner has the right to reproduce the concert on tape or some other medium. In the famous case *Sony Corporation of America v. Universal City Studios*, 464 U.S. 417 (1984), however, the U.S. Supreme Court held that private, noncommercial taping of television programs was permissible because the use was only for time shifting to watch the program at a later time.

Libraries and archives are granted exceptions to the exclusive right of reproduction so they can make copies of a work that is damaged or deteriorating. Generally, they are permitted to reproduce a work as long as their collections are open to the public and a copyright notice appears on the work.

To facilitate requests to reproduce copyrighted works, a nonprofit entity called Copyright Clearance Center (CCC) acts as a clearinghouse to permit individuals, teachers, and others to obtain permission to reproduce copyrighted works. CCC collects royalties for the use of these works and distributes them to the owners of the works. Companies that subscribe to trade journals often enter into arrangements with CCC so that they can make copies of articles in the journals and then distribute them to interested employees. CCC's Web site is www.copyright.com.

The Right to Create Derivative Works

As discussed in Chapter 8, only the author of a copyrighted work has the right to create derivative works based thereon or allow another to do so or adapt the work. Thus, you cannot translate *Tuesdays with Morrie* into another language, create a sequel to any of John Grisham's novels, or develop a television movie of the week based on a country–western ballad unless you have the copyright owner's permission to do so. Even if you have been given permission to create a sequel or other derivative work, your rights are limited to your particular newly created derivative work, and you have no rights to the underlying copyrighted work.

The Right to Distribute Copyrighted Works

The right of distribution allows the copyright owner the exclusive right to sell, transfer, or lease the work. Nevertheless, under federal law, once the original copyright owner sells the work, his or her distribution rights are exhausted, thus giving the new owner the right to further sell or lease that copy of the work. For example, assume you purchased the novel *Shipping News*. After your purchase, you may sell the book at a garage sale, destroy it, or lend it to a friend without violating the copyright owner's distribution rights. This is commonly called the first sale doctrine. The copyright owner retains other rights, however, including the right to prepare derivative works and rights to reproduce, display, and perform the work. Only the distribution right is eliminated upon the first sale of the work.

There are a few limitations to the general principle that once a copyrighted work is distributed, the copyright owner's rights of distribution are terminated:

▾ The doctrine applies only to lawfully made works. Thus, if a copyrighted item of jewelry is the subject of an unauthorized knockoff imitation, your purchase of it from a street vendor does not affect the author's distribution rights. You have no further right to sell, transfer, or lease the item to another because you did not obtain a lawful copy of the work.

▾ The doctrine does not apply to commercial rentals of records and certain computer programs. Thus, Shania Twain can prohibit a purchaser of her records or CDs from renting those items to another. Similarly, computer programs cannot be rented to another (even after they have been lawfully purchased by a consumer) unless they are incapable of being copied or are part of another product. Thus, videogames purchased by Blockbuster Video are routinely rented to its customers because consumers usually cannot copy the games. A computer program that is part of another product can be rented with the product. Consequently, when you lease a car from Hertz, the computer programs embedded in the car naturally accompany the car.

▾ The exceptions allowing libraries and archives to reproduce certain copyrighted material also allow them to distribute copyrighted matter.

In California, authors of fine art can share in the later appreciation of their work, even after they have sold it. California statutory law allows artists residing in California to collect 5 percent of the resale price of certain works, assuming the work is sold for at least $1,000 and assuming certain other conditions are met. For example, if an artist in California sells a painting for $5,000 and the purchaser later resells it for $10,000, the artist is entitled to $500 (5 percent of $10,000). Many foreign countries also recognize artists' rights to share in increased appreciation of their works, commonly called the *droit de suite* doctrine.

The Right to Perform the Work

Although copyright owners have the right to perform their works publicly, there are a number of limitations on that right, most of which allow certain performances for educational or charitable purposes or in small business establishments. The right granted to copyright owners is limited to the exclusive right to perform their works publicly. Thus, you may sing "My Way" or read a passage from the novel *Disclosure* to a small gathering of family and social acquaintances. However, you may not sing "My Way" in a nightclub or read a passage from *Disclosure* on a television program (unless you obtain consent from the copyright owner). Karaoke performances are acceptable if the owner of the player or club has paid a license fee to perform the songs.

Limitations for Charitable Purposes

The following activities do not constitute copyright infringement:

▾ Performances by teachers or pupils in the course of face-to-face teaching activities at a nonprofit educational institution.

▾ Performances of a nondramatic literary or musical work in the course of services at a religious assembly.

▾ Performances of a nondramatic literary or musical work for charitable, educational, or religious purposes (although notice must be given to the copyright owner so he or she can object). Thus, if Mary Chapin Carpenter plans to give a concert to raise money for cancer in which she will perform songs by Loretta Lynn and other country and western stars, Mary Chapin Carpenter will have to serve notice to Loretta Lynn and other copyright owners so they may object to use of their copyrighted works.

▾ Certain performances at agricultural fairs, performances for handicapped persons, and performances for veterans' organizations.

▾ Certain performances at stores, to allow stores such as Tower Records to play recorded music throughout the store specifically to promote sales of the work.

Most of the foregoing exceptions exist to allow noncommercial educational and charitable uses. Such performances are for the public good and generally do not deprive the copyright owner of revenue.

Limitations for Small Business Establishments

An important exception to a copyright owner's exclusive right to perform his or her works allows small business establishments to play the radio or broadcast television programs at the place of business. These businesses may play the radio or show television programs as follows: An establishment other than a food service or drinking establishment must have less than 2,000 square feet of space, and a food service or drinking establishment must have less than 3,750 square feet. If the establishment has more than the specified number of square feet, the number of loudspeakers or televisions at the location is limited to six and four, respectively, with no television having a screen larger than 55 inches, diagonally.

This exception allows a small restaurant or business to play the radio or show a televised sporting event for the enjoyment of customers without violating copyright law. The exception exists only for radio and television broadcasts. The business owner is not permitted to bring in his or her own CD player and play CDs throughout the business, no matter how small the establishment is. Businesses larger than the specified size (or with more than the designated number of speakers and screens) must obtain permission from the copyright owners to play the radio or television or CDs.

Although hotels can allow piped in music and the playing of video movies in private hotel rooms (the theory being that these are not public performances and are analogous to renting videotapes), playing music in lobbies and common areas is a performance that must be consented to by the copyright owner. Similarly, playing music (either via the radio or your own purchased CDs) while customers are on hold on the telephone is a copyright infringement. Performances in semiprivate places such as clubs, lodges, summer camps, and schools are also subject to copyright law, and permission must be obtained from the copyright owner before music or movies can be played or transmitted at those places.

One of the most common misconceptions about music is that anyone is free to play the radio or a purchased CD so the music can be heard throughout his or her place of business. This is not true, and in most cases the playing of music this way is a copyright infringement.

Performing Rights Societies

Because there are so many ways for a business to violate a copyright owner's right to perform his or her work, how does a business comply with copyright law while playing music on hold or playing music throughout a store or restaurant for customers' enjoyment? Most businesses enter into arrangements with one of the performing rights societies. The performing rights societies enter into contracts by which copyright owners allow the societies to license their works. The societies then enter into licensing arrangements with businesses, collect fees to allow the playing of music, and then distribute those fees to the artists and copyright owners. In recent years, performing rights societies have become quite vigilant in locating copyright violators, calling or visiting businesses anonymously to determine whether music on hold is played or music is played throughout the establishment without a license. If so, the organization generally demands that the business enter into a license arrangement, or the business can be sued for copyright violation.

The three best-known performing rights societies are Broadcast Music, Inc. (BMI), American Society of Composers, Authors, and Publishers (ASCAP), and SESAC. Among them, these organizations own rights to license millions of pieces of recorded music. The repertory of BMI alone is 4.5 million songs. Their repertories are viewable on their Web sites (www.bmi.com, www.ascap.com, and www.sesac.com), and information about the procedure for obtaining licenses is provided. License fees are collected annually and usually are moderate. Fees generally are based on the size of an establishment or the number of telephone lines it has. If a business owner intends to play music only by certain performers and these performers are exclusively affiliated with one performing rights society, obtaining one license from that society may be acceptable; however, most businesses must obtain licenses from all three organizations to ensure that a wide variety of music can be played. These organizations also enter into licensing arrangements with radio stations so that radio stations can play copyrighted music. Fees generally are a percentage of revenues of the station.

Limitations for Sound Recordings

The exclusive right given to authors to perform their works does not extend to sound recordings. The author of a sound recording does not have the exclusive right to prohibit others from performing his or her work. A sound recording usually is a specific arrangement or production of a song, and its author is the singer, record producer, or both. Thus, if the Dixie Chicks record a version of a song by Elton John, the Dixie Chicks' version can be performed by another artist without violating any of their rights. Their rights are limited to protection against duplication or physical misappropriation. However, permission must still be obtained from Elton John because, as the composer or author of the underlying work, he has the exclusive right to perform it. The exception allowing performance of sound recordings is likely meant to relieve radio stations and others from the burden of having to pay multiple royalties. If the exception did not exist, a radio station would have to pay a royalty to Elton John, the Dixie Chicks, and the record producer just to play one song.

The Right to Display a Work

Copyright owners have the right to display their works publicly. Although your purchase of a record or CD does not give you rights to perform the work publicly, if you buy a painting from an artist or a reproduction of such a work of art, you may display that work to the public directly or you may project no more than one image of the work to viewers present at the place where your copy is located. Thus, displaying a painting or sculpture you purchased at an art exhibit is permissible; however, showing multiple images of the painting or sculpture on more than one television screen at the art exhibit is impermissible.

Exceptions for Computer Programs

An owner of a computer program may make another copy of that program or may modify it without committing copyright infringement if the new copy or adaptation is created as an essential step in the utilization of the computer program or if the new copy or adaptation is for archival purposes only. Thus, the owner of a computer program can tinker with it to enhance its speed or add features to facilitate its use. However, the enhanced version cannot be sold to another; doing so would violate the author's right to create derivative works. The adaptation of computer programs is allowable so that the owner of a program can use it freely to obtain the greatest possible value from his or her purchase without committing infringement.

Makers of computer programs typically do not sell their programs to consumers but rather license the work, thereby retaining all rights to it. Such licenses are called shrink wrap licenses because they come into existence when the plastic shrink wrap on the product is opened. The extensive license agreement inside the package clearly states that the copyright owner is merely licensing the product to the consumer, and the consumer has limited rights to the product. If the consumer does not want to agree to the license, the consumer is instructed to return the product. These licenses often allow the consumer to make a backup or archival copy of the computer program. Nevertheless, they make it clear that copying or further distribution of the program is infringement. When software is licensed electronically, the license usually is called a click wrap license because it comes into existence upon the click of a mouse or computer key.

Moral Rights

Artists are always concerned that their works be attributed to them and that their works not be distorted or mutilated. Whereas continental Europe has recognized these rights for years, the United States has been slower to protect such rights of authors, generally called moral rights because they are independent of authors' economic rights in their works. The right to claim authorship of a work is known as the right of attribution, and the right to ensure that one's work is not mutilated is known as the right of integrity. These moral rights survive transfer of an author's work so that even after the author has sold his or her work, the work cannot be destroyed or mutilated.

In 1990, with the passage of the Visual Artists Rights Act, the United States specifically recognized certain moral rights of copyright owners. Moral rights in the United States are more limited than in Europe, primarily because the rights extend only to works of visual art such as sculptures, paintings, drawings, and prints that are produced in limited editions of 200 or fewer signed copies. Thus, if an artist authorized 500 prints of a work, there are no moral rights in the work. Moral rights do not extend to works such as posters and diagrams, generally because these works are not considered works of fine art.

An author's right of attribution means that he or she has the right to claim authorship of the work or to prevent the use of his or her name on a work he or she did not create and on a work that has been mutilated or modified such that having the author's name attached to the work would compromise the author's reputation. An author's right of integrity means that the author has the right to ensure that a work is not intentionally distorted, mutilated, or so modified that it would be prejudicial to his or her honor or reputation. Modifications and fading that occur as the result of the passage of time are permissible. Moral rights endure for the life of the author and cannot be transferred to another. However, moral rights may be waived by an author if the author expressly agrees to such in writing.

There are special rules for works of visual arts incorporated in buildings. For example, if the owner of a building wants to remove a mosaic from the building and removal is possible without destruction, the owner is required to give the author notice so he or she has the opportunity to remove it.

Fair Use

In general, a copyrighted work may be reproduced, distributed, or displayed for purposes such as criticism, comment, news reporting, teaching, and research without causing copyright infringement. Such a use is called a fair use. Because fair use generally is asserted as a defense in copyright infringement cases, it is discussed in Chapter 11.

10

The Copyright Application Process: Ownership, Registration, Notices, Duration, and Transfers

Filing a copyright application is a fairly simple process. An application form provided by the Copyright Office is completed and filed by the copyright owner or claimant for a filing fee of $30. The Copyright Office does not perform a substantive review of the application as the U.S. Patent and Trademark Office (PTO) does with trademark applications. The use of a copyright notice (© 1999 Gerald Trainor) is optional, but it affords certain advantages to copyright owners. Duration of copyright typically is for the author's life plus seventy years. Because copyrights are property, they can be sold to others. The transfer of all copyright rights is required to be in writing.

Copyright Ownership

Copyright vests initially in the author or authors of the work. Copyright also is transferable by agreement or by operation of law (as is the case in bankruptcy or when a copyright owner dies without leaving a will).

Ownership of a physical object does not carry with it ownership of the underlying copyright in the work. When you purchase the latest best-selling novel, you own the book itself. The author retains the rights to reproduce it, adapt it, and so forth. Unless the copyright owner expressly transfers all rights in writing, the exclusive rights given to copyright owners are retained, although a physical object (sheet music, a painting, a manuscript) is transferred.

Works may be jointly owned, as is the case when a work is prepared by two or more authors with the intention that their contributions be merged into a unitary whole. The parties' intention at the time the work is created governs ownership. Thus, if an author and illustrator work together on a book, it is a joint work. If the author of the book intended it to be complete at the time it was written but later decides to allow another party to add illustrations, the work is not a joint work. The author owns the copyright for the book and the illustrator owns the copyright in the derivative work, the illustrations.

It is important to determine whether a work is a joint one because the determination has long-ranging implications. First, unless the parties agree otherwise, courts presume that joint authors contributed equally, and thus profits will be divided equally. If the parties want some other arrangement, they must enter into an agreement specifying such. Second, the copyright for an author's work exists for the author's life plus seventy years. If the work is a joint one, copyright protection lasts until seventy years from the last surviving coauthor's death. Third, each joint author has the right to use the work, distribute it, adapt it, and so forth, without seeking the other's permission (although each must account to the other for profits arising out of such uses). Finally, any joint author has the right to grant a nonexclusive license to a third party to use the joint work without seeking permission of the other coauthors. However, the granting of an exclusive license does require consent of all coauthors.

The author of the work or the copyright claimant (or their agent) is entitled to submit an application form. A copyright author is either the person who created the work, such as the author of a book or the composer of a song, or, if the work is a work made for hire, the employer or other person for whom the work was prepared. A copyright claimant usually is one who gained the copyright through a transfer or through bequest by will. A copyright claimant can also be the owner of exclusive rights, such as the exclusive right to distribute or perform a work.

Works Made for Hire

Although the general rule is that the person who creates a work is the author of that work, there is an exception to that principle: works made for hire. If a work is made for hire, the employer (not the employee) or the party who commissioned the work is considered the author of the work.

Under copyright law, works created by employees during the course and scope of their employment are owned by their employers. To claim copyright rights, individuals often allege that they are not employees but are rather independent contractors who retain the copyright in their works. To determine whether an individual is an employee or independent contractor, courts examine a variety of factors. If the hiring party exercises control over the work by determining how the work is done, provides equipment and supplies, and provides a location at which the work is done, such tends to show an employment relationship. Similarly, if the hiring party exercises control over the hired party by controlling his or her schedule, assigning other projects to the party, hiring assistants for the party, or determining the method of payment, such also tends to demonstrate an employer–employee relationship. Finally, courts examine the status and conduct of the hiring party. If that party provides benefits, withholds tax from the hired party's payment, and is in business to produce works of the type created by the hired party, such tends to show that the hiring party is an employer. These factors are not exclusive, and courts are free to make other inquiries. In general, however, a regular, salaried arrangement supports an employer–employee relationship.

If the party is an employer, he or she is viewed as the author of any work created by the employee while on the job. Thus, if an employee in a department store's advertising group creates a new logo for the company, the company owns the work. However, if the employee writes a song over the weekend, the employee owns the song because it was not created in the scope of the employee's duties.

Companies or individuals who hire independent contractors to perform tasks may still own the works created by the independent contractor if two factors exist:

▾ The work is specially commissioned or ordered for use as a contribution to a collective work, a part of a motion picture or other audiovisual work, a sound recording, a translation, a supplementary work, a compilation, an instructional text, a test, answer material for a test, or an atlas.

▾ The parties expressly agree in writing that the work is made for hire such that the commissioning party owns it.

If the commissioned work does not fall within one of these categories, the party commissioned to create the work owns the copyright in it. Thus, if ABC Inc. retains Sally, an independent contractor, to paint a portrait of ABC's founder for the company lobby, Sally retains the copyright to the work. ABC owns the physical painting but Sally retains the exclusive rights to reproduce and make derivative works based on the portrait because paintings do not fall within the categories of works just listed. If ABC Inc. then orally retains Tim to prepare a test for prospective employees, Tim owns the copyright in the test. Although the test falls into one of the specially enumerated categories, the parties did not agree in writing that the work would be made for hire. Thus, Tim retains copyright rights in his work.

The effect of a work made for hire is that the employer or commissioning party is the author of the work (and should be identified as such in the copyright application) and is the owner of the copyright who possesses the bundle of rights discussed in Chapter 9, including the rights of reproduction, adaptation, distribution, performance, and display.

Companies should have employees and independent contractors who will be creating copyrightable works sign agreements verifying that any work created is made for hire. A good agreement should go beyond this and state that if for some reason it is later determined that the work is not one made for hire, the employee or independent contractor thereby automatically and irrevocably transfers and assigns the work to the employer or commissioning party. See Figures 19-1 and 19-2 for forms of clauses that can be used by employers or those who retain independent contractors to ensure that they own the copyright in works created for them.

Benefits of Copyright Registration

Because copyright protection exists from the moment a work is created in fixed form, registration with the Copyright Office is not required. However, registration is recommended for the following reasons:

▾ Registration provides public notice of an author's claim of copyright ownership.

- If registration occurs within five years of publication of a work, it is considered prima facie (literally, "on its face") evidence in a court of law of the validity of the copyright.
- Registered works may be eligible for statutory damages and attorney's fees in a successful infringement action.
- Registration is a prerequisite to bringing a copyright infringement action for works of U.S. origin.
- Registration allows the owner of the copyright to record the registration with the U.S. Customs Service, which will prevent the importation of infringing works into the United States.

Introduction to Copyright Applications

The U.S. Copyright Office is the only office in the United States that can accept copyright applications and issue registrations. To register a work, an author or copyright claimant must submit a completed application form, a nonrefundable filing fee of $30, and two deposit copies of the work to be registered (only one copy is required if the work is unpublished).

There is no need to conduct a search of Copyright Office records before filing an application. Copyright law protects original works, meaning works created through an author's creative process rather than those copied from another. There is no requirement that the work be the only one of its kind. Thus, the fact that an identical bracelet, poem, or song has been previously registered by another party does not preclude registration of a later work as long as it was independently created by its author. This theory is in contrast to trademark law, which precludes the registration of confusingly similar marks, even if they were created independently of each other. Although searching copyright records before applying is not required, searching will disclose whether a work has fallen into the public domain so that derivative works may be prepared based on the work. Some rudimentary searching can be done through the Copyright Office's Web site at www.loc.gov/copyright.

Searching online is difficult because the Copyright Office's system was developed in the 1970s, before the advent of current computer technology. The Copyright Office is developing software to replace its hard-to-use search system. Search tips are provided in free downloadable publications: Circular 22, "How to Investigate the Copyright Status of a Work," and Circular 23, "The Copyright Card Catalog and the Online Files of the Copyright Office." Alternatively, on request, the Copyright Office will search its records at the rate of $65 per hour. Records can also be searched in person at the Copyright Office at no charge. Finally, CCH Corsearch Inc. and Thomson & Thomson, the companies identified in Chapter 3 that conduct trademark searches, also perform copyright searches. Information can be obtained at the companies' respective Web sites at www.corsearch.com and www.thomson-thomson.com.

Although some public libraries have copyright application forms, the easiest place to obtain copyright forms is from the Copyright Office. Forms can be obtained through the Copyright Office's Fax on Demand service at (202) 707-2600, by telephone order placed with the Copyright Office's Forms Hotline at (202) 707-9100, and via the Internet at www.loc.gov/copyright. Application forms can be photocopied if they are copied back to back and head to head on a single sheet of $8^1/_2$- by 11-inch white paper.

Applicants must request and use different forms for different works. Applications are one page, front and back. The most commonly used forms are as follows:

- Form TX is used for literary works, including computer programs.
- Form PA is used for works of the performing arts (musical and dramatic works, motion pictures, choreographic works, and pantomimes).
- Form VA is used for works of the visual arts (pictorial, graphic, and sculptural works).
- Form SR is used for sound recordings.
- Form SE is used for serials (periodicals, newspapers, magazines, and so forth).

The Copyright Application

Completing the copyright application form is quite simple. The forms are accompanied by clear, detailed instructions, and examples of permissible wording often are included in the instructions. Generally, the following elements are required:

- *Title of the work.* Every work submitted for copyright registration must be given a title to identify it. Although it is easy to identify the title of a book, song, or movie, it is sometimes harder to identify the title of a work of the visual arts. It is acceptable to say "charcoal etching" or "jewelry design." If the work was known by previous or alternative titles, these should be given as well.

▾ *Author.* The full name of the author (or authors, if the work is a joint work) should be given. If the work is made for hire, the employer's or commissioning party's name is given. Additional information about the author, such as nationality or domicile, must be given. Finally, the nature of the authorship must be described briefly. For a book, it is sufficient to state "text." Other acceptable descriptions are "computer program," "three-dimensional sculpture," or "screenplay."

▾ *Creation and publication.* Every application for copyright registration must state the year in which creation of the work was completed. If the work is published, the complete date and nation of first publication must be given.

▾ *Claimant.* In most cases, the copyright claimant is the author of the work. However, it is possible that a work (or one of the exclusive copyright rights) has been transferred to another or inherited by will, in which case the claimant of the registration may be different from the author. If the copyright claimant is not the author, the Copyright Office requires a brief statement as to how the claimant obtained ownership of the copyright. Acceptable statements are "by written contract" or "by will."

▾ *Previous registration.* Generally, only one basic copyright registration can be made for the same version of a particular work. Thus, the Copyright Office inquires whether there was a previous registration for the work. If so, the Office will determine whether there is sufficient basis for a new registration. Generally, the application states that the work has been revised. If the work has been previously registered, the number and date of the registration must be given.

▾ *Derivative work or compilation.* The Copyright Office requires identification if the work is a compilation (for example, a collection of speeches or an almanac) or a derivative work (one based on an earlier work).

▾ *Miscellaneous information.* The application form includes spaces to indicate whether the fee is enclosed, to identify the party to whom the Copyright Office should direct inquiries, and for the author, claimant, or authorized agent to sign the form. Any person authorized to act on behalf of the copyright author or owner may sign the form, including an attorney.

Experienced applicants generally can complete the form within ten to fifteen minutes. The application may be typed or legibly printed, using black ink. Although many businesses use attorneys to prepare copyright applications, many others do not, primarily because the process is very straightforward.

Short Form Applications

The Copyright Office offers short forms for certain literary works, works of the performing arts, and works of the visual arts. These short forms are one page long and take only a few minutes to complete. Generally, the short forms may be used in the following circumstances:

- The author is the only author of the work, is living, and is the sole owner of the copyright.
- The work is completely new (rather than a derivative work or revised edition of an earlier work).
- The work is not one made for hire (thus, the work cannot be one prepared by an employee within the scope of employment or a specially commissioned work).

If these requirements are satisfied, the short form application may be used.

Filing the Application

After the application is completed it should be filed with the filing fee of $30 and deposit copies of the work.

Deposit Material

The Copyright Office requires a nonreturnable deposit of the work being registered. If the work is unpublished (meaning that it has not been distributed or offered to the public by sale or lease), one complete copy is sufficient. If the work has been published, two complete copies of the best edition of the work are required. For published books, two copies of the manuscript or finished text usually are submitted. For published musical compositions, two copies of the full score and parts usually are submitted. For three-dimensional works, such as sculptures or paintings, photographs of the work are submitted because the Copyright Office does not accept bulky objects.

Special deposit rules exist for computer programs. Whether the work is published or unpublished, the deposit requirement is one visually perceptible copy in source code of the first twenty-five and last twenty-five pages of the program. If the program is less than fifty pages, the entire source code should be submitted. If the source code contains trade secrets, the Copyright Office allows portions of the source code to be blocked out. A letter must accompany the application stating that the claimed matter contains trade secrets, and the deposit may then consist of any of the following:

- First twenty-five and last twenty-five pages of source code, with portions containing trade secrets blocked out
- First ten and last ten pages of source code, with no blocked-out portions
- First twenty-five and last twenty-five pages of object code plus any ten or more consecutive pages of source code, with no blocked-out portions
- For programs fifty pages or less in length, the entire source code with the trade secret portions blocked out

For computer programs, when the entire program is embodied in a CD-ROM, ordinarily the entire CD-ROM package must be deposited, together with a complete copy of any accompanying software and instructional manuals. Circular 61, "Copyright Registration for Computer Programs," provides detailed information about applying for a registration for a computer program.

Obtaining copies of another's work deposited with the Copyright Office is difficult. Only if the work is the subject of actual or prospective litigation, the copyright claimant of record authorizes its release, or a court orders its release, will the Copyright Office provide a copy of the deposited work.

Fees

Copyright application filing fees are $30 (effective through June 30, 2002) and are nonrefundable. Fees should be submitted in the form of checks, money orders, or bank drafts, payable to Register of Copyrights. Many businesses and law firms that file numerous applications maintain a deposit account with the Copyright Office against which fees are charged.

Examination of the Application and Registration

The Copyright Office does not send any notification that it has received an application. Thus, it is a good idea to send the application by registered or certified mail and request a return receipt from the Copyright Office. Once the application is filed, it is extremely difficult to obtain information on the status of the application. There is no tracking or monitoring system as is offered by the PTO for trademark and patent applications. If status information is critical, the Copyright Office will conduct an in-process search for $65 per hour.

Once the Copyright Office receives the application, an examination is conducted of the application and deposit material. The Copyright Office generally takes four to eight months to process an application. If further information is needed from an applicant, the Copyright Office will write or call the applicant. The examination of the copyright application is not nearly as in-depth as the examination of trademark and patent applications. In general, if the matter appears to qualify as copyrightable matter (it is not an idea, title, recipe, useful article, and so forth), the deposit material is acceptable, and the fee is included with the application, a registration is issued. The effective date of the registration is the date the Copyright Office receives the application, fee, and deposit material. For example, if you file an application on November 10 and the Copyright Office takes until May to examine the application, the registration date will be November 10. The Copyright Office sends a certificate of registration, which is merely a stamped copy of the application you submitted with a notation in the upper right corner that the copyright has been registered, the date of registration, and a registration number.

If expedited processing of an application is needed, the Copyright Office offers special handling. Special handling is granted only in special circumstances, such as pending or prospective litigation, customs matters, or contract or publishing deadlines that necessitate the expedited issuance of a certificate. Thus, if you need to register a copyright so that you can sell it to another or so that litigation can be instituted regarding the copyright, special handling is appropriate. Special handling generally results in issuance of a registration within one week rather than in four to eight months. The fee for special handling is $500 (plus the ordinary filing fee of $30). Consult Circular 10, "Special Handling," for more information about how to request expedited processing of a copyright application or other document.

If the Copyright Office refuses registration, a request for reexamination can be made. If registration is thereafter refused, the copyright applicant may seek judicial review in the U.S. District Court for the District of Columbia. In many cases, when the Copyright Office is unsure about the copyrightability of a work, it registers the work under its rule of doubt, meaning that although the Copyright Office has doubts about copyrightability, those doubts will be resolved in favor of the applicant. A court can later determine whether the work was actually copyrightable.

To correct an error in a copyright registration or to amplify information given in a registration (for example, to add another author's name to the registration), Form CA is used and a filing fee is $65 is required. See Figure 10-1 for a sample completed copyright application.

Notice of Copyright

Until March 1, 1989, notice of copyright was required as a condition of protection. The use of a copyright notice is no longer required under U.S. law. However, a notice is recommended because it informs the public that the work is protected by copyright, identifies the copyright owner, and provides the year the work was first published. Moreover, in the event that a work is infringed, if a proper notice of copyright appears on a published copy of the work to which a defendant had access, the defendant cannot assert that he or she was an innocent infringer. Typically, one who is an innocent infringer (meaning one who did not realize the work was protected) can mitigate actual or statutory damages.

The use of the copyright notice is the responsibility of the copyright owner and does not require advance permission from or registration with the Copyright Office. Thus, even an unregistered work should include a copyright notice.

The notice for visually perceptible copies should include the following three elements:

1. The symbol © (the letter "C" in a circle), the word *Copyright,* or the abbreviation *Copr.*
2. The year of first publication of the work
3. The name of the owner of the copyright (or an abbreviation by which the name can be recognized)

An example of a proper copyright notice appearing on a book would be "© 2000 Sandra Taylor."

Figure 10-1. Copyright application.

FEE CHANGES
Fees are effective through June 30, 2002. After that date, check the Copyright Office Website at www.loc.gov/copyright or call (202) 707-3000 for current fee information.

FORM TX
For a Nondramatic Literary Work
UNITED STATES COPYRIGHT OFFICE

REGISTRATION NUMBER

TX	TXU

EFFECTIVE DATE OF REGISTRATION

Month	Day	Year

DO NOT WRITE ABOVE THIS LINE. IF YOU NEED MORE SPACE, USE A SEPARATE CONTINUATION SHEET.

1

TITLE OF THIS WORK ▼

The Challenge

PREVIOUS OR ALTERNATIVE TITLES ▼

PUBLICATION AS A CONTRIBUTION If this work was published as a contribution to a periodical, serial, or collection, give information about the collective work in which the contribution appeared.   **Title of Collective Work** ▼

If published in a periodical or serial give: Volume ▼	Number ▼	Issue Date ▼	On Pages ▼

2

a NAME OF AUTHOR ▼
Andrea Rocca

DATES OF BIRTH AND DEATH
Year Born ▼ *1972*   Year Died ▼ *NA*

Was this contribution to the work a "work made for hire"?
☐ Yes
☑ No

AUTHOR'S NATIONALITY OR DOMICILE
Name of Country
OR { Citizen of ▶ *USA*
{ Domiciled in ▶

WAS THIS AUTHOR'S CONTRIBUTION TO THE WORK
Anonymous? ☐ Yes ☑ No
Pseudonymous? ☐ Yes ☑ No
If the answer to either of these questions is "Yes," see detailed instructions

NOTE

Under the law, the "author" of a "work made for hire" is generally the employer, not the employee (see instructions). For any part of this work that was "made for hire" check "Yes" in the space provided, give the employer (or other person for whom the work was prepared) as "Author" of that part, and leave the space for dates of birth and death blank.

NATURE OF AUTHORSHIP Briefly describe nature of material created by this author in which copyright is claimed. ▼
Text

b NAME OF AUTHOR ▼

DATES OF BIRTH AND DEATH
Year Born ▼   Year Died ▼

Was this contribution to the work a "work made for hire"?
☐ Yes
☐ No

AUTHOR'S NATIONALITY OR DOMICILE
Name of Country
OR { Citizen of ▶
{ Domiciled in ▶

WAS THIS AUTHOR'S CONTRIBUTION TO THE WORK
Anonymous? ☐ Yes ☐ No
Pseudonymous? ☐ Yes ☐ No
If the answer to either of these questions is "Yes," see detailed instructions

NATURE OF AUTHORSHIP Briefly describe nature of material created by this author in which copyright is claimed. ▼

c NAME OF AUTHOR ▼

DATES OF BIRTH AND DEATH
Year Born ▼   Year Died ▼

Was this contribution to the work a "work made for hire"?
☐ Yes
☐ No

AUTHOR'S NATIONALITY OR DOMICILE
Name of Country
OR { Citizen of ▶
{ Domiciled in ▶

WAS THIS AUTHOR'S CONTRIBUTION TO THE WORK
Anonymous? ☐ Yes ☐ No
Pseudonymous? ☐ Yes ☐ No
If the answer to either of these questions is "Yes," see detailed instructions

NATURE OF AUTHORSHIP Briefly describe nature of material created by this author in which copyright is claimed. ▼

3

a YEAR IN WHICH CREATION OF THIS WORK WAS COMPLETED   This information must be given in all cases. *2000* ◀ Year

b DATE AND NATION OF FIRST PUBLICATION OF THIS PARTICULAR WORK Complete this information ONLY if this work has been published. Month ▶ *June* Day ▶ *2* Year ▶ *2000*   *USA* ◀ Nation

4

COPYRIGHT CLAIMANT(S) Name and address must be given even if the claimant is the same as the author given in space 2. ▼

Andrea Rocca

TRANSFER If the claimant(s) named here in space 4 is (are) different from the author(s) named in space 2, give a brief statement of how the claimant(s) obtained ownership of the copyright. ▼

See instructions before completing this space.

APPLICATION RECEIVED

ONE DEPOSIT RECEIVED

TWO DEPOSITS RECEIVED

FUNDS RECEIVED

DO NOT WRITE HERE
OFFICE USE ONLY

MORE ON BACK ▶ • Complete all applicable spaces (numbers 5-9) on the reverse side of this page.
• See detailed instructions.   • Sign the form at line 8.

DO NOT WRITE HERE
Page 1 of .... pages

EXAMINED BY	FORM TX
CHECKED BY	
☐ CORRESPONDENCE Yes	FOR COPYRIGHT OFFICE USE ONLY

DO NOT WRITE ABOVE THIS LINE. IF YOU NEED MORE SPACE, USE A SEPARATE CONTINUATION SHEET.

PREVIOUS REGISTRATION Has registration for this work, or for an earlier version of this work, already been made in the Copyright Office?

☐ Yes ☑ No If your answer is "Yes," why is another registration being sought? (Check appropriate box.) ▼

a. ☐ This is the first published edition of a work previously registered in unpublished form.

b. ☐ This is the first application submitted by this author as copyright claimant.

c. ☐ This is a changed version of the work, as shown by space 6 on this application.

If your answer is "Yes," give: **Previous Registration Number** ▶   **Year of Registration** ▶

5

DERIVATIVE WORK OR COMPILATION

Preexisting Material Identify any preexisting work or works that this work is based on or incorporates. ▼

a

6

See instructions before completing this space.

Material Added to This Work Give a brief, general statement of the material that has been added to this work and in which copyright is claimed. ▼

b

DEPOSIT ACCOUNT If the registration fee is to be charged to a Deposit Account established in the Copyright Office, give name and number of Account.

Name ▼   **Account Number** ▼

a

7

CORRESPONDENCE Give name and address to which correspondence about this application should be sent.   Name/Address/Apt/City/State/ZIP ▼

Andrea Rocca
12 Elm Street
Edison, NJ 08512

Area code and daytime telephone number ▶ *(609) 271-9104*   Fax number ▶

Email ▶

b

CERTIFICATION* I, the undersigned, hereby certify that I am the

Check only one ▶

☑ author
☐ other copyright claimant
☐ owner of exclusive right(s)
☐ authorized agent of _____

of the work identified in this application and that the statements made by me in this application are correct to the best of my knowledge.

Name of author or other copyright claimant, or owner of exclusive right(s) ▲

8

Typed or printed name and date ▼ If this application gives a date of publication in space 3, do not sign and submit it before that date.

Andrea Rocca   Date ▶ *July 29, 2000*

Handwritten signature (X) ▼

X *Andrea Rocca*

		YOU MUST:
Certificate will be mailed in window envelope to this address:	**Name** ▼ *Andrea Rocca*	• Complete all necessary spaces • Sign your application in space 8
	Number/Street/Apt ▼ *12 Elm Street*	**SEND ALL 3 ELEMENTS IN THE SAME PACKAGE:** 1. Application form 2. Nonrefundable filing fee in check or money order payable to *Register of Copyrights* 3. Deposit material
	City/State/ZIP ▼ *Edison, NJ 08512*	**MAIL TO:** Library of Congress Copyright Office 101 Independence Avenue, S.E. Washington, D.C. 20559-6000

As of July 1, 1999, the filing fee for Form TX is $30.

9

*17 U.S.C. § 506(e): Any person who knowingly makes a false representation of a material fact in the application for copyright registration provided for by section 409, or in any written statement filed in connection with the application, shall be fined not more than $2,500.

June 1999—200,000
WEB REV: June 1999

⊕ PRINTED ON RECYCLED PAPER

☆U.S. GOVERNMENT PRINTING OFFICE: 1999-454-879/49

The notice should be placed such that it gives reasonable notice of the claim of copyright. For books and other printed matter, the notice usually appears on the reverse side of the title page or either side of the front or back cover. For two-dimensional works, such as photographs, the notice usually is placed on the front or back of the copy. For certain matter, such as jewelry or sculptures, the notice often appears on a tag attached to the work if placement on the work itself is impracticable.

For computer programs, the notice may appear with or near the title or at the end of the work, on printouts, at the user's terminal at sign-on, on continuous display on the terminal, or on a durable label affixed to the container used for the computer program.

It is common to see other matter with copyright notices, such as "all rights reserved." Although this notation is common in some foreign countries, it is not required under U.S. law and should never be used in place of the standard copyright notice (© 1998 West Group). Such additions generally are considered surplus matter that has no legal significance.

Duration of Copyright Protection

The duration of copyright protection depends upon when the work was created because over the years U.S. copyright law has been amended with regard to the term of copyright protection.

Works Created after January 1, 1978

Works created on or after January 1, 1978, are automatically protected from the moment of their creation and are given a term enduring for the author's life plus 70 years after the author's death. If the work was prepared by joint authors (who did not work for hire), the term lasts for 70 years after the last surviving author's death. For works made for hire and for anonymous works (works on which an author is not identified) or pseudonymous works (works on which the author uses a fictitious name), the term is 95 years from publication of the work or 120 years from creation, whichever is shorter.

Until 1998, these terms were 20 years shorter. In 1998, the Sonny Bono Copyright Extension Act amended previous law to extend each term 20 years.

Works Originally Created and Published or Registered before January 1, 1978

Under the law in effect before 1978, copyright was secured on the date a work was published or on the date of registration if the work was registered in unpublished form. In either case, the copyright lasted for a first term of twenty-eight years from the date it was secured. The copyright was eligible for renewal during the last (twenty-eighth) year of the first term. If renewed, the copyright was extended for a second term of twenty-eight years. If not renewed, the copyright expired at the end of the first twenty-eight–year term.

In 1998, the length of the second term was increased to sixty-seven years (thus affording those works a ninety-five–year protection term: twenty-eight years under the first term and sixty-seven years under the second term). If a renewal had been filed to claim the second twenty-eight–year term, the recent change in the law automatically extends the second renewal term from twenty-eight years to sixty-seven years. No other documents need be filed. For works in their first term of twenty-eight years, no renewal registration is required to secure the additional sixty-seven–year term. It exists automatically to afford the same ninety-five–year term of protection as newly created works have. Although there is no need to file a renewal application, federal copyright law affords some advantages to those who file renewals, primarily that the renewal certificate constitutes prima facie evidence of the validity of the copyright during the renewed term and of the facts stated in the certificate.

Additional information about duration of older works can be obtained in Copyright Office Circulars 15a and 15t.

Works Created before January 1, 1978, but Not Published or Registered by That Date

The duration of protection for works that were created before January 1, 1978, but that had not been published or registered by that date is the same as that for works created on or after January 1, 1978: life plus 70 years or the 95/120 year term used for works made for hire. Additional information about duration of copyright of such older works can be obtained in Copyright Office Circulars 15a and 15t.

Because copyright terms expire during a year rather than on a specific date, federal law provides that all terms of copyright run through the end of the calendar year in which they would otherwise expire.

Transfers of Copyright

Any or all of the copyright owner's exclusive rights may be transferred but the transfer of exclusive rights is not valid unless it is in writing and signed by the owner of the rights conveyed or the owner's duly authorized agent.

Because copyright owners have a variety of different rights (the right to reproduce, adapt, distribute, perform, and display their works), they may transfer all or any portion of these rights to another. Thus, author Tom Clancy can transfer the right to make a movie of one of his books to Paramount Pictures, the right to distribute his works to a certain publishing house, and the right to reproduce his books to another party. If the grant of any of these rights will be exclusive, meaning that no other party will be granted rights, the transfer must be in writing. Nonexclusive transfers of rights do not require a written agreement, although written agreements are recommended because they lend certainty in the event of a later dispute. Agreements for nonexclusive transfers of rights typically are called licenses, written documents that allow the licensee to engage in specified activities for the payment of a lump sum fee or for periodic royalty payments, usually a percentage of income earned by the licensee from the distribution, reproduction, or performance of the work.

The transfer of all of the rights of copyright ownership must be in writing. Although recording the transfer document, usually called an assignment, is not required, many people elect to record the assignment so that Copyright Office records correctly reflect the owner of the copyright. The fee to record a copyright assignment is $50. See Figure 10-2 for a sample copyright assignment.

Because it is an item of personal property, a copyright can be conveyed by operation of law (for example, in a bankruptcy matter, copyright may be automatically conveyed to a bankruptcy trustee, who then sells the copyright to raise money to pay creditors) or may be bequeathed by will.

Termination of Transfers

Copyrights that have been transferred or assigned can be recaptured by their original owners. Transfers of copyrights can be terminated after thirty-five years if the original owner serves written notice on the trans-

Figure 10-2. Copyright assignment.

WHEREAS William T. Taylor, an individual residing at 110 Elm Street, Phoenix, Arizona 22909 ("Assignor"), is the owner of all right, title, and interest in and to the copyright for the literary work known as *The Storm*, and copyright registration TX-180-792 therefor (the "Work"), and desires to assign the Work as hereinafter described;

WHEREAS Susan N. Nelson, an individual residing at 1010 Second Avenue, San Diego, California 92110 ("Assignee"), desires to acquire the Work and all rights thereto.

NOW, THEREFORE, for good and valuable consideration, the receipt and sufficiency of which are hereby acknowledged, Assignor hereby irrevocably transfers and assigns all right, title, and interest in and to the Work throughout the world to Assignee.

Assignor represents and warrants that he created the Work independently, that no other party has any right, interest, or title in or to the Work, that he has the legal right to assign the Work to Assignee and that such assignment does not infringe the rights of any other party. Assignor further represents and warrants that there are no pending claims or actions relating to the Work.

Assignee shall have the right to file appropriate documents with the U.S. Copyright Office to ensure that title to and ownership of the Work are registered in Assignee's name, and Assignor shall cooperate with Assignee with regard thereto. Assignee shall have the right to sue for and retain all damages for any past, present, or future infringements of the Work.

This Assignment shall be binding on and inure to the benefit of the parties hereto and their respective successors and assigns.

Executed this 30th day of November, 2000, at Phoenix, Arizona.

William T. Taylor

---

feree within a five-year period beginning at the end of the thirty-fifth year. The process is somewhat complex, but if the appropriate documents and notices are filed, the original copyright reverts to its owner. After a notice of termination is given, the parties often renegotiate the transfer.

These provisions allowing the termination of earlier transfers contradict all other principles of contract law. When a person sells a house, stock, or jewelry, he or she does not have a right to recapture the sold item. Once a sale is made, it generally cannot later be set aside, except in extraordinary circumstances, such as those involving fraud. The theory underlying the unusual law allowing copyright owners to later recapture their works is that copyright owners (especially musicians and other performers and artists) often sell their copyrights in their early, struggling years, before they understand the value of the copyrights. The ability to terminate an earlier transfer is an effort to level the playing field. Works made for hire are not subject to rights of termination.

International Copyright Protection

There is no such thing as an international copyright. Protection of a work in another country requires compliance with that country's laws. The United States (with nearly 140 other nations) is a party to a treaty called the Berne Convention for the Protection of Literary and Artistic Property. This treaty requires signatories to treat nationals of other member countries like their own nationals for purposes of copyright.

Because copyright protection in other nations is governed by their laws, one should not publish or distribute a work in another country without first checking those laws. Most business owners cannot secure copyright forms from other countries unless they retain an attorney. United States law firms that engage in intellectual property work have established relationships with foreign counsel and can easily facilitate this process. For the text of the Berne Convention, Paris Convention of 1883, other treaties, and useful information on international copyright protection, access the home page of the World Intellectual Property Organization (WIPO) at www.wipo.org. WIPO is a specialized agency within the United Nations whose goal is to promote intellectual property throughout the world.

11

Copyright Infringement

The nearly insatiable demand of consumers for books, movies, music, and software has led to increasing copyright infringement, estimated to cost copyright owners more than $20 billion each year. Copyright infringement occurs when a work derives from another and shows substantial similarity to the first work. Infringement does not require intent. Even an innocent use can be infringement. There are a variety of defenses to infringement, chief among them that of fair use, meaning a use for scholarship, educational, or news reporting purposes, or as a parody. Remedies include damages, injunctive relief, and seizure of the infringing goods.

Introduction to Copyright Infringement: Access and Substantial Similarity

Infringement occurs when one or more of the exclusive rights granted to copyright owners (reproduction, adaptation, distribution, performance, or display) is violated, whether the violation occurs innocently or with intent. Because two identical works can coexist as long as they were independently created, the accused work must derive from the copyrighted work for infringement to exist. Even if two works are identical in every respect, if they were independently created, there can be no infringement.

Because it is difficult to find direct evidence that a work has been infringed (there are seldom witnesses who have observed any copying), courts generally infer that infringement exists if the defendant had access to the copyrighted work and the two works are substantially similar. Access can be proven by showing that the defendant had an opportunity to view or hear the work. Thus, if a company displays its copyrighted marketing materials at a trade show attended by the defendant, and the defendant's later-developed marketing materials show a substantial similarity to the company's, a court probably will find infringement. In general, the greater the similarity of the works, the less important access becomes. For example, if Company A's forty-page employee handbook is an exact duplicate of Company B's, access is presumed because of the near impossibility of two companies independently creating such identical works. There are a number of famous cases involving infringement of maps in which the original mapmakers inserted deliberate mistakes in their maps. When the mistake occurs in the accused work, infringement is readily found.

Similarity between the two works need only be substantial. Although literal copying, such as making duplicate copies of a videotaped movie, is clearly infringement, infringement also exists when less than an entire work is taken. The question often arises as to how much of a work must be taken before infringement exists. There is no clear answer to the question. Courts examine the two works and determine whether an ordinary observer would believe that the heart of the accused work has been taken from another. Although ordinarily taking just a few lines of a work such as a movie might not constitute infringement, if a famous line from a book or movie, such as "You complete me" or "Hasta la vista, baby," is taken and placed on clothing and accessories, infringement probably exists.

Whereas it is easy to determine that infringement exists when the copying is literal, as when one photocopies chapters of a book or makes unauthorized videos or CDs, more difficult cases arise from paraphrasing or nonliteral copying. If an ordinary observer would perceive the second work as deriving from the first, infringement generally is found. Thus, paraphrasing is not a defense to an infringement charge. Otherwise, one could make a few minor changes in a work and be protected from infringement.

Finally, infringement does not require willfulness or intent. Even an innocent infringer is still an infringer. It is the violation of any of the copyright owner's exclusive rights that gives rise to the action for infringement. Violation of federal copyright law has been found even in cases in which the infringement was subconscious, as a court held in finding that former Beatle George Harrison's song "My Sweet Lord" infringed the song "He's So Fine." The court determined that although Harrison did not intend to infringe the song but rather subconsciously recollected the earlier song, infringement existed nevertheless. Marketing and design professionals are particularly vulnerable to such subconscious copying because they see numerous clever slogans and ads. In many cases, and without intent, they subconsciously incorporate such preexisting material into later material they design.

Moreover, one can be liable for contributory infringement. In a number of cases, copy shops have been found liable for copyright infringement in allowing students to photocopy copyrighted textbooks and articles. Similarly, operators of flea markets and swap meets are liable for contributory infringement by allowing the sale of copyrighted videos and CDs. Employers can also be liable for the copyright infringements of their employees because the employer is in a position to direct and control the activities of employees and has a duty to do so.

The Fair Use Defense

The most commonly asserted defense to a claim of infringement is that the accused work is a fair use of the copyrighted work. Under federal law, the fair use of a copyrighted work for purposes such as criticism, comment, news reporting, teaching, scholarship, or research is not an infringement of copyright. The fair use defense allows reviewers to quote from novels, movie critics to show clips of films, and teachers to distribute portions of a poem. Congress has determined that the benefit to the public from such uses outweighs any harm to the copyright owner.

In determining whether a use is fair, courts consider the following four factors:

• *The purpose and character of the use, including whether the use is of a commercial nature or is for nonprofit educational purposes.* Although a commercial use is not automatically an infringement, such a use tends to show infringement. Furthermore, even nonprofit uses can constitute infringement, as occurs when a nonprofit charity event uses copyrighted music without permission.

• *The nature of the copyrighted work.* Courts tend to afford less protection to informational works than to highly creative works. Thus, a novel generally receives more protection than a highly technical article published in a scientific journal or factual information, as is found in historical accounts or biographies. The use of such factual material for purposes of scholarship and research is favored under federal law.

▾ *The amount and substantiality of the portion used.* Although there is no perfect test for determining when too much has been taken from an existing work, if the amount taken is substantial or is the heart or central focus of the copyrighted work, infringement generally is found. Thus, courts analyze not only the quantity of work taken but also the quality.

▾ *The effect of the use on the potential market for the copyrighted work.* Courts typically view this factor as the most important, reasoning that if the accused work adversely affects the copyright owner's market for his or her work, infringement probably has occurred. Thus, scooping a work before it is published or publishing so much of the work that consumers refrain from buying it usually are found to be infringements because they deprive the copyright owner of revenue. In one of the more famous modern copyright cases, the U.S. Supreme Court held in 1981 that the sale of videocassette recorders by Sony Corporation was not a violation of copyright because allowing consumers to record copyrighted television shows for private viewing at a later time did not affect the potential market for the copyrighted works. Such time shifting was thus held to be a fair use. Moreover, because the videocassette recorders had numerous uses other than infringing uses, the products could not be deemed to have been created solely for the purposes of copyright infringement. Conversely, a company's purchase of a few copies of a journal and routing of them to its employees (who then photocopied the articles of interest to them) was found to be infringement because such use diminished the market for the journals.

Other Defenses

Although fair use is the most commonly asserted defense in copyright infringement actions, a variety of other defenses exist. Chief among them are the following:

▾ *Parody.* Parodies of movies, songs, and novels are considered to be useful forms of social commentary and criticism and thus are generally permissible. Parody is a form of fair use of a work, namely a use for the purposes of criticism. In a recent case, the rap group 2 Live Crew parodied the famous song "Oh Pretty Woman." The court held that the parody was a permissible form of fair use. Although the work was commercial, the parody added new material. Furthermore, the parody was unlikely to supplant the original work. Persons interested in the original song were unlikely to purchase the parody version as a substitute.

▾ *Reproduction by libraries*. Libraries are allowed to reproduce works to distribute to the public and for archival purposes. Additionally, they are insulated from liability for infringement for unauthorized photocopying by others if they display notices on or near the photocopy equipment that the making of copies may violate copyright law.

▾ *Archival copying of computer programs*. As discussed in Chapter 9, owners of computer programs may make one copy of the program for backup or archival purposes and may adapt the program as an essential step in utilizing the computer program.

▾ *Invalidity of copyright*. Defendants often assert that the work the plaintiff seeks to protect is not copyrightable. Although the existence of a copyright registration issued by the Copyright Office gives rise to a presumption that the copyright is valid, the presumption can be defeated. Defendants often assert that the work is not original, is a useful article, or is merely factual.

▾ *Statute of limitations*. Under federal law, no civil action can be maintained for copyright infringement unless it is brought within three years after the infringement occurs.

▾ *Equitable defenses*. Defendants can assert a variety of other defenses as well, including laches, asserted when a plaintiff has so unreasonably delayed in bringing an action that the defendant has been prejudiced thereby. Laches can be asserted before the three-year statute of limitations has expired. Typically, a defendant raising a laches defense argues that the plaintiff knew about or acquiesced in the defendant's use of the copyrighted matter and the defendant then incurred great expense in using, marketing, or distributing the matter, such that it would be inequitable to preclude the defendant from using the copyrighted matter. A defendant can assert that the plaintiff has "unclean hands" in that the plaintiff has misused the copyright or has engaged in unlawful activity such as requiring those who would license the copyrighted matter to purchase licenses for other matter also, such that the plaintiff should be precluded from recovery.

Infringement Actions

As in trademark actions, copyright owners typically send a cease and desist letter to the accused copyright infringer before initiating litigation for infringement. The cease and desist letter shown in Figure 6-1 can be modified easily for copyright violations. If the letter fails to bring about a resolution, the plaintiff can bring action in federal court *if the copyright has been registered.* If the Copyright Office refused registration, an action for infringement can still be brought if the plaintiff notifies the Copyright Office so it can participate in the action regarding the issue of registrability of the copyright. Only U.S. works are subject to the requirement of registration; works originating in most other nations need not be registered before action for infringement can be brought.

Once the plaintiff files the lawsuit, the defendant answers the complaint and asserts various defenses. Discovery commences and depositions are taken, documents are produced, and interrogatories (sets of written questions) are sent to each party for response. If the parties do not settle the dispute themselves, the case proceeds to trial. Plaintiffs are entitled to a jury trial, if desired. Courts can award the following remedies:

▾ *Injunctive relief.* Courts can order that the defendant cease use, distribution, reproduction, performance, or display of the copyrighted matter. Courts issue restraining orders only if the plaintiffs show that they are likely to prevail at trial and that money damages are insufficient to protect them.

▾ *Impoundment.* Courts can order the impounding of the infringing goods while an action is pending. After the action is concluded, a court may order the destruction or other disposition of infringing materials.

▾ *Damages and profits.* An infringer is liable for the actual damages suffered by a copyright owner and any profits of the infringer that are attributable to the infringement. Instead of actual damages and profits, copyright owners can elect to recover statutory damages, namely, damages not less than $500 and not more than $20,000 for each infringement, as a court considers just. If the infringement was willful, the court can increase the award to $100,000. Generally, plaintiffs elect statutory damages when it may be difficult to prove actual damages. In one recent case, a court determined that a plaintiff should receive more than $70,000 for each act of infringement of a defendant who had violated the plaintiff's copyright in 440 separate unauthorized airings of a television program. The damage award, nearly $32 million, is believed to be the highest ever awarded for copyright infringement. Statutory damages are available only if the work was registered within three months after publication, thus providing a powerful incentive for prompt registration of copyrights.

▾ *Attorney's fees and costs.* Courts, in their discretion, may award attorney's fees and costs to the prevailing party. Typically, costs and attorney's fees are awarded only in cases of willful misconduct or infringement, or if a contract provides for them.

▾ *Criminal sanctions.* Copyright violators can be subject to fines and even imprisonment in cases of serious infringement. The statute of limitations for criminal proceedings is five years.

▾ *Fines.* The use of a fraudulent copyright notice or the fraudulent removal of a copyright notice may subject the violator to fines up to $2,500.

Top Ten Copyright Myths

Because the penalties for copyright infringement can be severe, it is critical for all those in a business enterprise to take affirmative action to avoid infringement. Following are the ten most common misunderstandings and myths about copyright infringement:

▾ *If I attribute material to its author, there can be no infringement.* Because copyright law provides the exclusive right to copyright owners to reproduce, adapt, distribute, display, and perform their works, any violation of any of these rights is an infringement. Although giving credit to an author may help show that one is not a willful infringer and may reduce damages, merely attributing material to its author does not insulate one from a claim of copyright infringement. Do not just give attribution. Get permission.

▾ *If it's on the Internet, it's free for all to use.* A common misconception is that material posted on the Internet is available for all to use and disseminate. Check the legal terms for each site. In some cases, Web owners give permission for materials to be used. Without such express permission, use of material posted on the Internet probably is infringement.

▾ *If I paraphrase, there can be no copyright violation.* Courts protect copyright owners against literal and nonliteral copying. Thus, paraphrasing can constitute copyright infringement.

▾ *If I just take a little, it's okay.* Although courts examine the amount of material taken, even a little infringement goes a long way. If what is taken is the heart or central focus of the copyrighted material, infringement can occur. Thus, merely taking the eight words "Yesterday, all my troubles seemed so far away" from the famous song "Yesterday" would constitute infringement.

▾ *I can freely play the radio or television at my business for the enjoyment of my customers.* Unless the business establishment is very small (generally, less than 2,000 square feet for non–eating establishments and less than 3,750 square feet for food service or drinking establishments), playing the radio or television is an infringement. Similarly, playing CDs or other forms of recorded music on hold or throughout the establishment without obtaining a license is an infringement.

▾ *Once I own a work I can do anything I want with it.* Although an owner of a copyrighted work can later distribute it to another (as by selling it or lending it to another), copyright owners retain other rights even after their works are sold. Thus, reproducing several chapters of a book or magazine or making duplicate copies of a CD or video are infringements, even if there is no commercial motive. Similarly, under the Visual Artists Rights Act, works of fine art cannot be mutilated or destroyed. Finally, as discussed in Chapter 9, because most computer programs are licensed rather than sold, you do not own the software you bought; you are a licensee with very limited rights of use and no rights of copying (other than for backup purposes) or distribution.

▾ *Any nonprofit use is permissible.* Although noncommercial use may show lack of willfulness and thus help reduce damages, use need not be commercial for infringement to occur. Even a nonprofit use of copyrighted work can be an infringement, particularly where such use affects the market for the copyrighted work.

▾ *If it's just for me it's okay.* Whereas using a VCR to record an episode of *Friends* to watch later in the week is permissible time shifting, making a copy of the rented video *The Sixth Sense* for a friend is a copyright infringement even though there is no commercial exploitation of the movie.

▾ *I didn't know what I did was wrong, so there can be no violation.* As discussed earlier, even an innocent copyright violation is a copyright violation nonetheless. Innocence and intent have a bearing on the amount of damages a defendant may be liable for; they do not excuse copyright infringement.

▾ *I didn't do it.* As mentioned earlier, copy shops have been held liable for contributory infringement for allowing students and others to use their equipment to reproduce copyrighted matter. Similarly, photo shops have been held liable for infringement for allowing patrons to make reproductions of copyrighted photographs, and employers can be liable for the acts of their employees. Thus, merely allowing someone else to use your equipment does not insulate you from liability. Liability attaches to those who violate copyright and to those who assist them or are in a position to control their wrongful conduct.

12

Emerging Copyright Trends: Software Usage and Internet Policies

Most cutting-edge copyright issues relate to two distinct fields: computer programs and the Internet. Courts have struggled with some of the newer copyright issues, and the law continues to shift and evolve with technology. Similarly, the use of the Internet and computer programs can lead to liability for a company that allows employees to disseminate the company's or others' information on the Internet or to use unlicensed software. Although companies cannot protect themselves against every electronic threat, establishing and enforcing software and Internet usage policies affords significant protection. Sample policies are found throughout this chapter.

Ten New Issues in Copyright Law

Computer Programs

Computer programs are protectable under copyright law and can be registered with the Copyright Office as literary works, regardless of their medium. Thus object code, source code, disks, and CD-ROMs can all be protected. Because of the ease of registration and modest filing fees, numerous authors have registered their computer programs with the Copyright Office. Only one registration per work is required, and computer screen displays and accompanying instruction manuals are considered part of the computer program so that only one registration need be sought for the work.

As discussed in Chapter 10, because a computer program can include trade secrets, the Copyright Office allows the copyright claimant to block out portions of the program to protect such trade secrets.

Because some courts have given little or no protection to computer programs, based on the programs being utilitarian products, and other courts have allowed reverse engineering or decompiling of computer programs in some instances, many computer program creators have interpreted these cases as indicating a trend toward limiting the scope of copyright protection for computer programs and have thus begun seeking patents for them. In fact, the U.S. Patent and Trademark Office (PTO) witnessed a doubling in patent applications for software-related inventions between 1995 and 1997. Because copyright protects only original works, if a second computer program creator independently develops a program similar or identical to the first, there is no infringement. Patent law, on the other hand, provides a patent owner with an exclusive right to prohibit the making, using, or selling of a patented invention. Thus, although securing a patent is far more expensive and complex than securing a copyright registration, patent protection is much broader than copyright protection (during the term of patent protection).

The reverse-engineering cases have held that if disassembly is the sole means to gain access to the ideas and functional elements embodied in a computer program (namely, the nonprotectable elements) and if there is a legitimate reason for seeking such access, reverse engineering of the program is not an infringement. Because courts seem to be giving narrower protection to computer programs, owners of programs should draft their written contracts carefully to expressly preclude any reverse engineering, disassembly, or decompiling of computer programs sold, licensed, or used by others.

Computer Programming Languages

In spring 2000, the Sixth Circuit Court of Appeals held that computer programming languages are protected by the First Amendment. The controversy arose out of a Case Western Reserve professor's placement of an encryption code on his Web site to help his students understand computer programs. Under current federal law, programs that can scramble electronic messages must be licensed before being exported, and the government contended that the professor's encryption program needed such a license. The court held that the encryption computer program was protected by the First Amendment because the source code is a means of communication or speech.

The Shrink Wrap License and Electronic Signatures

Recall that the first sale doctrine allows one who owns a copyrighted work to distribute it: After your purchase of the memoir *Angela's Ashes*, you can sell it to a friend. Due to the first sale doctrine and the great ease of duplication of computer programs, makers of software programs decided not to sell their goods outright but rather to license them. If goods are licensed, the first sale doctrine does not apply. Moreover, the licensor can impose a variety of terms and conditions on use of the software pursuant to a license agreement.

Thus, the shrink wrap license was born. Most software makers do not sell their software but merely license its use under a written license agreement. The license agreement springs into existence when the shrink wrap surrounding a package containing software is opened. A notice appears on the box warning that the goods are not being sold but rather licensed, and a procedure is described for returning the goods if the would-be purchaser does not consent to the license terms. When software is licensed electronically, the transaction is called a click wrap license. Courts have generally held that such licenses are enforceable just like any other licenses as long as their terms are not unconscionable.

In June 2000, Congress enacted legislation (which became effective October 1, 2000) providing that electronic signatures and documents will have the same force in law as their pen-and-ink counterparts. Under the Electronic Signatures in Global and National Commerce Act, consumers will be able to choose whether to use an electronic or handwritten signature, although the law requires certain documents (such as notices canceling water, heat, and health and life insurance, eviction notices, court documents, and product recall notices) to be sent in paper form. The electronic signature can consist of a keystroke. The new law allows some records to be stored electronically and requires consistent rules for authenticating electronic signatures, thus boosting consumer confidence and promoting uniformity in transacting business electronically.

The Uniform Computer Information Transaction Act

The Uniform Computer Information Transaction Act (UCITA), a proposed piece of legislation, was released in 1999, and its proponents hope to convince each of the fifty states to adopt its provisions, which are aimed at strengthening licenses for software and digital information. As originally envisioned, the act was meant to promote fair transactions in the electronic age and thus assist companies wanting to sell goods and software electronically. As drafted, however, the act gave far too much protection to the software industry, according to many consumer groups. Its critics include the Federal Trade Commission, Consumers Union, twenty-eight state attorneys general, and the American Library Association, all of whom contend that the legislation is anticonsumer. For example, under UCITA, software makers could include backdoors in their programs that would allow them to disable a user's software and could monitor a user's computer to ensure that all license requirements are obeyed. UCITA's critics contend that much of the act is unnecessary and that there is no valid reason for treating digital transactions differently from paper transactions. At the time of writing of this book, only Virginia and Maryland, with their strong high-tech industries, had adopted UCITA, and the act continues to be subject to much debate and controversy.

Automated Databases

An automated database is a body of facts, data, or other information assembled into an organized format suitable for use in a computer and comprising one or more files. Thus, collections of maps, federal antitrust cases, or film reviews collected on a CD-ROM are automated databases, protectable as literary works under copyright law. Although the elements in the database may not qualify for copyright protection (for example, federal cases are in the public domain), the particular selection and arrangement of those materials may allow the material to qualify for protection as a compilation. Registration of automated databases is made using Form TX. Information can be found in the Copyright Office's Circular 65, "Copyright Registration for Automated Databases."

One of the newer issues confronting Congress is the extent of protection that should be allowed for databases. In *Feist Publications, Inc. v. Rural Telephone Service Co.*, 499 U.S. 340 (1991), the Supreme Court held that a telephone directory was not entitled to copyright protection because it did not reflect sufficient creativity in its mere alphabetical arrangement of names. *Feist* has been interpreted as refuting the sweat-of-the-brow doctrine, which held that any works that were the subject of a great deal of time and effort should be copyrightable. After *Feist*, it is clear that no matter how much effort is put into a work, if it does not reflect some minimum threshold of creativity, it is not copyrightable. Thus, although telephone white pages are not ordinarily copyrightable, other directories, such as the Yellow Pages, may be if there was care and selectiveness in determining how to arrange the entries and which entries to use.

Because of the enormous increase in collections of information available on the Internet, such as stock quotes, weather reports, sports statistics, and real estate listings, the purveyors of such information have lobbied for copyright protection for those collections. The 106th Congress (H.R. 354) considered legislation that would protect such databases—created through the "sweat of the brow"—so that their owners could preclude others from using or copying them. Exceptions would be allowed for scientific, educational, research, and news reporting uses. Nevertheless, the topic of whether and how much protection should be afforded such automated databases is subject to vigorous debate, with the creators asking for copyright protection and consumers often opposing such protection on the basis that such factual information should be free for all to use and that current law is sufficient to protect against piracy. The protection of such databases is a key issue in other countries as well.

Online Works

Works transmitted online and accessed via World Wide Web sites are protectable under copyright law. Thus, a company's Web site is fully protectable under copyright law. Text, artwork, music, audiovisual material (including sounds), online newsletters, and sound recordings all qualify for copyright protection. Although copyright registration is not required for these works because they are protected from the time of their creation and fixation, registration affords important benefits. Registration is accomplished using the pertinent forms (for example, Form TX is used to protect written text, Form VA is used to protect pictorial and graphic works, and Form PA is used to protect audiovisual material, including sounds).

One of the difficulties in protecting online works lies in the frequent updating of such works. There is no blanket copyright registration available to cover revisions made on various dates. Separate copyright registrations are needed for the original work and then for each revision of it. Group registration may be available for serials and newsletters, eliminating the need for hundreds of separate copyright applications. See Circular 62, "Copyright Registration for Serials," or Circular 62a, "Group Registration of Daily Newspapers and Newsletters" for more information.

Deposits for the works may consist of a computer disk containing the entire work, a printout, an audiocassette, or a videotape.

All Web sites should include a copyright notice. Such notices and Web site disclaimers and policies are discussed later in this chapter.

Multimedia Works

A multimedia work combines authorship in two or more media. For example, a textual presentation of PowerPoint® slides may be accompanied by artwork or music, photography may be accompanied by music, or music may be accompanied by choreography. Registration for such works is made by using the pertinent forms. For example, Form PA is used if the work contains an audiovisual element, such as slides, film, or videotape (regardless of whether any sounds are included). See Circular 55, "Copyright Registration for Multimedia Works," for additional information.

Internet Transmissions

Congress passed the Digital Millennium Copyright Act in 1998 to provide that search engines and online providers such as America Online are liable for copyright infringement that occurs through the use of their services only when they have actual knowledge of infringement, profit from it, and fail to stop it. In this way, Internet service providers are somewhat analogous to telephone companies, which do not have liability when defamatory material is spoken over the telephone or when individuals use telephones to commit crimes such as wire fraud. The Internet service providers are mere conduits for information rather than publishers who would be liable for infringement under the Copyright Act. Most experts believe that Congress was reluctant to make Internet service providers responsible for ensuring that all transmissions that occurred through their systems were legal. Similarly, in late 2000, a court in San Francisco held that online auctioneer eBay Inc. was not liable for the sale of pirated audio recordings offered on its Web site. Other similar cases are pending.

The act also prohibits the circumvention of encryption measures, thus making it illegal for hackers to pierce through encrypted material, and requires that the U.S. Copyright Office consult with nonprofit educational institutions and others and submit to Congress recommendations on distance learning.

One of the newer issues confronting courts is whether providing links to facilitate copyright infringement is itself a violation of copyright law. In early 2000, a company was ordered to stop posting certain DVD descrambling software; it did so but then merely posted links to other sites where the descrambling software was available. In mid-2000, the Southern District of New York enjoined the linking because it was equivalent to abetting copyright infringement. Search engines are particularly concerned after this ruling because if linking to copyrighted material leads to liability, those search engines would be forced to review every link and determine whether it led to copyrighted material, a process so time-consuming and expensive that it would arguably paralyze the Internet. Cases enjoining linking have turned on their specific facts. In each case, the defendant's acts were willful and intentional and followed acts of actual infringement.

Book Publishing

A defining event occurred in the book publishing world in mid-2000 when author Stephen King sold a serialized novel exclusively online. Although other authors have published material online, King's publication marked the first time a hugely popular author entered the electronic publishing world. The book was downloaded by users who paid a $2.50 fee for viewing the book on their computer screens. Although the text was protected by encryption technology to guard against dissemination to unauthorized users, a hacker managed to crack the code, causing the publisher to adopt stronger encryption technology. In November 2000, King suspended the project because too many people downloaded the work without paying for it.

In a related issue, courts have recently been called upon to decide whether magazines and newspapers have the right to reprint or relicense articles and photos in electronic databases from freelancers without seeking permission. In one case, the National Geographic Society was sued by writers and photographers after the Society compiled works from its magazines into a CD-ROM without seeking permission from (or paying royalties to) the writers and photographers for those articles. In another case, a court held that unless a contract provides otherwise, online publishing is a new use of copyrighted materials, and thus the publisher must seek permission from the copyright holders. The issue remains unsettled, however, because the U.S. Supreme Court has agreed to consider the appeal of the publishers. A ruling is not expected until mid-2001.

In the wake of numerous lawsuits, some publishers have begun either contractually requiring authors to allow later online publishing or have entered into royalty payment arrangements with the authors.

Another recent issue relates to whether a publisher can be liable for a false statement made on a book cover. In several cases, plaintiffs have alleged that claims made on a book cover (such as how to receive a 24 percent return on your stock market investment) are a form of speech that must comply with truth in advertising laws. While some courts have ruled that because such commercial statements are advertising, they are not protected under the First Amendment if they are false, other courts have reached the opposite conclusion, causing concern among publishers and broadcasters as to how to promote their products. The issue remains unsettled.

Finally, the issue of ownership of college professors' lecture notes has caused concern in academia. In many cases, students have taken notes in class and then offered them for sale on the Internet. Oral, nonfixed lectures are not protected by copyright law. Moreover, although universities generally own the work produced by their employees, professors, and teachers, they have not typically enforced their ownership rights. Some experts have suggested that the professors arguably possess moral rights in their works so that any lecture notes must be attributed to them. The American Association of University Professors is studying the issue and has formed a strike force to craft a proposal for adoption by the universities that would clarify the ownership issues surrounding lectures.

Online Music

A new technology, called MP3 and offered by MP3.com, allows users to download music from the Internet and play it over their computer speakers. MP3 is a digital compression standard used to shrink music files for easier and clearer transmission over the Internet. One service offered by MP3.com, called My.MP3.com, allows users to listen to digital copies of songs when they verify that they already own the CDs on which the songs appear. In essence, the service functions as an online locker room, allowing users to access music from any online connection. In May 2000, in an action brought by various record labels and the Recording Industry Association of America, the Southern District of New York held that the service constituted copyright infringement. Just a few days after the court issued its decision, MP3.com reached a licensing agreement with Broadcast Music, Inc. (BMI), to pay license fees for the use of the music in BMI's repertory. MP3.com then agreed to pay Warner and BMG Entertainment, other record labels, $20 million each and pay a fee each time the labels' songs are downloaded. Other licensing arrangements with other record labels are being negotiated.

Of perhaps even greater significance to record labels and artists is Napster, the brainchild of a former student at Northeastern University in Boston. Napster is a software program that allows users to share music files with others online. The software can be downloaded at no cost, and users are then matched up with others who have the songs they want. Napster itself does not store any music on its servers but connects users to each other. The songs can be played through the computer's speakers, recorded onto a CD-ROM, or transferred to a portable MP3 player.

The band Metallica and rap artist Dr. Dre have sued Napster for copyright infringement of their songs. After a number of universities were also sued by Metallica, which alleged that the universities contributed to copyright infringement by allowing university-owned computers and computer services to be used to transmit music in violation of copyright law, the universities either blocked or sharply curtailed the use of Napster on their campuses. Some schools have discovered that as much as 60 percent of traffic on campus computer systems was related to the use of Napster technology to capture music from the Internet. Boston University, the University of Chicago, Indiana University, Northwestern University, and the University of Texas are among more than 120 schools that have banned the use of Napster to download music.

In addition to the Metallica and Dr. Dre suits, Napster has also been sued by the Recording Industry Association of America and several record labels for copyright infringement. Although Napster initially claimed that it should be entitled to the safe harbor provided to Internet service providers, a federal judge ruled that the Digital Millennium Copyright Act was not applicable because Napster was not transmitting or providing connections through its system.

Although Napster was originally enjoined from further infringing activity, the injunction was stayed pending an appeal. In late 2000, Napster announced a partnership with media giant Bertlesmann AG to develop a system that would guarantee payment to artists for music shared through Napster. Many experts predict that eventually the dispute over Napster and peer-to-peer music and entertainment sharing will be settled through similar arrangements.

The results in these early cases, which may be on appeal for several years, are likely to transform the way music is purchased and licensed in the electronic age. In mid-2000, members of Metallica testified before

Congress at a hearing convened to explore whether Congress needs to enact legislation to protect copyrighted music against Napster and similar Internet music services.

Napster is the fastest-growing program in the history of the Internet, easily demonstrating the potential for copyright piracy on a scale unknown in previous years. Other Internet music distribution systems exist along with Napster, and their future is also uncertain. Although some artists and record labels are convinced that Napster and similar services will destroy the music industry, others are quick to point out that although Universal attempted to shut down use of videocassette recorders, the use of VCRs has done nothing but increase the revenue of movie studios.

Movie studios are also concerned about Napster-like technology being used to make movies available over the Internet, which would adversely affect box office ticket sales and video rentals. The president of the Motion Picture Association has testified before Congress about the growing threat such technology presents to artists' and owners' rights in movies.

Copyright and the Internet

The Internet poses both enormous promise and great risk for companies. Although the Internet opens a vast array of new business opportunities to customers without the need to establish brick-and-mortar stores, a company's valuable trade secrets and other assets can be disseminated easily to millions of others with just a keystroke. Moreover, improper use of a company's resources can lead to liability for infringement, defamation, and harassment.

Perhaps the three most significant issues confronting businesses in the electronic age are the use of unlicensed software, which can subject a company to civil and criminal liability; improper use of the Internet by employees, which can also subject a company to liability; and protection of a company's Web site. Although companies cannot predict or avert every possible danger, they can go a long way toward protecting themselves from liability by establishing and enforcing software compliance and Internet usage policies. Samples of policies are found in this chapter. Similarly, companies can protect their Web sites from infringement by implementing and posting a legal notice or disclaimer section on their Web sites confirming the terms and conditions for use of their sites, verifying that no warranties are being made, and stating that links to others' sites do not constitute endorsement of products or services offered at those sites. Further discussion of Web site terms and conditions policies is found later in this chapter.

The Risk of Using Unlicensed Software

One of the most alarming trends today is the use of unlicensed software. Experts estimate that the use of unlicensed software causes a loss of revenue of nearly $3 billion annually in the United States. The proliferation of unlicensed software is easy to understand because improper use is so readily accomplished. No additional product need be bought, and software can be copied easily or accessed by multiple users through a network. The ease of copying and access itself leads to the misconception that the purchase of one software package for a company is sufficient for companywide use.

Software makers have become increasingly vigilant about ensuring that their software is not pirated or used without license. Because it is quite common for employees to make copies of software and install it on another computer for home use, for a friend, or for a coworker, software makers often join associations to protect their proprietary rights. One of the best known associations is the Software Information Industry Association (SIIA, formerly known as the Software Publishers Association), which has established an antipiracy division devoted to locating cases of retail, corporate, and Internet piracy. In many instances, former disgruntled employees report piracy to SIIA. Microsoft has become especially effective in locating software pirates and maintains an office in Florida dedicated exclusively to combating software piracy in South Florida and Latin America. Penalties for the use of unlicensed software have included back payments for the unlicensed software, injunctions ordering audits of a company's computers to locate pirated software, and imprisonment. In 1999, a father and son were sentenced to five years and one year in prison, respectively, for engaging in a conspiracy to sell more than $20 million of pirated Microsoft software.

One issue confronting many companies today is the use of software by employees who work at home either exclusively or on a flexible telecommuting schedule. Although some software companies allow their software to be used both on company premises and at home, in many instances loading a copy of a software program licensed to an employer onto a home computer is a violation of the software license and of copyright law. Thus, companies need to make sure that software used at home for business use is properly licensed. Additionally, the use of unlicensed software promotes viruses, which can readily destroy a company's valuable information stored on a computer.

How can a company protect against piracy? SIIA offers an audit program to identify whether a company's software is properly licensed. Access SIIA's Web site at www.siia.net and search for "Audits" or "Software Management Tools." Companies should also implement and enforce a software compliance program that clearly notifies employees that software used by employees must be properly licensed and must not be copied for home use and that employees should report any violations or piracy to a designated company representative. Policies related to software usage can be presented to employees as separate agreements or can be included in the company's employee handbook, which employees should be required to sign, confirming that they have read the handbook and agree to its terms. See Figure 12-1 for sample software usage policy.

Internet Policies

Because a company's electronic communication systems are owned by the company, it must ensure that those systems are used for business purposes only. Improper use of the Internet during business hours not only results in a loss of productivity but can also lead to liability, as a court recently ruled in holding that Continental Airlines could be liable for defamatory and harassing remarks about an employee that were posted in a chat room that Continental Airlines knew about and could have controlled. Thus, companies should implement Internet usage policies to ensure that employees understand that use of the Internet during business hours must be for business purposes only and that improper use can lead to discipline, including termination.

How does a company determine that its electronic communication systems are being used improperly? Generally, companies have a right to monitor use of their online communication systems as long as employees are notified that the company might engage in such monitoring. Implementing and enforcing an Internet usage policy is the easiest way to help protect a company from liability for improper Internet usage during business hours. Such policies can be provided to employees as separate agreements or can be incorporated into a company's employee handbook. Monitoring of phone conversations by employers is generally illegal. (Customer service and telemarketing calls can be monitored if it is disclosed

Figure 12-1. Software usage policy.

1. **General Statement of Policy.** It is the policy of ABC, Inc. (the "Company"), to respect all computer software copyrights and to adhere to the terms of all software licenses to which the Company is a party. The Company will take all steps necessary to prohibit users from duplicating any licensed software or related documentation for use on the Company's premises or elsewhere unless the Company is expressly authorized to do so. Unauthorized use or duplication of software may subject users and the Company to civil and criminal penalties under the U.S. Copyright Act. The Company does not permit any user to use software in any manner inconsistent with applicable license agreements, including giving or receiving software from clients, contractors, customers, and others.

2. **Acquisition of Software.** All software acquired by the Company must be purchased through the Information System (IS) Department. Software acquisition channels are restricted to ensure that the Company has a complete record of all software that has been purchased for the Company's computers and can register, support, and upgrade such software accordingly. This includes software that may be downloaded or purchased from the Internet.

3. **Registration of Software.** The IS Department is responsible for completing registration and inventory requirements before installing software. Because of personnel turnover, software will be registered in the Company's name rather than in the name of an individual user.

4. **Home Computers.** The Company's computers are owned by the Company and must be kept both software legal and virus free. Only software purchased through the Company's procedures described in this policy may be used on the Company's computers. Users are not permitted to bring software from home and load it onto the Company's computers. Similarly, Company-owned software cannot be taken home and loaded on a user's home computer unless express permission is received from the Company's software manager. If a user is to use software at home, the Company will purchase a separate package that will be owned by the Company and registered to it. Nevertheless, because some software companies allow home use under their license agreements with the Company, home use may be permitted. Use of Company-owned software at home is permissible for business use only. Users should consult with the Company's software manager to determine whether home use is appropriate. In the event a user ceases to work for the Company, any Company-owned software must be removed from a user's home computer, and related documentation and materials must be returned to the Company.

5. **Use of Software.** Software can be used only in accordance with the terms of applicable license agreements. Unless otherwise authorized in the license, any duplication of copyrighted software, except for backup and archival purposes by the Company's software manager, is a violation of copyright law. Additionally, such unauthorized duplication is a violation of the Company's policies. Thus, all users are subject to the following rules:

   a. All users must use all Company-owned software strictly in accordance with Company license agreements and this policy. All users acknowledge that they do not own this software or its related documentation and, unless expressly

Figure 12-1. (Continued).

authorized by the software owner, may not make additional copies except for archival purposes.

b. The Company does not tolerate the use of any unauthorized copies of software. Any person illegally reproducing software may be subject to civil and criminal penalties, as well as discipline according to the Company's Employee Handbook, including termination of employment.

c. Users cannot use software within the Company that has been brought in from any unauthorized location, including but not limited to the Internet, home, friends, and colleagues.

d. Any user who determines that there may be a misuse of software within the Company must notify the Company's software manager.

e. All software owned by the Company must be used solely for the Company's business purposes and must be purchased through the procedures set forth in this policy.

_____   Date: _____
Signature

each and every time at the beginning of the call. See Figure 12-2 for a sample Internet usage policy.

Web Site Considerations and Policies

The use of a Web site is an easy and inexpensive way for a company to provide information to customers and potential customers and achieve national and even global recognition. Even if a company does not sell goods or services through its Web site but merely uses the site as an information and marketing tool, a number of legal considerations are involved, and the company's Web site should be reviewed periodically to ensure that it does not infringe the rights of others.

The following tips can help companies ensure that their Web site increases business rather than liability.

Ownership of Web Site Content

Make sure your company owns its Web site content. If a company engages another to create its Web site, appropriate language should be included in the contracting documents to ensure that the company will own the finished product and all content. Otherwise, the party who created the site may own the content, and the commissioning company will not be able to revise the content because such would violate the creator's

Figure 12-2. Internet usage policy.

The following policy applies both to the Company's internal network and electronic mail (e-mail) system and to that of any electronic communication provider, such as America Online, to which the Company affords access ("Systems").

1. The Systems, documents stored thereon, and electronic messages are owned by the Company.
2. E-mail, network, and Internet access is restricted to authorized business use only. Company personnel may use the Company's Systems and computer and data communication resources solely for the furtherance of the Company's business activities. Personnel should not use these resources for nonbusiness matters.
3. Confidential Company or client materials may not be copied, reproduced, republished, uploaded, posted, transmitted, or distributed in any way. Modification of such materials or use of them for any other purpose, except as permitted herein or with the Company's prior written consent, is a violation of the Company's copyrights and other proprietary rights.
4. Use of the Company's computer and data communication resources is subject to periodic monitoring, and there is no expectation of privacy regarding online activities, regardless of how material is sent, received, or created.
5. The Company expressly prohibits the transmission of any discriminatory, offensive, harassing, or threatening communications of any kind or nature, including pictures or other images.
6. All e-mail messages are automatically stored in backup or archival files, regardless of an employee's "deletion" of a message.
7. All stored e-mail messages and all material downloaded from the Internet are subject to periodic review at the discretion of management.
8. Company personnel may not print, upload, transmit, or disseminate another party's copyrighted materials, including software programs.
9. Deliberately wasting computer resources, knowingly interfering with the normal operation of the Company's Systems, using the Systems to gain unauthorized access to any computer system, attempting to monitor or tamper with another employee's communications or files, knowingly running or installing a program intended to cause damage or place an excessive load on the Systems, and using the Systems in any way to adversely affect the Company or its customers are prohibited.
10. Employees are provided individually selected, confidential passwords for the protection of the Company and not to ensure any privacy unique to the employee. Employees are expected to keep their passwords secure and should safeguard their logon ID and password from disclosure.
11. Penalties for violation of any of the terms of this Internet Usage Policy may range from a warning to suspension of Internet privileges to probation to termination of employment, depending upon the nature of the violation.
12. Access to and use of the Company's Systems constitute consent for Company recording and monitoring of all electronic material and acceptance of the terms of this policy.

rights to create derivative works. Moreover, the contract should provide that the designer will use only original material and will indemnify the company if a claim is made that the company's Web site infringes material owned by another. If the company's Web site has already been created, the company should confirm that the company owns the content and, if necessary, obtain an assignment of copyright from the Web site creator. See Figure 10-2 for a sample copyright assignment form.

Use of a Copyright Notice

Because the material on a company's Web site can be protected by copyright, a copyright notice should be displayed prominently on the home page of the company's Web site. Although copyright registration affords a number of benefits, registration may be impractical for companies whose Web sites change continually and include new material, which would then necessitate repeated copyright applications. The use of a notice, though not required, will defeat a claim of innocent infringement, so companies should place the notice prominently on their Web sites. Such a notice should take the following form: © 2000 Alliance Consulting, Inc.

Linking to Others' Sites

As discussed in Chapter 7, linking to others' sites can be risky. To eliminate risk, ask permission before linking to another's Web site. At a minimum, use only narrative instruction (for example, "Further information can be obtained at ABC Inc.'s Web site at www.xxx.com") and refrain from using another company's trademarks or logos. Deeplinking, which bypasses another's home page to information deep within the site, is perhaps the most risky conduct of all and should be avoided. To further reduce risk, appoint one individual who has the sole authority to make changes to the company's Web site.

Terms and Conditions Sections

Most companies provide a link on their home pages to their terms and conditions, privacy policies, legal terms, or disclaimer sections. Most users probably will not read these in depth, if at all, but such policies can protect a company by allowing it to assert that it adequately notified users of company policies, and a user is thus liable for actions violating such policies. To review sample terms and conditions, check the legal disclaimers used on the Web sites of large companies such as www.ibm.com, www.ford.com, and www.microsoft.com.

At a minimum, the terms and conditions should include the following:

- A statement that use of the Web site is deemed to be an agreement to the Web site owner's terms and conditions and that if a user does not agree to the terms and conditions, the user should not continue to use the site
- A reminder that the Web site design, text, and illustrations are owned by the company and that material from the site cannot be copied, reproduced, republished, uploaded, posted, transmitted, modified, or distributed in any way
- A statement that links to another's site are not endorsements or approvals of those sites or of products or services offered at those sites and are provided only for the user's convenience
- A statement that material posted or transmitted to the site will be treated as nonconfidential and that users who transmit materials to the company's site agree that the company may use the material for any purpose, including reproduction, publication, transmission, and posting
- A disclaimer that the materials on the site are provided as-is, without warranties of any kind, and that the Web site owner will not be liable for any damages arising out of or in connection with use of the site, including losses caused by viruses, communications delays, or failures
- A statement that by accessing the site, users agree that jurisdiction for any disputes arising between the parties will be where the company has its principal place of business
- A notice that any trademarks of the company shown on the site are owned by the company and cannot be used by others without prior written consent
- A copyright notice

Doing Business on the Web

Although conducting business on the Web presents enormous opportunities to reach customers, doing business on the Internet also entails some risks for most companies. The most significant areas of concern are as follows:

▾ *Jurisdiction*. Injuries and damages based on electronic transactions and communications can subject the sender of the information to jurisdiction in venues in which the sender does not physically do business. Generally, the more interactive a Web site, the more likely that a court will require the sender to submit to jurisdiction in the locale where the message is received. If a Web site is passive, merely presenting text and information, the sender probably will not be subject to jurisdiction in the locale where the message was received. Web sites at which customers can order goods and services and interact with the sender typically have resulted in jurisdiction being imposed on the sender in any location where the message is received, even though the sender maintains no physical presence or office at that location. Although it is uncertain whether such a technique will be successful, companies should post a statement on their Web sites that parties doing business with the company automatically agree that venue will be in the state where the company's principal offices are located.

▾ *Contracts*. If a company does business on the Internet and accepts orders and business, the contracts used should be as nearly identical as possible to the ones used by the company for conventional paper transactions (assuming that such contracts have been approved by legal counsel). Because online contracts generally are held to be just as valid as conventional paper contracts, the use of similar or identical documents helps a company ensure that its contracts are enforceable. Customers can be asked to review the contract and click an "I accept" bar. Under new legislation passed in 2000, such a click-through is a signature as valid as a signature on a paper document.

▾ *Linking*. Courts are divided as to whether linking to a page with defamatory or illegal material subjects the linker to liability. In some cases it has been held that intentionally sending a person to a site offering pirated software constitutes contributory copyright infringement. The safest course of action is to routinely monitor the pages and sites to which a company links to review the sites for offensive, harassing, defamatory, or illegal material. If such material is present, immediately remove the link. Typically, Internet service providers such as America Online have a safe harbor such that they are not liable for harmful material sent through their systems unless they know of the material and refuse to stop it. Using such a policy as an analogy to linking by businesses suggests that innocent linking may be a defense. Linking to sites containing known pirated information is considerably more risky.

▾ *Metatags.* The use of metatags (hidden codes that allow search engines to find a Web site) to divert traffic to one's Web site probably is unlawful where another party's trademark is used.

▾ *Licenses.* The licenses required to operate a brick-and-mortar business apply with equal force to cyberbusinesses. Thus, if the sale of wine requires a license in a jurisdiction, offering the wine for sale over the Internet requires compliance with licensing regulations. Similarly, conducting contests over the Internet is highly regulated.

▾ *Privacy issues.* Sending unsolicited advertisements (spamming) is subject to intense scrutiny, and at least one company that sent such advertisements was found guilty of trespass. The Interactive Services Association provides information about marketing through unsolicited e-mails at its Web site at www.isa.net. Similarly, tracking, collecting, and using information gained from customers using a Web site raises privacy concerns. The Terms and Conditions section of the Web site could indicate that users have no expectation of privacy and that the Web site owner can use the information submitted for any purposes it likes. Because such policies are objectionable to most consumers, many companies state that the only information collected and stored for normal Web site use is the identity of the Internet service provider, the Web site that referred the user, the pages requested, and the time and date of that request. Most companies also state that for normal Web site usage, personally identifiable information such as name, mailing address, phone number, e-mail address, and social security number are not collected, stored, or passed along to any other company and that such information is collected only when needed to fulfill a customer's request. The Federal Trade Commission offers a variety of information and publications about ensuring Internet privacy on its Web site at www.ftc.gov. Although there is no legal requirement that a company adopt a privacy policy, such policies often provide reassurance to consumers.

13

Patent Basics

A patent is a grant from the federal government conferring the right to exclude others from making, selling, or using an invention for the term of patent protection. Like copyrights, patents are governed exclusively by federal law. Whereas rights in trademarks arise from use and copyright rights arise from the moment a work is created, and neither requires federal registration, patents must be issued by the federal government to be protectable. There are three types of patents: those for useful objects, those for the ornamental design of an object, and those for asexually reproduced plants. This book focuses primarily on patents for useful objects, called utility patents, because they are by far the most common type of patent.

Whereas trademarks can last forever if properly protected and maintained, and copyrights have a long term of duration (generally the author's life plus seventy years), patent protection lasts only twenty years from the application date for utility and plant patents (and fourteen years from the grant date for design patents). After this period of protection, the exclusive monopoly given to the patent owner expires and the invention falls into the public domain, free for all to use. Moreover, during the term of utility patent protection, fees are due at various intervals to maintain the patent in force.

No patent gives its owner the right to make, use, or sell the invention; rather, the right granted is only to exclude others from making, using, or selling the patented invention. Thus, if one obtains a patent for a new widget and the widget would infringe another's patented invention or sale of the widget requires a license, the inventor has no right to make, use, or sell the widget (unless permission from the first inventor or a license is obtained).

What Can Be Protected under Patent Law

Three broad categories of inventions can be protected by patents: inventions for useful items are protected as utility patents, inventions for designs are protected as design patents, and new varieties of asexually produced plants are protected as plant patents.

Utility Patents

Utility patents are by far the most common type of patent and cover what we generally think of as inventions, such as the cotton gin, the automobile, the airplane, and the computer. The category of utility patents is quite broad, however, and also covers any new and useful process, machine, manufacture, composition of matter, or any new and useful improvement thereof. These classes taken together include practically everything that is made by humans as well as the processes for making the products. Thus, golf balls, cameras, gene sequences, genetically altered mice, and pharmaceutical drugs can all be patented, as can the processes for making such items.

There are three basic requirements for utility patents: the invention must be useful, it must be novel in relation to the prior art in the field, and it must not be obvious to a person of ordinary skill in the field.

The term *useful* means that the subject matter of the invention must have a useful purpose. Thus, a machine that contradicts scientific principles, such as a perpetual motion machine, is not useful and cannot be patented. Utility is also found lacking if the invention's sole purpose is illegal or immoral, as was the case in 1990 when a patent was refused for a process of making a cheap cigar wrapper tobacco leaf that resembled superior products.

The novelty requirement means that an invention cannot be patented if either of the following exists:

▾ The invention was known or used by others in this country or patented or described in a printed publication before the applicant invented it. This requirement refers to the acts of others and ensures that a patent is granted only to the first to invent. If another person has described the invention, used it, or patented it, it cannot be novel.

▾ The invention was patented in any country, described in a printed publication anywhere in the world, or in public use or on sale in this country more than one year before the application for patent in the United States. This requirement refers to the acts of the inventor and allows the inventor a one-year grace period to file a patent application after patenting the invention in another country, describing the invention in a printed publication, or using or offering the invention for sale in the United States.

The printed publication may be a scientific journal or even a conference paper. Thus, if the inventor gives a presentation at a conference and describes the invention in materials distributed at the conference, the inventor has only one year thereafter to file a patent application in the United States. Similarly, if the inventor begins publicly using the invention in the United States, he or she has one year thereafter to file a patent application. If the inventor's use is for experimental or testing purposes, the one-year grace period does not begin to run until actual public use has commenced. Finally, if the inventor sells or offers to sell the invention in the United States, he or she has a one-year grace period (called the *on-sale bar*) to file a patent application. If the inventor does not file a patent application within one year after any of these events, any right to a patent is lost.

The requirement of nonobviousness means that not all new and useful inventions can be patented. The subject matter sought to be patented must be sufficiently different from what has been used or described before, called the prior art, that it is nonobvious to a person having ordinary skill in the area of technology related to the invention. Thus, substituting one material for another or making mere changes in size ordinarily does not result in a patentable invention.

Determining nonobviousness is difficult, and courts have struggled to develop guidelines. In general, courts consider the following factors in determining whether an invention is nonobvious:

▾ *Prior art.* Courts examine the prior art in the pertinent field to determine whether an invention is nonobvious. Journals, publications, previously issued patents, and other sources of public knowledge are examined.

▾ *Differences between prior art and the invention.* If the invention is superior to prior art and performs better than other similar inventions, such tends to show nonobviousness.

▾ *Level of ordinary skill in the prior art.* If the invention would be obvious to one possessing ordinary skill in the technology to which the invention relates, the invention cannot be patented.

Courts also consider whether the invention is a commercial success (reasoning that inventions that are commercially successful tend to be nonobvious) and whether the invention has satisfied a long-felt commercial need (reasoning that if there has long been a need for the invention that was unsatisfied, the invention must have been nonobvious; otherwise, numerous other people would have been able to meet the need by inventing the item).

As mentioned earlier, utility patents remain in force for twenty years from the date on which a patent application is filed in the United States. Previously, the term was seventeen years from the date the patent was granted. In 1995, the law was changed to motivate inventors to move their applications through the U.S. Patent and Trademark Office (PTO) as quickly as possible to obtain the maximum benefit of the patent term. Until the change in the law, many inventors delayed the process while they gathered funds, conducted marketing, and so forth, leading to a backlog in the PTO. Patent terms are extended under certain circumstances, such as for pharmaceuticals when there is a delay in granting the patent because of the time taken for approval by the Food and Drug Administration.

Fees to maintain utility patents are due $3^1/_2$, $7^1/_2$, and $11^1/_2$ years after the original grant for all utility patents. After the patent expires, anyone may make, use, or sell the invention without liability.

Design Patents

A design patent is granted to any person who has invented any new and nonobvious ornamental design for an article of manufacture. In general, a utility patent protects the way an invention is used and works, whereas a design patent protects the way an article looks. Both design and utility patents may be obtained on an article if there is inventiveness in both its utility and its ornamental appearance. Thus, a camera tripod or a computer mouse may be eligible for both a utility patent and a design patent. The design patent protects only the appearance of an article, not its structural or functional features. Design patents can be obtained for containers such as trash receptacles, jewelry, furniture, clothing, embossed eating utensils, burial urns, and many other items. The design must be ornamental rather than primarily functional. Although trash receptacles and eating utensils clearly serve a useful purpose, if there are numerous ways in which an item could be designed and still remain functional, then any one design for it probably is ornamental rather than functional. Thus, because a chair can be designed in a variety of ways (with or without rolled arms, a high back, curved legs, and so forth), a design for a chair qualifies for design patent protection. If there is only one way in which the article could be designed, it is primarily functional and does not qualify for design patent protection.

Like utility patents, design patents must be novel and nonobvious to a designer of ordinary skill who designs articles of the type applied for in a design patent application. The requirements for novelty and nonobviousness apply equally to design patents. Design patents have a term of fourteen years from the date of their grant, and no maintenance fees are charged to maintain a design patent in force.

There is some overlap between copyright and design patents. For example, jewelry can be protected under copyright or patent law. In many instances, matters of cost and strategy dictate the method of protection sought. For example, copyright applications are inexpensive ($30) and easily obtained, whereas patents are expensive (generally several thousand dollars) and can take up to two years to issue. Moreover, copyright protection generally lasts for the life of the author plus seventy years, whereas design patent protection lasts only fourteen years from the date of grant. Because an item of jewelry may go out of style after a season or two, the designer may well elect to protect the item under copyright law rather than seek a patent for it. On the other hand, patent law protects against the unauthorized making, using, or selling of a patented invention and would thus prohibit a later infringing use even if it were independently created. However, copyright law would allow a later independently created work.

Plant Patents

Since 1930, federal law has allowed for the granting of a patent to anyone who has invented or discovered and asexually reproduced any distinct and new variety of plant or cultivated nontuberous plant. Asexually reproduced plants are those reproduced by means other than from seeds, such as by grafting or the rooting of cuttings. The new variety can be different from previous plants in its resistance to disease or drought, color, scent, flavor, or productivity. Thus, a new color of rose, drought-resistant corn, and disease-immune orange trees are all available for protection. The on-sale bar applies to plant patents such that if the inventor has used or sold a plant variety in the United States, he or she has only one year thereafter to seek a patent for it. The term of a plant patent is identical to that for utility patents: twenty years from the date on which the application for the patent is filed with the PTO. Unlike utility patents, no fees are charged during the term of the plant patent to maintain it in force.

How Patent Rights Are Acquired

Patents are governed exclusively by federal law, and rights in patents arise from Article I, Section 8 of the U.S. Constitution, which provides that "Congress shall have power to promote the progress of science and useful arts, by securing for limited times to . . . inventors the exclusive right to their . . . discoveries." There is no such thing as a state patent. Whereas rights in trademarks arise from the moment a trademark is used, and copyright rights arise the moment a work is created in fixed form, patent rights do not arise unless the PTO grants a patent after an application is filed. Patent statutes are found in Title 35 of the United States Code, Sections 100, et seq. (www4.law.cornell.edu/uscode).

Exclusions from Patent Protection

Under federal law there are a number of exclusions from patent protection, including the following:

- Inventions useful solely in the use of special nuclear material or atomic energy for atomic weapons
- Laws of nature (for example, the law of gravity or pure mathematical formulae)
- Products of nature, such as naturally occurring plants (because inventions such as genetically altered mice and oysters are made by humans rather than naturally occurring products, they are patentable)

- ▾ Printed matter
- ▾ Abstract ideas or suggestions

For 200 years, the conventional wisdom has been that business methods were not patentable. In 1998, the Federal Circuit Court issued an opinion allowing a patent for a business method, holding that business methods, mathematical algorithms, and software are patentable as long as they produce useful, tangible, and concrete results. In the wake of this case, the PTO reported an increase of approximately 700 percent in the number of patent applications containing claims for business methods. Patents have issued for Amazon.com's one-click shopping method and Priceline.com's method for letting prospective customers propose a price for a product or service, leading experts to question whether the issuance of such broad patents ultimately will stifle innovation and competition in the marketplace. Business method patents a discussed further in Chapter 16.

The U.S. Patent and Trademark Office

The PTO, the same government agency that is responsible for examining trademark applications and issuing registrations, is responsible for examining patent applications and granting patents. Patent applications are examined by those skilled in the art to which the patent application relates. The process is expensive, often costing between $5,000 and $20,000, and lengthy, usually taking eighteen to twenty-four months.

Perhaps reflecting the impact of technology and the Internet, the PTO Patent Examining Division is one of the busiest of government departments. In 1999, the PTO granted a record 169,154 patents, with U.S. inventors receiving 56 percent of all patents and residents of foreign nations receiving 44 percent of patents issued. Japan, Germany, and Taiwan led foreign applicants. Whereas only twenty-two inventions related to the Internet received patents in 1990, by 1998 the number of Internet-related patents had exploded to 2,193. The PTO Web site is www.uspto.gov, and its general information services number is (800) PTO-9199 or (703) 308-4357.

Invention Development Organizations

Invention development organizations are private and public consulting and marketing businesses that exist to help inventors bring their inventions to market. The PTO advises that although many of the organizations, also called patent promotion organizations, are legitimate, many are not. Some recommend that an inventor use their services to pursue patent protection with little regard for the value of a patent that may ultimately issue. Most experts advise extreme caution in dealing with invention development companies, particularly those that charge fees in advance of any services. The PTO does not provide information about the organizations and recommends that inventors contact the Better Business Bureau in the city in which the organization is located to determine whether it is reputable.

In fact, the American Inventors Protection Act of 1999 protects inexperienced inventors from unscrupulous invention developers by requiring promotion companies to disclose the number of inventions they have evaluated positively and negatively and their customers' success in receiving financial profits and licensing arrangements as a direct result of the promotion firm's activities. Inventors also can withdraw from contracts made with invention developers within a certain period of time. The PTO limits its assistance in the marketing and use of inventions to publishing in the *Official Gazette*, for $25, a notice that the patent is available for sale or licensing.

14

Patent Searching, Patent Applications, Duration, and Transfers

Because obtaining a utility patent depends on an invention being novel and nonobvious, conducting a search before applying for a patent is critical. A search of the prior art and U.S. Patent and Trademark Office (PTO) records will disclose whether the invention is sufficiently novel and nonobvious to qualify for patent protection. Once the search has been conducted, an application for the patent is filed, disclosing the method of making and using the invention. Like the trademark process, patent prosecution involves examination by the PTO and responses by the applicant to any PTO objections until the application is finally approved or rejected. As noted in Chapter 13, once a utility patent is issued, it remains in force for twenty years from the date the application was filed as long as all fees are paid during the term of the patent to maintain its existence. As items of personal property, patents can be sold or licensed to others and can be bequeathed by will. Any assignment or transfer of an application for a patent or an issued patent must be in writing. An inventor who wants patent protection in other countries must comply with the laws and requirements of those countries because the rights granted by a U.S. patent extend only throughout the United States.

The Need for a Patent Search

Because of the expense and time involved in preparing and filing a patent application, inventors should not risk filing an application only to have it rejected for lack of novelty or for obviousness. Thus, examining the prior art is critical before filing an application for a patent. Filing a patent application without conducting a search of the prior art is like leaving home for a long road trip without a set of directions. Additionally, searching patent records provides an overview of the competition and usually provides meaningful guidance on preparing the patent application so it meets with the fewest possible objections from the PTO.

Although the PTO provides a public search room for patent searching, searching prior art takes a great deal of experience, expertise, and familiarity in the field to which the invention relates, so searches generally are conducted by experts. Nevertheless, suggestions for searching are provided on the PTO's Web site at www.uspto.gov, and the site affords access to the PTO's own collection of more than 6,500,000 patents issued since 1790, which can be searched by inventor name, patent number, or topic field. Additionally, the PTO maintains Patent and Trademark Depository Libraries throughout the United States, which include collections of issued patents. The PTO Web site provides addresses for these approximately eighty libraries. Free sources for searching issued patents are provided at www.delphion.com and www.lib.utexas.edu. Coverage includes all U.S. patents since 1971. Users can search by keywords describing the invention, inventor name, or patent registration number.

Although searching these databases will disclose issued and expired patents, it will not disclose references to inventions in publications such as journals and conference papers. Thus, most inventors retain the services of a law firm or professional search firm to review not only patent records but also publications that may bear on novelty and nonobviousness. Engaging legal counsel affords additional advantages because not only are the actual results of the search provided to an inventor, but the lawyer or firm issues a written availability opinion discussing the chances of obtaining a patent for the invention.

In addition to the novelty search, many inventors request that an infringement search be conducted. An infringement search is more involved than a novelty search, and the results detail whether the invention might infringe that of another party. A formal written opinion discussing both novelty and infringement often costs between $1,000 and $5,000 but may well be worth the cost, particularly because obtaining advice of competent counsel may protect an inventor from having to pay punitive damages in a later infringement action because it shows that the inventor acted with due diligence rather than willfully and recklessly. Professional patent searchers can be found by using telephone directories. Most are located in the Washington, D.C., and northern Virginia because of the greater accessibility of PTO records and publications maintained at the Library of Congress.

Some inventors adopt a middle course, searching the free PTO or IBM databases as much as they can. If their preliminary search shows that the invention may qualify for patent protection, they then retain the services of a law firm to broaden the search and provide an availability and infringement opinion.

The Utility Patent Application Process

If the search reveals that the invention probably qualifies for patent protection and does not infringe that of another inventor, a patent application should be prepared and filed with the PTO. Unlike trademark and copyright applications, which can be prepared and filed easily by their owners, patent applications are highly technical and nearly always require expert assistance. Although inventors can prepare their own applications, approximately 80 percent of inventors retain patent attorneys or agents to prepare and file their patent applications. Patent attorneys generally have science or technical degrees in addition to law degrees. Many law firms have groups of patent attorneys, each devoted to a certain field of art, such as for mechanical, electrical, biotech, chemical, or computer inventions. Patent agents can also file patent applications for others. Patent agents generally are engineers and scientists who have passed very difficult exams given by the PTO but are not attorneys. Although patent agents can file applications, they cannot give advice or represent an inventor in a court proceeding. The PTO Web site maintains a list of registered patent agents and attorneys. Additionally, the American Intellectual Property Association, located in Arlington, Virginia, an organization of intellectual property attorneys, has a referral service as well as a directory of members by city and state. Its Web site is www.aipla.org, and its phone number is (703) 415-0780.

The process of shepherding a patent application through the PTO is called prosecution, just as it is for the trademark registration process. During the initial stages of prosecution, all material relating to an application is held in confidence, and no information relating to a pending application can be disclosed without the applicant's authority. Eighteen months after the patent is applied for or as soon as the patent is issued by the PTO, however, the entire patent file and any correspondence leading up to issuance of the patent, called the file wrapper, is available to the public for review.

The publication of patent applications eighteen months after their priority date represents a significant change in U.S. patent law. For more than 200 years, patent applications were maintained in strict secrecy until issuance. The change was made in late 2000 to harmonize U.S. practice with that of most foreign countries. For foreign applications, the priority date is usually the date the application was first filed abroad, and for U.S. applicants, the priority date is usually the filing date of the inventor's first provisional or complete application.

The applicant can avoid publication by certifying that no foreign applications have been or will be filed. It is not easy, however, to avoid publication, and the PTO practice is now to publish patent applications whenever possible.

The PTO has initiated a system called Patent Application Information Retrieval (PAIR) to allow the general public to access information about issued patents and to allow patent applicants to obtain secure information about the status of their patent applications. Applicants are given a secure customer number that they can use to access the system and obtain information about their pending patent applications. The system is designed to maintain the initial confidentiality of applications, and PAIR is accessible only to patent applicants and their designated representatives. Information about accessing PAIR is available at the PTO Web site at www.uspto.gov. Alternatively, one can call the PTO for general patent information at (703) 308-HELP or can call (703) 557-INFO for automated recorded patent information.

The Patent Application

The Patent Applicant

Under federal law, only the inventor may apply for a patent (with certain exceptions). The inventor is the person who furnishes the ideas, not the employer or the person who furnishes money for building and testing the invention. Because the true inventor must sign the application, nearly all applications are signed by individuals. If the individual has made an invention on behalf of his or her employer, the employer therefore owns the invention, so the individual inventor assigns the application to the employer simultaneous with filing the patent application. Thus, although John Doe signs the application, the patent issues to his employer. If the inventor refuses to apply for the patent or cannot be located, a joint inventor or person having a proprietary interest in the invention (such as the employer) may apply on behalf of the nonsigning inventor. Two or more persons can be joint inventors if each had a share in the ideas forming the invention; the patent issues in both their names. On the other hand, if one person merely gives suggestions or follows the instructions of another who provided the underlying idea, the owner of the patent is the person who contributed the idea. See Figure 19-1 for a form of agreement by which employees assign all inventions to their employers.

The Patent Application

There are two types of utility patent applications: provisional and nonprovisional. A provisional application is a less formal type of application and is usually filed when an inventor is in a race with a competitor. Filing a provisional application allows the inventor to establish an early effective filing date. The provisional patent application includes no claims, and the filing fee is moderate ($150). Within twelve months after filing the provisional application, the inventor must file a standard or nonprovisional patent application. The twelve-month period can be used to assess the marketability of the invention and gather funds to promote and sell the invention. Additionally, the twenty-year term of a patent begins with the filing of the standard nonprovisional patent application, not with the earlier provisional application. The only disadvantage to filing a provisional application is that the application will not be examined during the twelve-month period, thus giving the inventor no idea as to whether the invention qualifies for patent protection.

There are three elements to a nonprovisional patent application: a written document comprising a specification of the invention and an oath of declaration of the inventor, a drawing of the invention (when necessary), and a filing fee. The PTO prefers that transmittal forms or cover letters accompany the application and the fee. Free downloadable forms are provided on the PTO Web site.

The PTO has fairly detailed requirements for the paper application in terms of its size, margins, spacing, and appearance. The requirements can be found on the PTO Web site. The most important part of the patent application is the specification, the written description of the invention and of the manner and process of making and using it. The specification must be in such full, clear, concise, and exact terms as to enable any person skilled in the art or science to which the invention pertains to make and use the invention. In return for this full disclosure to the federal government as to the best way of making and using the invention, the government issues the patent, giving the inventor a twenty-year monopoly to exclude others from making, using, or selling the invention.

A specification must include at least one claim. Claims define the scope of the invention and are the most critical part of the specification. Claims are similar to the legal description of a parcel of real estate, setting forth all its boundaries and limits. During prosecution, the claims are compared against the prior art to determine whether the invention is novel and nonobvious. If there is a later infringement, the claims in the patent are compared against the accused device to determine whether infringement has occurred. Thus, the claims must be drafted with great care because they play a part not only in determining whether the patent will issue but also in defining the scope of its protection against infringers.

The specification includes the following elements:

- The title of the invention
- Cross-references to any related applications
- A description of the background of the invention, including descriptions of the known prior art
- A summary of the general idea of the claimed invention, pointing out its advantages
- A description of the drawings (if any)
- A detailed description of the invention along with the best mode of making and using the invention so that a person of ordinary skill in the relevant art or science could make and use the invention
- Claims, namely the subject matter that is regarded as the invention
- An abstract or brief summary of the invention (limited to 150 words), enabling the PTO and public to quickly determine the nature of the invention

Patent applications typically include drawings if such are necessary for understanding the subject matter to be patented. The drawings show the invention from a variety of angles and views. Nearly all patent applications include drawings, usually in black ink, and most of the drawings are prepared by artists retained by patent attorneys and agents. The PTO ordinarily does not accept photographs. The patent application concludes with the oath or declaration of the actual inventor, identifying the address and citizenship of the inventor and providing an address for correspondence with the PTO.

Preparing the application is time-consuming and costly. Many attorneys take forty hours or more to draft a patent application, craft the claims as carefully as possible, and coordinate the preparation of the drawings.

Once prepared, the application is filed with the PTO together with a filing fee. The PTO has developed an Electronic Filing System to allow the submission of utility patent applications electronically via the Internet, available at www.uspto.gov/ebc/index.html. Two types of fees are assessed by the PTO: a standard fee and a reduced fee, called a small entity fee, for independent inventors, registered practitioners, nonprofit organizations, or small business concerns. A small business concern is one with fewer than 500 employees. Most fees for these individuals or businesses are reduced by 50 percent. The standard filing fee for a utility patent application is $710. The small entity fee is $355. See Figure 14-1 for patent fees.

Examination of the Patent Application

Patent applications can be filed in person or mailed to the PTO. All applications received in the PTO are assigned a serial number, and the applicant is given a filing receipt several weeks after filing to verify the serial number and filing date.

Patent applicants owe a duty of candor to the PTO and are required to disclose to the PTO any information that pertains to the patentability of an invention. Thus, known prior art and other patents must be disclosed. Applicants use an Information Disclosure Statement (IDS) identifying material that bears on patentability. The IDS is filed with the application or within three months thereafter.

The application is assigned to an examining attorney skilled in the area of technology related to the invention. The examining attorney reviews the application for compliance with legal requirements and a search of U.S. patents, foreign patent documents, and available literature and

Figure 14-1. Patent fees.

	Basic Fee	Small Entity Fee
Utility patent filing fee	$ 710	$ 355
Provisional patent application filing fee	$ 150	$ 75
Design patent filing fee	$ 320	$ 160
Plant patent filing fee	$ 490	$ 245
Reissue filing fee	$ 710	$ 355
Utility patent issue fee	$1,240	$ 620
Design patent issue fee	$ 440	$ 220
Plant patent issue fee	$ 600	$ 300
Maintenance fee due at 3½ years	$ 850	$ 425
Maintenance fee due at 7½ years	$1,950	$ 975
Maintenance fee due at 11½ years	$2,990	$1,495
Surcharge for late payment of maintenance fee (if late payment made within six months)	$ 130	$ 130
Surcharge for late payment of maintenance fee (if late filing is unavoidable)	$ 700	$ 700
Surcharge for late payment of maintenance fee (if late filing is unintentional)	$1,640	$1,640

publications to determine whether the claimed invention is new, useful, and nonobvious.

Nearly all applications are subject to an initial rejection by the PTO. The examining attorney sets forth the examiner's objections by a written communication called an office action specifying the reasons for the objections and any action required of the applicant. The applicant must respond within a prescribed time limit. The maximum period of response is six months, and the usual period for response set by the PTO to an office action is three months. A fee usually is required if the response period is extended beyond the time set by the PTO. If no response is filed within the appropriate time period, the application is considered abandoned, although it can be revived upon a showing that the failure to respond was unavoidable or unintentional. Because the patent will expire twenty years from its filing date, it is in the best interests of the applicant to respond as quickly as possible to any PTO objections.

An applicant may amend a patent application in response to a rejection. Claims may be canceled, modified, deleted, or added. Added and amended claims cannot include new matter and must be supported by the original specification. If two or more distinct inventions are claimed in a single application, the examiner issues a restriction, requiring the applicant to limit or restrict the application to one of the inventions. The other invention may be made the subject of a new application, entitled to the benefit of the filing date of the original application, often called the parent application. Similarly, an applicant may not obtain two patents for the same invention. In some instances, a new patent application shows subject matter that is a duplication, obvious improvement, or variation on an invention already applied for by the inventor. In those cases, the double patenting principle requires that one set of identical claims be canceled. If the claims are not identical but are related, the PTO requires that the inventor agree that the term of the second patent will not extend beyond the term of the first. Otherwise, inventors could make successive applications for slight variations on a single invention and thereby obtain continual patent protection beyond the twenty-year term set by law.

If some claims are allowed by an examiner and others are refused, the applicant can elect to go forward with the allowed claims and continue to pursue the rejected claims in a newly created continuation application. This strategy allows the inventor to obtain a patent on the allowed claims. Otherwise, delays in the issuance of the patent caused by troublesome claims will begin to eat into the twenty-year term of patent protection.

If the PTO determines that an application being examined would conflict or interfere with a pending application or existing issued patent, the PTO declares an interference, a proceeding designed to determine priority of the inventions. In the United States, patents are granted to the first to invent. Generally, the first to invent is the one who first reduces the invention to practice, either actually (by making the invention) or constructively (by filing a patent application therefor). To verify the time and date of conception to practice, inventors should maintain laboratory notebooks containing detailed entries of work on the item that, if possible, are witnessed by others. The notebooks then provide a record of the progress and date of invention for purposes of proving priority. The PTO also provides a service called the Document Disclosure Program that allows inventors to file a document with the PTO as evidence of the date of conception of an invention. The Disclosure Document should contain a clear and complete explanation of the manner and process of making and using the invention and should include drawings or sketches. The PTO maintains the Disclosure Document for two years, and it helps ensure that information about an invention is properly safeguarded.

In an interference action, the Board of Patent Appeals and Interferences, a department of the PTO, reviews evidence and statements of the parties and issues a decision resolving the issue. Disappointed parties may appeal to the Court of Appeals for the Federal Circuit located in Washington, D.C., or bring an action in federal district court.

The Board of Patent Appeals and Interferences also hears appeals from applicants whose patent applications have been rejected by the PTO. If the board rules against the applicant, the applicant may appeal to the Court of Appeals for the Federal Circuit or may institute a civil action in the U.S. District Court for the District of Columbia.

The PTO maintains a Patent Assistance Center to answer general questions about patent examining policy and procedure at (800) PTO-9199 or (703) 308-HELP.

Allowance, Issue, Correction, and Reissue of Patent

Once the patent application is found to be allowable, a notice of allowance is sent to the applicant (or its attorney or agent), and a fee for issuing the patent is due within three months from the date of the notice of allowance. At present, the issue fee for utility patents is $1,240 ($620 for small entities). If the fee is not paid in time, the application is considered abandoned unless delay is unavoidable or unintentional.

When the issue fee is paid, the patent issues as soon as possible thereafter, depending on the backlog of patents being granted. The patent grant, the official document granting the patent, is mailed to the applicant (or its attorney or agent). A patent number is assigned to the patent. On the date of the grant, the patent file becomes open to the public, and records are viewable at no cost through the PTO Web site. The PTO typically grants about 65 percent of the patents for which applications are filed, and the time from filing to issuance generally is eighteen months to three years. Once granted, there is a presumption that a patent is valid. Although the presumption can be defeated, typically one asserting patent invalidity must prove such by clear and convincing evidence.

If a clerical error is made in the printed patent grant document, a certificate correcting the error is issued without charge. If the patent is defective in more substantive respects (for example, the patentee realizes that she could have stated the claims more broadly), the patentee may apply for a reissue patent. The application for a reissue patent must be made within two years of the date of grant of the original patent. The reissue patent, if granted, replaces the original patent and is granted for the balance of the unexpired patent term. A reissue patent is an appropriate way to enlarge claims, but no new matter can be added. The filing fee for a reissue patent is $710 ($355 for small entities).

Patent Marking

Once a patent application is filed, the applicant can mark articles with the terms "patent applied for" or "patent pending." Because patent protection does not start until a patent is granted, these phrases have no legal effect but merely give notice that a patent application has been filed. Once a patent is granted the patentee may mark articles with the word "patent" and the number of the patent, for example, "Patent No. 5,586,991." Although patent owners are not required to mark their inventions or articles, the patentee may not recover damages from an infringer unless the infringer was duly notified of the infringement and continued to infringe thereafter. Marking the invention constitutes notice such that the patentee can recover damages from the time of first infringement. Marking an item as patented when it is not is illegal.

Patent Duration and Maintenance

Under present law, utility patents remain in force for 20 years after the filing date of the application. Under a 1999 federal law, patent terms are extended to compensate for certain PTO processing delays and for delays in the prosecution of applications pending more than three years. The three-year guarantee provides that an original patent will not be delayed more than three years from the date of its actual filing (assuming the applicant is not responsible for delays). Thus, diligent applicants are guaranteed a minimum seventeen-year patent term. Extensions of patent terms are also available for delays in issuance of a patent because of delays caused by other government agencies (such as the FDA), interference proceedings, secrecy orders issued by the government precluding issuance of a patent for national security reasons, and appellate review.

All utility patents are subject to maintenance fees, which must be paid to maintain the patent in force. Maintenance fees are not charged for design or plant patents. The PTO does not provide reminder notices to patent owners that the maintenance fees are due. These fees are due at $3^1/_2$, $7^1/_2$, and $11^1/_2$ years after the date the patent is granted. Maintenance fees should be paid within six months before their due date, although they can be paid (with a surcharge) within a six-month grace period thereafter. Failure to pay the maintenance fee on time or within the grace period may result in expiration of the patent and entry of the invention into the public domain. The patent may be revived thereafter if the failure to pay was unavoidable or unintentional. The current maintenance fees are as follows:

Anniversary Date	Fee	Small Entity Fee
3½ years	$ 850	$ 425
7½ years	$1,950	$ 975
11½ years	$2,990	$1,495

Design and Plant Patent Applications

The process of filing and prosecuting applications for design and plant patents is similar to that for utility patents. Owing to their shorter economic life, the PTO has created an expedited procedure for design applications upon payment of a $900 fee. Design patents have only one claim, and the drawing should clearly depict the appearance of the article because the drawing defines the scope of patent protection for design patents. Their term of duration is fourteen years from the date of grant, and no maintenance fees are due during the term. Design patents are designated with the letter *D*, as in "D395,122."

An application for a plant patent consists of the same parts as utility applications, with the addition of a plant color coding sheet to show the color of the plant. A duplicate of the application is required so it can be sent to the Agricultural Research Service within the Department of Agriculture for an advisory report on the plant variety.

The specification for a plant patent must provide a detailed description of its characteristics that distinguish it from other known varieties and its antecedents and must identify where and in what manner it was asexually reproduced. Because a plant patent is granted on the entire plant, only one claim is permitted or necessary. The term of a plant patent is twenty years from the date on which the application was filed, and no maintenance fees are due during the term to maintain the plant patent in force. Plant patents are designated with the introductory letters *PP*, as in "PP10,401."

Patent Transfers and Licenses

A patent is personal property and therefore may be sold to others or bequeathed by will. The transfer of a patent is called an assignment, and the transfer must be in writing to be valid. When the patent is assigned, the assignee becomes the owner of the patent and has all of the rights and obligations that the original owner had. Patents can also be transferred in part, such that the original owner retains a fractional part of ownership, and can be transferred only for a specified region or part of the United States. Typically, such limited transfers are called licenses, whereas a transfer of all of the rights in and to a patent is called an assignment.

Although recording of the assignment with the PTO is not required to make the assignment valid, recording provides public notice of the chain of title of the patent. The PTO provides forms for recording patent assignments, just as it does for recording trademark assignments. See Figure 14-2 for a sample patent assignment form.

Patents often are owned jointly, as is the case when there are two or more coinventors or a patent is bequeathed by will to several people. Any joint owner of a patent, no matter how small the part interest, may make, use, offer for sale, sell, and import the invention without regard to the other owners and may sell the interest (or a part of it) or grant licenses to others, without the consent of and without accounting to the other owners unless there is an agreement providing otherwise. Thus, it is critical that joint owners of a patent enter into a written agreement specifying their rights and duties. Many agreements include a right of first refusal so that if one of the owners receives an offer from a third party to buy his or her interest, the owner must allow the other owners to match the offer.

Patent owners can grant licenses to others to make, use, sell, or import the invention. Licenses can be restricted as to time, with licensing rights granted to a party for only a portion of the term of the patent. Licenses can be restricted geographically, with rights granted to different parties who have the right to use or sell the invention in various defined geographic areas or regions. Licenses can be restricted as to activity, with one party being granted the right to make the invention and another the right to sell it. Finally, licenses can be exclusive (with one party being granted sole rights) or nonexclusive (with several parties granted rights). The licensor may elect to retain rights to make, use, or sell the invention. Some licenses are for a fixed lump sum payment; others may require periodic royalty payments based on sales of the patented item. No particular form of license is required, and the form of trademark license provided in Figure 5-3 can be modified easily for patents. The license agreement should provide detailed information about the parties' rights and obligations in the event of a claim of infringement. Generally, the owner of the patent has a duty to maintain the patent in force, pursue infringers, and defend

Figure 14-2. Patent assignment.

PTO/SB/41 (08-00)
Approved for use through 05/31/2002. OMB 0651-0027
U. S. Patent and Trademark Office; U.S. DEPARTMENT OF COMMERCE
Under the Paperwork Reduction Act of 1995, no persons are required to respond to a collection of information unless it displays a valid OMB control number.

ASSIGNMENT OF PATENT	Docket Number (optional)

Whereas, I, _____ of _____ , hereinafter

referred to as patentee, did obtain a United States Patent for an improvement in _____

_____

No. _____ , dated _____ ; and whereas, I am now the sole

owner of said patent, and,

Whereas, _____

of _____

hereinafter referred to as "assignee" whose mailing address is _____

_____

City of _____ , and State of _____ .

is desirous of acquiring the entire right, title and interest in the same;

Now, therefore, in consideration of the sum of _____ dollars ($ _____), the receipt whereof

is acknowledged, and other good and valuable consideration, I, the patentee, by these presents

do sell, assign and transfer unto said assignee the entire right, title and interest in and to the said

Patent aforesaid; the same to be held and enjoyed by the said assignee for his own use and

behoof, and for his legal representatives and assigns, to the full end of the term for which said

Patent is granted, as fully and entirely as the same would have been held by me had this

assignment and sale not been made.

Executed this _____ day of _____ , 20 _____ ,

at _____ .

_____
(Signature)

State of _____)
County of _____)   SS:
Before me personally appeared said _____
and acknowledged the foregoing instrument to be his free act and deed this _____ day
of _____ , 20 ____.

_____

Seal   (Notary Public)

Burden Hour Statement: This form is estimated to take 0.1 hours to complete. Time will vary depending upon the needs of the indivdual case. Any on the amount of time you are required to complete this form should be sent to the Chief Information Officer, U. S. Patent and Trademark Office. Washington, DC 20231. DO NOT SEND FEES OR COMPLETED FORMS TO THIS ADDRESS. SEND TO: Commissioner of Patents and Trademarks, Washington. DC 20231.

claims of infringement, and the licensee has a duty to cooperate in any lawsuit and promptly provide notice of any infringing activity or claim to the owner.

Patent owners are free to impose whatever restrictions they want on licensees, and these restrictions travel to downstream users and transferees as long as the restrictions do not violate federal law. An outright sale of a patented item generally exhausts the patent owner's rights to control further use of the item.

Patents can also be used as collateral to secure performance of some obligation. In the most common scenario, a company borrowing money pledges some of its patents as security for its promise to repay the debt. If the debt is not paid, the lender then seizes the security and becomes the owner of the patents. Licensing and collateralizing patents are both effective ways for companies to use their patents to produce revenue. For a $25 fee, the PTO will publish a notice in its weekly publication, the *Official Gazette*, that a patent is available for sale or licensing.

International Patent Protection

Patents granted by the PTO have effect only in the United States. To protect an invention in other countries, an inventor must obtain a patent in those countries, which often impose a patchwork quilt of laws, fees, and processes. There are three fairly expeditious methods by which U.S. inventors can pursue patent protection in other countries: by using the benefits of the Paris Convention, the Patent Cooperation Treaty, and the European Patent Organization.

Paris Convention Priority

Chapter 4 discussed the fact that under the Paris Convention, a trademark applicant in the United States or other Paris Convention country has six months after filing a trademark application in another member nation to capture the earlier filing date for purposes of establishing priority to a mark or application. The same principle is true for patent applications, except that the priority period is one year for utility patents (six months for design patents). Thus, an inventor who files a utility patent application in the United States has one year to file an application in any of the more than 135 member nations of the Paris Convention; the application will be viewed as having been filed on the date the U.S. application was filed.

Capturing the priority of the earlier filing date can be extremely useful for circumventing prior art that has come into existence between the U.S. filing date and the date of the foreign filing. The Paris Convention thus allows U.S. inventors to file a patent in the United States and then use the next twelve months to evaluate whether the invention will be successful in other countries and gather funds to market the discovery. The text of the Paris Convention is available at the World Intellectual Property Organization (WIPO) Web site at www.wipo.org.

The Patent Cooperation Treaty

Because pursuing multiple applications in multiple countries is expensive and time-consuming, the Patent Cooperation Treaty (PCT) came into force in 1978 to provide a centralized way to file, search, and examine patent applications simultaneously in numerous countries. Nearly 100 nations are members of the PCT. The PCT allows the filing of one international patent application, which is then searched, examined, and later prosecuted in the countries designated by the applicant. The application is filed, together with a filing fee, with the inventor's home patent office (for U.S. inventors, this is the PTO), listing the countries in which the applicant desires patent protection. The application is effective in all designated nations, saving the costs of preparing and filing separate applications for all those countries. A PCT application can claim priority under the Paris Convention of an earlier-filed patent application. The application is then subjected to an international search, which provides no opinion on the value of the invention but cites prior art, thereby indicating whether the patent will be novel and nonobvious in other countries. The applicant can amend the application in response to the prior art citations.

The applicant then has the option to have an international preliminary examination of the application performed for a fee. The results of the examination are set forth in a report, which provides a strong indication as to whether the patent will be granted in the various designated nations. If the applicant wants to pursue the application in the designated countries, prosecution is commenced in each country, and each country then determines whether to grant the patent. The international patent application does not automatically achieve registration or grant in each designated country; however, the search and examination phases provide strong indications as to what objections will be made in various countries, thus allowing the applicant to marshal evidence to meet those objections or drop certain countries from the application. One of the most desirable results of the PCT is that it affords patent applicants significant time, up to thirty months, to evaluate the possible success of the invention in other countries, gather funds to prosecute applications and market the invention internationally, and then determine in which countries to pursue the patent. The PCT is administered by WIPO in Geneva, Switzerland (www. wipo.org). PCT forms, statistics, fee schedules, lists of contracting nations, and tutorials are all available on the PTO Web site, and the PTO provides a PCT Help Desk at (703) 305-3257.

European Patent Organization

The European Patent Organization was founded in the early 1970s to provide a uniform patent system in Europe. A European patent (covering nearly twenty European nations, including Austria, France, Germany, Greece, Italy, Spain, and the United Kingdom) is obtained by filing a single application. Once granted, the patent is valid for twenty years (from the filing date of the application) in any of the contracting nations. A European patent can be combined with a PCT patent so that a United States inventor can designate all of the European Patent Organization as a single entity rather than specifically enumerating member countries, such as Denmark, Germany, and Portugal. Additional information can be obtained on the Web site of the European Patent Office at www.epo.co.at/epo/.

Foreign Filing Licenses

Under federal law, for purposes of national security, it is necessary to obtain a license from the commissioner of the PTO before applying for a patent for a U.S.-made invention in a foreign country, and the commissioner has the authority to refuse to issue the license. Filing an application in the United States constitutes an automatic request for such a license, and the official filing receipt provided by the PTO will indicate whether the request has been granted or denied. Six months after the U.S. application is filed, the applicant may file an application in a foreign country. The six-month waiting period allows the PTO to determine whether the invention affects matters of national security.

The PTO also has the authority to issue a secrecy order forbidding patent issuance in the United States for national security reasons. Until the secrecy order is lifted, no patent can issue; however, the inventor can obtain compensation from the federal government for damages caused by his or her inability to obtain a patent for the invention.

15

Patent Infringement

Patent infringement is an invasion of a patentee's right to make, use, or sell a patented invention. Because patent infringement actions involve an examination of the claims of an issued patent and comparison of the patented article and the accused article, experts generally are required. The complexity of patent law and of the technology underlying most patents makes patent litigation extremely costly. Patent infringement can lead to damages in the millions.

Reexamination of Patents

Before a trademark registration is issued by the Patent and Trademark Office (PTO), the trademark is published in the *Official Gazette* so that parties who believe they may be damaged by registration of the mark can oppose registration. Similarly, after a trademark is registered, it can be canceled upon the petition of one who can prove that he or she is damaged by continued registration of the mark. No analogous procedures exist for opposing or canceling patents in the United States. Nevertheless, any person (including the patentee) can file a request with the PTO that it reexamine the patent on the basis of prior art (consisting of patents or printed publications) the person believes has a bearing on the patentability of any claim. A request for reexamination can be made at any time during the life of the patent. The reexamination fee is $2,520. There is no reduced fee for small entities.

179

Within three months the PTO determines whether a question of patentability is raised by the request. If so, a reexamination of the patent is ordered to resolve the question. The patentee may file a statement regarding patentability and may amend the patent or propose new claims to distinguish the issued patent from the prior art cited in the request for reexamination. Reexamination is conducted under the rules and proceedings that govern initial issuance of any patent. The PTO then issues and publishes a certificate canceling any claim of the patent finally determined to be unpatentable or confirming any claim determined to be patentable.

Reexamination can be a prelude to patent infringement litigation or can be conducted simultaneously with litigation. Because federal law requires that patent reexamination proceedings be conducted "with special dispatch," reexamination may afford a practical alternative to litigation, affording both a patentee and one who believes a patent has been improperly issued to obtain PTO review of patentability.

Patent Infringement

A patent can be infringed only after it has been issued. Making, using, or selling an invention before a patent has been issued for an invention is nonactionable. Similarly, once the patent has expired, anyone is free to make, use, or sell the invention. Thus, there is a limited period during which patents are protected.

Similar to copyright infringement, patent infringement does not require intent to infringe. An innocent infringement is infringement nonetheless, although knowledge of infringement has a bearing on damages assessed. Infringement may be direct, as occurs when another wrongfully makes, uses, or sells the patented item, or infringement may be indirect, as when a party sells a component that is used in a patented item for infringing purposes when the component has no significant noninfringing use or when one actively induces infringement. Thus, if a critical element for a patent is item X, a party cannot make or sell item X to another, knowing that the other will use item X to infringe the patent.

For example, in July 2000, Mattel Inc. and Toys "R" Us, Inc. each agreed to pay several million dollars to a party who held an exclusive license for making scrunchies (cloth-covered elastic ponytail holders). The companies had sold kits for making the scrunchies at home. The scrunchies were subject to a design patent, and the kit was created for no other purpose other than to make infringing scrunchies and was marketed with complete instructions as to how to make the infringing product. Patent infringement also occurs when one party induces or encourages infringement. For example, if an employer instructs an employee to make an infringing device, the employer is liable for actively inducing infringement.

The First Sale Doctrine

In copyright law, sale of a copyrighted work, such as a book, exhausts the copyright owner's right to further distribute the work, thus allowing the buyer to sell or lend the work. Known as the first sale doctrine, the principle also applies to patent law. The first authorized sale of a patented item exhausts the patent owner's exclusive right so that the buyer can further use, repair, and resell the invention. Repair may extend to replacement of worn-out parts so that the item can be further used, but a purchaser cannot reconstruct the invention to create a new device. Although patent owners can certainly enter into contractual arrangements with users and licensees of the patented item that restrict future use and sale, an unconditional sale of a patented item exhausts the patent owner's right to control the purchaser's further use of the item.

Claim Construction

In determining infringement, the claims of the patented device are interpreted and reviewed against the accused device. If the accused device falls within the language of the patent's claim there is literal infringement. If the accused device differs somewhat from the patented device, there can be no literal infringement because every claim has not been copied; however, under the doctrine of equivalents, infringement exists if the accused device is equivalent to the patented device in that it performs substantially the same function in substantially the same way to reach substantially the same result. Thus, a device may infringe even if it would not be precluded by the claims of the patent if it is equivalent to the patented product. The doctrine of equivalents also requires a determination of the significance of the patented device. If the patented invention is a pioneer patent in that it is wholly new, it will be given a broad scope of protection, and infringement is more readily found than if the patented device is a minor improvement of other patented devices.

In interpreting claims, the entire file wrapper and all correspondence and responses to office actions made during prosecution of the patent application are reviewed. The inventor is bound by the prosecution history of the patent and cannot later argue that a claim was intended to be broader than it is actually set forth in the issued patent and cannot take a position inconsistent with that taken during prosecution of the patent. This principle, variously called prosecution history estoppel or file wrapper estoppel, is meant to ensure that applicants who disagree with an examiner during the prosecution of a patent fully protect their own interests. They are therefore bound by actions they take, arguments they submit, and amendments to their patent claims.

Patent Infringement Actions

Before filing an action for infringement, a patent owner typically sends a cease and desist letter to the infringer, setting forth pertinent information about the patent and demanding that the infringer cease making, using, or selling the patented device. The cease and desist letter provided for trademark matters in Figure 6-1 can be modified easily for use in patent matters.

   If the cease and desist letter does not produce favorable results, the patent owner should initiate an action in federal court for infringement. Patent matters are exclusively within the jurisdiction of federal courts. The plaintiff files a complaint and the defendant files an answer, which typically denies that any infringement has occurred and asserts a variety of defenses. Discovery commences and the parties thereby obtain information about when the patented item was invented, who worked on the device, what laboratory notebooks exist detailing the progress of work on the invention, experts who may be called, and any other information that may be relevant to proving or disproving infringement. If the matter cannot be resolved amicably, it proceeds to trial. Either party may request a jury. Although juries answer the ultimate question as to whether infringement occurred, to ensure uniformity in patent law, judges determine claims construction. A disappointed litigant may appeal to the Court of Appeals for the Federal Circuit, specifically created in 1982 for patent cases. Further appeal may be made to the U.S. Supreme Court if it, in its discretion, decides to take the case. Government and municipal entities can also infringe patents. Actions against the federal government for infringement must be brought in the U.S. Court of Federal Claims located in Washington, D.C.

Defenses to Patent Infringement

The first defense asserted by most defendants in patent infringement actions is that there was no infringement, either literal or under the doctrine of equivalents. Defendants also assert the following defenses:

▾ *Invalidity of patent.* Defendants often allege that the patent is invalid and should not have been granted because it was not useful, novel, or nonobvious. Because issued patents are presumed to be valid, one challenging the validity of a patent must prove invalidity by clear and convincing evidence.

▾ *Fraud.* Misconduct or fraud by an applicant during the patent application process invalidates the patent.

▾ *Misuse.* If the patent owner has misused the patent, the owner may be precluded from enforcing it. One of the most common examples of misuse is collecting license fees for use of a patent after its term has expired.

▾ *Experimental use.* Generally, making or using a patented invention for research or experimental use is not infringement.

▾ *Laches.* Although there is no statute of limitations for bringing an action for patent infringement, a patent owner may not recover damages for infringing acts committed more than six years before the lawsuit is begun. The patentee may recover other remedies such as an injunction prohibiting further making, use, or sale of the accused device, but no damages can be recovered once this limitation period has expired. Moreover, an unreasonable delay in initiating litigation that causes prejudice to a defendant may bar a patentee from bringing suit under the doctrine of laches. There is no specific time period that must pass for laches to occur. Generally, if a patentee knows of an infringement and does not bring action promptly, and the infringer thereafter incurs great expense in making, using, or selling the invention, believing that the patentee has acquiesced in such acts, the patentee may be barred from bringing an action for infringement.

▾ *First inventor defense for business method patents.* Under new legislation enacted in 1999, one accused of patent infringement can successfully defend an infringement action if he or she can prove commercial use of the business method for a year before a patent application for it was filed. This defense is allowed only in actions alleging infringement of business methods. The first inventor defense is discussed further in Chapter 16.

Remedies for Infringement

A variety of remedies are available to injured patentees, including the following:

▾ *Injunctive relief.* Courts can order injunctive relief to prevent unauthorized making, using, or selling of a patented invention. In many cases, although plaintiffs desire damages for prior infringements, they are more interested in ensuring that the infringing activity ceases. If the usual factors for obtaining an injunction are met by the plaintiff (a showing of likelihood of success on the merits, irreparable harm that cannot be compensated for by money damages, more harm to the patentee if relief is not granted than to the alleged infringer if relief is granted, and public interest favoring relief to the patentee), a temporary restraining order can be granted immediately, a preliminary injunction can be granted during pendency of the lawsuit, and a final or permanent injunction can be ordered as the judgment in the case.

▾ *Compensatory damages.* A patentee who proves infringement is entitled to damages adequate to compensate for the infringement. Damages include the patentee's lost profits. In no event can the damages be less than a reasonable royalty rate for the use of the invention as used by the infringer. Typically, if damages would be difficult to prove (often because the patentee has not yet made any profit on the invention and thus cannot prove what his or her lost profits or damages are), patentees elect to recover a reasonable royalty from the infringer based on what licensees of similar devices pay.

▾ *Punitive damages.* Courts have the authority under federal law to increase compensatory damages up to three times the amount found or assessed. Generally, such increased or punitive damages are not assessed unless the defendant acted willfully or in bad faith. One with actual notice of another's patent rights has a duty to avoid infringement; thus, continuing infringement after notice may constitute such bad faith as to lead to the imposition of punitive damages.

▾ *Interest, costs, and attorneys' fees.* Courts can award prejudgment interest to compensate patentees fully for their losses. Attorney's fees, costs, and expenses can be awarded to the prevailing party; however, generally they are not awarded unless the other's conduct has been reckless, willful, or intentional, or a contract provides for such.

Modern Infringement Practice and Infringement Avoidance

Patent litigation often is considered to be the riskiest variety of litigation. Damages can run into the millions, and litigation can take years because of the complexity of many technical inventions. Moreover, there is always the chance that a judge or jury will not fully understand the complex scientific evidence that often forms the basis of the case. Damages can run into the millions. For example, the largest judgment awarded nationwide in 1999 in a patent infringement case was nearly $170 million in damages for infringement of a patent on heat-shrinkable films used for packaged meat and poultry. To this sum, the judge added $20 million for willful infringement, $5.5 million for supplemental damages, and nearly $40 million for prejudgment interest, for a total of nearly $240 million.

Companies can take two actions to reduce the threat of infringement claims and costly judgments:

▾ Companies should investigate the possibility of obtaining patent infringement insurance. Just as doctors and lawyers insure against malpractice, companies engaged in technology research and engineering should investigate the availability of patent infringement insurance. Although willful and fraudulent activities can never be insured against, acts of innocent infringement may be covered under certain intellectual property insurance policies. Moreover, even if the ultimate damages are not covered by insurance, having insurance for the costs of defending an infringement claim is extremely valuable. The costs of such insurance can be very high, depending on the technology involved, but companies engaged in making, using, or selling certain items and devices would be foolish not to obtain such insurance.

▾ Companies should retain competent legal counsel as soon as a claim of infringement is made against them. Although obtaining advice of counsel seldom provides blanket immunity for one's acts, acting on counsel's advice may well shield an infringer from a claim of willful infringement (which itself can lead to triple damages). Some courts have held that absence of counsel suggests willfulness.

Just as companies need to be cautious to ensure that they do not commit acts of infringement, companies should also be alert to ensure that their own patents are not infringed. Thus, businesses owning patents should attend trade shows in the field to which the patent pertains and review trade and technical publications to remain vigilant in protecting their patents. Because the PTO does not publish patents for opposition purposes and because patent applications are initially confidential, companies are often unaware that an infringing invention exists until it has been patented and marketed.

16

Emerging Patent Trends

The newest trends in patents are the emergence of patents for methods of doing business and the use of patents in the biotechnology field. Patents are now available for methods of doing business, leading to a 700 percent increase in U.S. Patent and Trademark Office (PTO) filings for software and business method patent applications. Because many of these patents have yet to be tested in court, a wave of litigation is expected as courts attempt to determine whether such patents are enforceable.

Patents in the biotech field involve serious considerations of the need to reward private inventors as well as the need of society to ensure that important inventions such as those for the production of food and the cure of diseases are available for all to use.

Patent Protection for Computer Programs

As discussed in Chapter 8, the cost of obtaining a copyright registration for computer software is minimal, and the period required to obtain the registration can be as short as four months. Unfortunately, however, courts have signaled a reluctance to afford broad copyright protection to computer programs, in many cases holding that the program or many of its elements are useful articles undeserving of copyright protection. Although patent protection affords greater protection, the prosecution costs are significant (between $10,000 and $30,000 in many cases), and the patent may take up to thirty months to issue, during which time the program may become obsolete. Some experts have suggested that only groundbreaking software should be patented. The costs and time involved may well be justified because the patent owner can license the software to others and collect royalties for its use. Perhaps because the rewards more than compensate for the costs and time involved, Microsoft received nearly 200 patents for software in 1998 alone.

Patent protection for computer programs affords significantly broader protection than does copyright law. Recall from Chapter 8 that copyright law protects original works; thus, if two authors independently create the same work, such as a computer program, both works are protected. Under patent principles, however, the patent owner has the exclusive right to preclude others from making, using, or selling his or her patented invention. Thus, patent law protects against independent creation of the same or equivalent computer program. Creators of software programs thus need to consider a variety of factors in determining whether to seek copyright or patent protection (or both) for their computer programs, including costs, life span of the program, and whether it is likely to be independently developed by others.

Patent Protection for Business Methods

No area of patent law has caused as much controversy as the recent rush of Internet-related patents and patents for business methods. For years, the governing principle, and indeed federal law, disallowed patents for methods of doing business. In 1998, however, in *State Street Bank & Trust Co. v. Signature Financial Group Inc.*, 149 F.3d 1368 (Fed. Cir. 1998), the Federal Circuit allowed a patent for a data-processing system designed to make financial calculations because the calculations produced a useful, concrete, and tangible result. The court's decision opened the floodgates for similar patents, most of which are related to methods for doing business. Because most business methods arguably produce some tangible and useful result, the number of patent applications for software related to such business methods has skyrocketed. Similarly, in 1990 the PTO granted 22 patents for inventions related to the Internet; by 1998, that number had grown to 2,193.

Many of these patents have engendered significant criticism, with experts alleging that many of the recently granted business method patents are so broad as to stifle competition, are obvious ideas that should be unpatentable, or are mere minor variations of known inventions. For example, there are now patents on the method of holding a golf putter, on a method of teaching janitors how to clean a building more efficiently, on a wagering solitaire game, on allocating assets in a divorce settlement, and one on what appears to be a method of making toast (see Patent No. 6,080,436 relating to refreshing bread by toasting it). Many companies have sought business method patents in a defensive strategy approach, reasoning that if they do not rush to protect their business methods, other companies will patent those methods and then prevent the first user from continued use of the method. Realizing that many companies had not patented their business methods because they preferred to maintain them as trade secrets, a tactic that could result in later claims of infringement, Congress enacted the First Inventor Defense Act in 1999 to provide a new defense in infringement actions involving business methods. Under the new law, one who can prove that he or she commercially used a business method for one year before a patent application for it was filed cannot be sued for infringement. This defense is available only for cases involving alleged infringement of business methods, not for other types of patent infringement.

The avalanche of new patents has inevitably led to litigation. For example, in 1999 Amazon.com obtained an injunction against barnesandnoble.com preventing it from using Amazon's patented one-click system for repeat orders, and Priceline.com sued a Microsoft subsidiary for infringement of its patented reverse auction system in which customers make bids and state prices they are willing to pay for commodities such as airline tickets. Priceline.com has alleged that Microsoft's Expedia service, which lets customers name their own prices for hotel rooms, infringes on its patent. Microsoft has responded that the patent is such an obvious business method that it is overbroad and invalid. Similarly, FantasySports.com has sued Yahoo!, ESPN, and two other sites for misappropriating online fantasy football concepts.

In spring 2000, Jeff Bezos, CEO of Amazon.com, proposed a patent reform plan to help ensure that patents are granted only to nonobvious business method inventions. Perhaps in response, in March 2000 the PTO announced new guidelines and procedures in the application process for business method patents, including an automatic second level of review for business method patents and additional training for its examiners in banking, finance, online commerce, insurance, and the Internet. The PTO has also announced plans to hire more examiners with computing backgrounds and plans to convene a forum to discuss the history behind computer-implemented business method patents and to identify ways to improve the PTO's examination approach of such patent applications.

Because the field of business method patents is so new, there has been little testing of these patents in the courts. The First Inventor Defense enacted by Congress may prove to be an effective shield against liability. Additionally, it is expected that those accused of infringement will allege that based on prior art, the business method patent is neither new nor nonobvious and thus the patent should be held invalid.

Not only has litigation increased because of the new business method patents, but the method of calculating damages for infringement has also been affected. A patentee who proves infringement is entitled to damages to compensate for the infringement, in no event less than a reasonable royalty rate for the use of the invention by the infringer. Traditionally, recovering a royalty was less lucrative than recovering actual damages or lost profits. One catch for the new online commerce patent holders is that only those who have been successful in marketing a product can show lost profits. Thus, because many of the owners of the new business method patents have yet to turn a profit, they may be forced to elect a reasonable royalty rate, based on licenses of similar inventions by other parties.

Biotechnology Patents

The other emerging trend in patent law is the increased interest in biotechnology patents. The seminal case in the field of biotechnology is *Diamond v. Chakrabarty*, 477 U.S. 303 (1980), which held that bioengineered bacteria were patentable. Since that decision, patents have issued for genetically altered mice, genetically altered food, and inventions involving human genes and DNA.

In one recent case, *Pioneer Hi-Bred International Inc. v. J.E.M. Ag Supply Inc.*, 33 F. Supp. 2d 794 (N.D. Iowa 1999), the U.S. District Court for the Northern District of Iowa held that seeds, as well as the plants grown from them, are patentable. Although the PTO had been granting plant and seed patents, the ruling in *Pioneer* firmly established patentability of seeds. The decision has far-reaching implications for combating world hunger by developing seeds that produce insect-resistant corn and potatoes and those that tolerate a wide range of weather, pesticides, and other adverse conditions.

Opponents are concerned that the genetically modified plants and seeds could spawn newly resistant predators or pose threats to other species. Another concern is the cost of obtaining licenses to use plant and seed patents. For example, because some of the "miracle rices" in Asia depend on parent strains from many different countries, it would be prohibitively expensive to obtain licenses for each type of seed involved in the final rice seed. In response to such concerns, in mid-1999 Monsanto agreed to delay its plans to produce its patented "Terminator" seeds, which would protect the company's patents by producing sterile plants. Because the technology would thus force farmers to buy seed each season rather than save seed from harvest to harvest, the company bowed to public pressure and postponed commercialization of the technology.

Other interesting topics in the field of biotechnology are as follows:

▾ In 1999 the PTO rejected a patent application for a chimera (a mixture of a human and animal). The inventors have claimed that they have no true intention of making the chimera but filed the application to force public debate and obtain judicial certainty on the limits of patentability of human genetic material. The inventors have announced they intend to appeal the rejection to the U.S. Supreme Court, if necessary.

▾ Indigenous peoples from nine South American countries successfully petitioned the PTO in late 1999 to cancel a patent issued to a U.S. citizen for the ayahuasca vine, a plant used in religious and healing ceremonies, part of a continuing trend in developing countries that want to prevent foreigners from patenting their native plants. The basis for the patent cancellation was that the plant was known and available before the patent application. Some experts have been disappointed with the PTO rationale, preferring that the PTO directly confront the issue of whether it is ethical for private patent applicants to claim rights in a plant or knowledge that is sacred to a particular ethnic or cultural group.

▾ The largest settlement in a biotech infringement matter occurred in late 1999 when Genentech Inc. agreed to pay the University of California $200 million.

▾ Patented pharmaceuticals such as Viagra® and Claritin® are in high demand and are advertised with the same commercial fanfare as cars and appliances. The significant costs drug and pharmaceutical industries invest in developing, testing, and marketing products, some of which never make it to market, are well justified when such companies are granted the exclusive monopoly of patent protection. Nevertheless, society can be harmed if one company has the exclusive right to sell and commercialize certain products of great importance. Some experts believe that there is more financial incentive for companies to develop incremental advances in treatments for diseases such as cancer and AIDS, each of which can be patented, than to develop actual cures.

These new issues in patent law provide no easy answers, leading to thought-provoking public debate on the balance between the need to reward companies for inventions and the need of society to ensure that certain types of knowledge and technology are in the public domain.

17

Trade Secret Basics

Companies generally have a wealth of information that is valuable to them that, if known to their competitors, would afford those competitors an advantage in the marketplace. This information is known as trade secrets, and nearly any type of information may qualify for protection, from customer lists to product sales information, financial forecasts, and the methods by which the company conducts its business.

Moreover, the ease with which such information can be misappropriated and then disseminated via the Internet resulted in a more than 300 percent increase in acts of economic espionage from 1990 to 1995. Thus, because such intellectual capital is more important to companies than ever before and because it can be misappropriated more easily than ever before, protecting such information should be a top priority for all companies. The advantage for companies is that protecting trade secrets entails no registration or government formalities. As long as reasonable efforts are made to protect the information, it can be protected forever.

Definition and Governing Law

The commonly accepted definition of a trade secret is any information (including a formula, pattern, compilation, program, device, method, technique, or process) that derives independent economic value, whether actual or potential, from not being known to the public or others and is the subject of reasonable efforts to maintain its secrecy. Thus, both information that is valuable to a company and information that has potential value can be protected.

Trade secrets are governed by a patchwork of various state laws. There is no specific federal trade secret law (although there is a federal Economic Espionage Act that criminalizes theft of trade secrets), and each state has been free to enact its own statutes governing trade secrets. The very first trade secret case in the United States, in 1837, involved the protection of recipes and manufacturing techniques for making chocolate. In 1979, a Uniform Trade Secrets Act (UTSA) was drafted by the National Conference of Commissioners on Uniform State Law, an independent group of scholars of the law who envisioned that each state would adopt the act. Although the majority of states have adopted the act, most revised it, resulting in a great variance among states as to the treatment of trade secrets. Although there is significant discussion of the need for an overriding federal law relating to trade secrets, at present trade secrets are governed primarily by differing state statutes and cases interpreting those state statutes.

What Can Be Protected under Trade Secret Law

Most state statutes do not specifically list the type of information that can qualify for trade secret protection but rather provide that any information that might be valuable to a competitor is protectable. Thus, nearly any type of information qualifies for trade secret protection, including chemical formulas and compounds, customer lists, methods of doing business, sales techniques, financial forecasts and models, marketing plans, and lists of potential acquisition targets. Information need not be technical or scientific to be protected. As long as the information is subject to reasonable efforts of protection and as long as the information would be valuable if known by competitors, it generally qualifies for trade secret protection. Even "negative" information, such as a report discussing a method of doing business that is not profitable or a line of products that is not marketable, is protectable. Moreover, the information generally is protected regardless of the medium in which it is stored. Thus, written documents, computer files, and even an employee's memory of various items can be protected from unauthorized disclosure.

Because trade secret law expressly protects processes and methods, it readily coexists with patent law. Under patent law, the owner of an invention or process or useful business method essentially obtains a twenty-year monopoly to exclude others from making, using, or selling the invention, in return for which the owner fully discloses the information to the U.S. Patent and Trademark Office (PTO). In contrast, trade secrets can be protected in perpetuity as long as they are not disclosed to the public or competitors. Thus, the owners of various useful and tangible business methods, recipes, and inventions have a choice. They can seek the exclusive monopoly of patent protection, in return for which they are required to fully disclose their information and allow it to enter the public domain after the period of patent protection. Alternatively, they can maintain the information as a trade secret, in which case they are charged with the responsibility for maintaining confidentiality, but can protect the information forever. If another independently discovers the trade secret, however, protection is lost.

The classic example given to illustrate this principle is the recipe for Coca-Cola®, which is rumored to be placed under lock and key, with no one person having access. If the recipe or process for making the beverage had been patented, its owner would have enjoyed exclusive rights for only a limited time, after which the recipe or process would enter the public domain. In contrast, maintaining the recipe and process as trade secrets results in protection in perpetuity, as long as reasonable efforts are made to safeguard the confidentiality of the information. Thus, companies need to consider whether they will be served best by patent protection or trade secret protection. A final consideration is that because a patent gives its owner the exclusive right to make, use, and sell the patented item, patent law protects an inventor against the independent development or reverse engineering of his or her invention. Generally, trade secret law merely protects against the misappropriation of information. Thus, if a party independently develops or reverse engineers a patented item, infringement has occurred. In contrast, independent development does not and reverse engineering might not constitute a violation of another's trade secrets.

Because trade secrets are a form of property, their use can be licensed to others (although clear provisions should be set forth in a written agreement prohibiting misuse or disclosure of the information by the licensee) and can be sold to others.

Maintaining Secrecy

It is axiomatic that the law helps those who help themselves. Thus, companies can obtain protection for their trade secrets only if they have engaged in reasonable efforts to keep the information confidential. What constitutes reasonable efforts varies from case to case. In general, however, many courts consider the following factors (none of which is determinative) in resolving whether information qualifies for trade secret protection:

• *The extent to which the information is known outside the business.* Information that is known to the public or competitors generally does not qualify for trade secret protection. Information that is commonly known within an industry cannot be appropriated by one company for its own exclusive use. Thus, once information is known to others or publicly disseminated, it usually loses its status as protectable trade secret information.

• *The extent to which the information is known within the company.* To be protectable, information should be known or disclosed only to those with a legitimate need for the information. If companies disclose information in a company newsletter or on the company bulletin board, protection usually is lost. On the other hand, selected disclosure to employees and customers who have a demonstrated need for the information does not negate the information's status as a trade secret.

• *The extent of measures taken to protect the secrecy of the information.* Companies that use visitor sign-in logs, restrict access to confidential materials, and control the dissemination of important information are more likely to prevail in arguing that information is a protectable trade secret. Although companies are not required to go to extraordinary lengths to protect information, reasonable efforts are required. Thus, keeping important information in locked cabinets, stamping documents as confidential, and ensuring that only those with a definite need for the information have access to it help safeguard the protectable status of the information. Conversely, if a new process or information is viewed as highly critical to the company's success, posting such information on the company's Web site, analyzing it in company newsletters, and discussing it at company meetings or trade shows usually militates against a finding that such information is protectable as a trade secret.

• *The value of the information to the company and its competitors.* Generally, the more valuable the information is, the more stringent the efforts to protect it should be. Similarly, the effort a company makes to protect information tends to show that the information has value to the company. Information that is common and well known is subject to a lower standard of protection, and half-hearted efforts to protect information suggest that the information is not particularly valuable to the company.

▾ *The effort expended in developing the information.* If information is developed at great cost, time, and effort to a company, it is more likely to be protectable. Information that is easy to obtain and develop is subject to a lower standard of protectability.

▾ *The ease with which other companies could develop the information.* If information can be easily duplicated, reverse engineered, or discovered, it is subject to far less protection than information that is difficult to develop or obtain. Trade secret law may not protect against reverse engineering and generally does not protect against independent development of information. However, a patent gives its owner the exclusive right to use, sell, and exploit the patented invention and thus protects against reverse engineering or independent development. If the trade secret information can be reverse engineered but only with significant time and effort, courts may still protect the information, especially if the "engineer" has acted in bad faith.

Trade Secret Protection Methods

Because the key factor in determining whether information constitutes a trade secret is the secrecy of the information, it is critical for companies to develop programs to protect valuable information. There are two ways for companies to protect trade secret information: physical measures and written agreements.

Physical Measures

Because all companies own information that is valuable to them that, if known to a competitor, would cause damage to them, companies need to implement a variety of physical measures to protect proprietary information. For example, to gain access to Microsoft's Florida office devoted to combating software piracy, one must first give one's name to an office receptionist. Then one is personally escorted to another floor where all doors are unlabeled, locked, and monitored. In fact, some experts believe that it is becoming a director-level responsibility to ensure that a corporation implements an information security program.

The following are commonly used methods of protecting trade secrets:

▾ Restricting access to confidential materials. Confidential materials should be provided only to those within the company who have a legitimate interest in them. Thus, sales forecasts may be distributed to the sales, marketing, and accounting departments but not to the company's rank and file employees.

▾ Stamping documents with legends such as "confidential," "proprietary information of ABC Inc.," or "may not be reproduced without written consent of ABC, Inc." Such legends should be restricted to truly sensitive information. Marking all company documents as confidential suggests that nothing is truly confidential.

▾ Maintaining logbooks indicating which employees have been provided sensitive materials such as managers' handbooks or disks with company forms.

▾ Providing secure passwords for company computer systems, requiring periodic backups of sensitive documents, monitoring computer use (after providing written notice to employees of the company's right to monitor its electronic systems), and write-protecting documents to ensure that employees can read but not modify certain documents.

▾ Destroying or shredding sensitive written documents or samples on company premises.

▾ Permanently erasing or purging materials from company computers of departed employees or computers that will be discarded or sold.

▾ Providing locked cabinets for proprietary materials, locked doors for offices of personnel who maintain sensitive documents, and security and alarm systems for company office premises.

▾ Encrypting documents before sending them via electronic systems.

▾ Logging in visitors to company premises, requiring visitors to wear badges that are logged in, and accompanying them throughout their visits to the company's offices.

▾ Restricting access to photocopiers, placing notices near copiers reminding employees of their obligations to protect the company's proprietary information, and requiring keypad entry of employee identification numbers and client or customer account numbers for documents being copied.

▾ Holding meetings at which sensitive information is discussed offsite to reduce the possibility that employees who observe closed-door sessions with groups of well-dressed visitors start rumors that the company might go public, be sold, or merge with another entity.

▾ Ensuring that company premises are adequately protected by alarms, security systems, and security personnel.

Written Agreements

All employees have duties to their employers to protect information gained in confidence, whether or not the employee has signed a written agreement. Similar duties arise in partnerships and other fiduciary relationships. The duty not to disclose or misuse confidential information exists during the term of employment and thereafter.

For the best protection, all employees should be required to sign simple agreements confirming that they understand that the company's information is confidential and agreeing not to disclose it during or after their employment. Similarly, employees should be required to sign the company's software and Internet usage policies (see Chapter 12 for sample policies). These agreements and policies should be signed during the employee's orientation (or should be included in the company's employee handbook as long as the employee is required to verify in writing that he or she agrees to the handbook's terms), and then employees should be reminded of their obligations during their exit interviews. Independent contractors retained by the company should also sign such policies. See Figure 17-1 for a sample confidentiality policy.

Although some companies use formal written employment agreements detailing all the terms of employment for all employees, such an approach is too burdensome for most companies. Therefore, most companies use employment agreements only for their most senior employees and those who will have intimate knowledge of the company's processes and business. Three key components of such agreements relate to trade secrets and other intellectual property:

▾ A nondisclosure section requiring employees to hold the company's proprietary information in confidence

▾ A section confirming that work created by employees is owned by the company

▾ Restrictive covenants, which prohibit an employee who leaves the company from soliciting other employees or competing against the company for some limited period of time in some geographic area

See Chapter 19 for additional discussion of such topics.

A new concept in the intersection of employee rights with trade secret law is the doctrine of inevitable disclosure, which holds that if it is inevitable that an employee will disclose trade secret information to a new em-

Figure 17-1. Employee confidentiality policy.

It is the policy of ABC, Inc. ("Company") to develop necessary guidelines and controls to protect confidential Company information. The Company's confidential information must be held in the strictest confidence to protect the Company, its clients, and its employees. Similarly, confidential information gained during prior employment should be maintained in confidence and not used during employment with the Company.

In the course of employment, employees may have access to or work with information or data that must be kept confidential. Employees are reminded that information such as financial data, customer lists, customer records and requirements, personnel and payroll data, and other similar records are confidential and may be disclosed only to those within the Company who have a need to know such information.

To protect the confidentiality of such information, employees must
- Protect or secure confidential information from unauthorized use or disclosure
- Avoid displaying confidential materials where they can be easily observed
- Avoid discussions about confidential information except when required to perform their jobs
- Refrain from photocopying or reproducing or disseminating in any manner any confidential information except when necessary to perform their jobs
- Immediately inform a supervisor of any loss of confidential information

The provisions of this policy apply not only during the term of your employment with the Company but also thereafter.

Employee signature   Date

---

ployer that he or she gained during employment with a previous employer, the previous employer can obtain an injunction to prohibit the employee from going to work at the new place of employment. Because such a remedy is extreme and has a chilling effect on an employee's mobility and right to earn a living, courts do not enter such injunctions unless there is substantial evidence that the employee will inevitably rely on trade secrets in the new job. Typically, the employee and the second employer argue that the employee will be relying only on his or her general knowledge and skill and not on trade secrets gained while working for the first employer. The inevitable disclosure doctrine provides a compelling argument for screening prospective employees to determine whether they are subject to noncompete or nondisclosure agreements and whether they had access to trade secrets at their previous place of employment. Moreover, new employees should be advised that they must not use trade secret information gained from previous employers.

Thus, companies not only should protect against the disclosure of their information by their employees but should ensure that newly hired employees will not disclose trade secret information learned during previous jobs. Applicant screening should be used to determine whether a candidate has signed a previous nondisclosure or noncompete agreement and whether the employee's anticipated position in the company would entail the use or disclosure of such information. If so, the candidate should be rejected.

Samples of clauses to ensure that employers own the work created by their employees and independent contractors, sample restrictive covenants, and nondisclosure clauses are found in Chapter 19.

Innocent Receipt of Trade Secrets

Liability for trade secret theft requires that the party acquiring the information have done so through improper means or through breach of a confidential relationship. Improper means include theft, bribery, wiretapping, using one's own employees to become employees of a competitor for the purpose of obtaining confidential information, and inducing others to disclose valuable trade secret information. Confidential relationships include the employer–employee relationship and can arise either by express agreement or by the conduct of the parties. Thus, if under the circumstances parties would ordinarily believe information was confidential, a duty to protect it arises. For example, if a company official discloses financial information to an employee of a bank, even without an agreement to protect the information, the bank would be liable for disclosing it because the company's expectation would reasonably be that the information would be maintained in confidence, and the bank and its employees should have inferred the same. Moreover, courts seek to promote morality in the marketplace and would thus not reward the bank's unethical conduct.

In many instances, parties acquire trade secret information innocently, as when confidential materials are mistakenly sent to a competitor, when materials are inadvertently left at another's office, or when a party who is subject to a duty not to disclose the information acts wrongfully and discloses it to an innocent recipient. Generally, the recipient has no duty with regard to the information and can use it and disclose it to others until he or she receives notice that the information is claimed as a trade secret. After receiving notice that the information is a trade secret, however, the recipient cannot further use or disclose it unless he or she in good faith paid for the information or has already changed his or her position in reliance on the information, such that requiring cessation of use would be inequitable. For example, if an innocent recipient hires new employees, retools a plant, and begins selling a new product based on information innocently acquired, it may be inequitable to require the recipient to cease such use. In many cases, courts then require the innocent recipient to pay some reasonable royalty to the trade secret owner.

The key question in determining whether one is an innocent recipient is whether under the circumstances the recipient knew or should have known that the information was a trade secret.

Innocent receipt can be prevented to some extent by adding notices to fax cover sheets and e-mail communications indicating that the communication is intended only for the designated recipient and that anyone who receives information by mistake must return it to the sender.

Using Nondisclosure Agreements

While conducting its business, a company inevitably will need to disclose some proprietary information to potential customers or others. Such disclosure does not negate the trade secret status of the information as long as proper measures are taken to protect the use and confidentiality of the information. Thus, before demonstrating critical software or other products to potential customers or discussing volume pricing or other sensitive matters, a company should require those customers to sign a nondisclosure agreement, agreeing to maintain the information in confidence, usually for one or two years. If the negotiations ripen into a contractual relationship, the company's standard contract should include additional provisions safeguarding its information. Some companies include deliberate typographical errors in materials provided to third parties to make it easier to monitor the source of unauthorized disclosures. Information disclosed without the safeguard of a nondisclosure agreement from the recipient probably will lose its trade secret status, not only for that particular recipient but for all others as well. Once lost, trade secrets are lost forever. See Figure 17-2 for a sample nondisclosure agreement.

If the company enters into a licensing arrangement with others, it should ensure that the licensing agreement includes clear terms on the permitted uses of the information or product licensed, restrictions against reverse engineering or decompilation of the product, restrictions against

Figure 17-2. Mutual nondisclosure agreement for use with clients.

This Mutual Nondisclosure Agreement ("Agreement") is made between Technology Consulting, Inc. ("TCI"), a company incorporated under the laws of New York, with its principal office address at _____, and _____("Company"), with an office at _____. The parties wish to engage in discussions with a view to entering into a business relationship between them and, in the course of or for the purpose of facilitating such relationship, each party will disclose confidential information (such party being referred to as the "Disclosing Party") to the other party (such receiving party being referred to as the "Receiving Party"), as defined below. For good and valuable consideration, the receipt and sufficiency of which are acknowledged by each of the parties hereto, this Agreement sets out our respective obligations with respect to Confidential Information, as defined below, which Receiving Party receives from the Disclosing Party.

1. "Confidential Information" means any business or technical information, whether or not stored in any medium, relating to the Disclosing Party's business (and those of its suppliers and customers) including but not limited to equipment, software, designs, technology, technical documentation, product or service specifications or strategies, marketing plans, pricing information, financial information, information relating to existing, previous, and potential suppliers, customers and contracts, inventions, applications, methodologies, and other know-how that is identified as confidential at the time of disclosure or that a reasonable person would consider, from the nature of the information and circumstances of disclosure, to be confidential. Confidential Information includes original information supplied by the Disclosing Party, as well as all copies and any reports, analyses, products, and other materials derived from or containing such original information.

2. Receiving Party agrees to treat the Confidential Information as confidential to and as the property of the Disclosing Party and to use an appropriate degree of care which, in any case, will not be less than the degree of care it uses with respect to its own information of like nature to prevent disclosure of the Confidential Information of the Disclosing Party. Receiving Party will not disclose this Agreement or Confidential Information at any time during the Term hereof (as defined in Paragraph 12) or thereafter, except to Receiving Party's directors, officers, employees, and contractors who have a need to know for the purpose of carrying out the purpose of the Agreement and, in the case of contractors, who have acknowledged receipt of a copy of this Agreement and agreed in writing to comply with its terms.

3. Receiving Party will use the Confidential Information only for the purposes of evaluating the proposed business relationship with the Disclosing Party, and neither party will use the Confidential Information for purposes of competition with the other party. Neither party will circumvent or otherwise try to avoid, directly, indirectly, or otherwise, any terms or provisions or intent or purpose expressed herein. Neither party will disassemble, decompile, or reverse engineer any Confidential Information of the other. Nothing in this Agreement is to be construed as granting Receiving Party any title, ownership, license, or other right

Figure 17-2. (Continued).

or interest with respect to the Confidential Information of the Disclosing Party. Confidential Information will be held in trust by Receiving Party for the Disclosing Party.

Confidential Information will be returned by Receiving Party to the Disclosing Party upon termination of discussions between TCI and Company in relation to matters in respect of which Confidential Information was disclosed if a business relationship is not entered into, and upon request by the Disclosing Party at any time.

4. Except as permitted under this Agreement and except upon prior written consent of the other party, neither party shall disclose to any other person or entity the existence or terms of this Agreement or that the parties have engaged in or are engaging in discussions with respect to a potential business relationship or have entered into a business relationship.

5. The Disclosing Party may mark all Confidential Information with the legend "Confidential" on the top of the first page of Confidential Information that is in written form. The Disclosing Party will prominently declare as "Confidential" all Confidential Information made available by the Disclosing Party other than in written form at the time of disclosure and may provide to the Receiving Party a written summary of such Confidential Information within thirty (30) days of disclosing said Confidential Information. Receiving Party will not copy or reproduce the Confidential Information except as reasonably required for the purposes contemplated in this Agreement and will ensure that any confidentiality or other proprietary rights notices on the Confidential Information are reproduced on all copies.

6. This Agreement does not apply to or restrict the parties from using or disclosing Confidential Information that
   a. Is or becomes public other than through a breach of this Agreement
   b. Is known to Receiving Party before the date of this Agreement and that Receiving Party has received without the breach by any person of any obligation of confidentiality
   c. Is independently developed by Receiving Party without a breach of this Agreement
   d. Is disclosed, without obligation of confidentiality, to Receiving Party by a person or entity who is not party to this Agreement and who is entitled to disclose such information without breaching an obligation of confidentiality
   e. Is required to be disclosed by law, whether under an order of a court or government tribunal or other legal process, so long as a party receiving such order provides notice thereof to the other party within three (3) days after receipt of such order so the other party can take appropriate action to protect its Confidential Information

7. The parties do not make any representation or warranty as to the accuracy or completeness of the Confidential Information. Both parties agree that neither shall have any liability to the other resulting from use of the Confidential Information except as may otherwise be provided in a definitive agreement that may be executed by the parties.

8. Nothing in this Agreement is to be construed as obligating any party to continue any discussions or business relationship. Each of the parties has the unilateral right,

exercisable at its option, to terminate the discussions at any time without notice and without any further obligations except as intended in this Agreement. This Agreement does not create any agency or partnership relationship between the parties and neither party may bind nor is responsible for the acts of the other party or the other party's directors, officers, employees, contractors, or agents.

9. Notices delivered in connection with this Agreement must be in writing and delivered to the address set out in the first paragraph of this Agreement to the attention of the individual executing this Agreement on behalf of such party, or as changed by the parties by notice in writing delivered to each other from time to time in accordance with this Agreement. Each party will designate in writing to the other the individual(s) in their respective organizations who are authorized to disclose and receive Confidential Information and to receive notices under this Agreement.

10. Delay, failure, or partial exercise by a party of any right or remedy under this Agreement will not constitute a waiver of any right or remedy. Any waiver must be in writing, but any such waiver will be limited to its terms and will not constitute waiver of any other provision or breach of this Agreement. Receiving Party acknowledges and agrees that money damages may not be an adequate remedy for any breach of this Agreement and that the Disclosing Party shall be entitled to an injunction or specific performances as a remedy for any breach and that such remedies will not be deemed to be exclusive but in addition to any other remedies available at law or in equity.

11. If any part of this Agreement is invalid, the invalid provision will be severed, and the remaining provisions will continue in effect unamended.

12. This Agreement shall remain effective for a period (the "Term") beginning on the date signed by both parties (the "Commencement Date") and ending on the date that is the later of two (2) years from the Commencement Date or two (2) years from the date on which all business relationships entered into by the parties with each other are terminated. All Confidential Information disclosed during the Term shall continue to be governed by these provisions after expiration of the Term or other termination of this Agreement.

13. Neither party to this Agreement shall solicit or hire, directly or indirectly, any employees or personnel of the other during the Term and for one (1) year thereafter without the prior written consent of the other party.

14. The Agreement sets out the entire agreement of the parties concerning the matters described above and supersedes all prior written or oral agreements and understandings. This Agreement may be amended only by consent in writing of both parties.

15. This Agreement binds the parties and their respective successors and permitted assigns. Neither party shall assign this Agreement without the prior written consent of the other.

16. This Agreement is governed by the laws of the State of New York, and the parties agree to the nonexclusive jurisdiction of the courts of the State of New York in relation to this Agreement.

17. This Agreement may be signed in facsimile or in counterparts, each of which will be deemed to be an original and all of which together will be deemed to be one and the same document.

Figure 17-2. (Continued).

Technology Consulting, Inc.	Company
By: ————————————	By: ————————————
Title: ———————————	Title: ———————————
Name: ——————————	Name: ——————————
Date: ———————————	Date: ———————————

unauthorized disclosure, and a requirement that the licensee return all materials upon termination of the license.

The departments within the company that will interact with competitors should be trained carefully to ensure that confidential information is not disclosed inadvertently. For example, marketing employees who attend a trade show that competitors also attend should be trained not to provide too much detail about the company's proprietary products or operations. Similarly, speeches given or articles written by employees should be reviewed before presentation or publication to protect against inadvertent disclosure.

The Economic Espionage Act of 1996

In 1996 Congress enacted the Economic Espionage Act to provide that misappropriating trade secrets is a federal criminal offense subject to forfeiture of property, fines, and imprisonment. One part of the act applies to theft of trade secrets by those intending to benefit any foreign government (for which individuals can be imprisoned up to ten years and fined up to $500,000); another prohibits the misappropriation of trade secrets with the intent to convert the trade secret to the economic benefit of another (for which individuals can be imprisoned up to fifteen years and fined up to $500,000). The act broadly defines trade secrets to include nearly any kind of business, technical, scientific, or financial information and covers information regardless of how it is stored, collected, or memorialized. Thus, even personal recollection is protected, and the act makes it clear that theft of trade secrets by electronic means is prohibited. Finally, the act prohibits receiving, buying, or possessing trade secret information of another knowing that it was stolen, misappropriated, or obtained without its owner's consent. The act provides penalties for attempts and conspiracies to violate it.

The Economic Espionage Act is the first federal recognition of the importance of trade secret rights and the potential for harm to companies through theft of their trade secrets. For some companies, computer source code and chemical formulas are as valuable as an entire automobile manufacturing plant. Because employees can readily download a company's trade secrets from its computer system, put it on a disk, and later disseminate it throughout the world with a click of a keystroke, a company can lose all its assets in minutes. Until the act was enacted, the only remedy for theft of a trade secret was civil litigation (although wire and mail fraud statutes often were used to prosecute some trade secret thefts). With its stiff criminal penalties and authorization for the U.S. Attorney General to apply for a court order to intercept communications, the act should be a significant deterrent in preventing trade secret theft. In fact, in spring 2000, a former Intel Corporation employee was indicted for allegedly having stolen files related to the design and testing of Intel's next-generation Itanium brand microprocessor chip and taking them to his new employer.

Trade Secret Litigation

A company harmed by trade secret theft can initiate a civil action for damages in court. An action is commenced by the filing of a complaint describing the defendant's wrongful conduct. The action should be commenced as soon as possible after the theft is discovered. Failure to act promptly not only weighs against the ability to obtain an injunction but suggests that the information is not sufficiently valuable to its owner to be protected aggressively. The defendant typically asserts some or all of the following defenses:

- The defendant did not do the acts complained of.
- The defendant independently developed the information or product without any act of misappropriation.
- The defendant innocently received the information without any act of misappropriation.
- The defendant received the information by proper means (such as with the consent of the owner) and with no restrictions on its use.
- The information has entered the public domain or is generally known in the trade.

- ▾ The trade secret owner failed to protect the information and keep it secret.
- ▾ The defendant reverse engineered the information from products or materials properly obtained.
- ▾ The trade secret owner has unclean hands (his conduct is improper, even if not strictly illegal, and he should, therefore, not be allowed to recover anything) or has unreasonably delayed in bringing suit such that the defendant has been prejudiced thereby, or the defendant relied on some action or representation by the trade secret owner that no action would be taken for misappropriation.

Memorization typically is not a defense; thus, the fact that a defendant memorized a formula or process rather than copied it or physically took it is no defense to a claim of trade secret theft.

A successful plaintiff can obtain injunctive relief to prevent further misappropriation (or, under the inevitable disclosure doctrine discussed earlier, to prevent threatened misappropriation), monetary damages to compensate the trade secret owner for harm suffered (which may include both the owner's lost profits and the defendant's wrongful profits), seizure of goods wrongfully obtained, and punitive damages, attorneys fees, and costs (in cases in which the defendant's conduct is wanton and willful).

One of the issues that inevitably arises in trade secret litigation is whether and how much of the trade secret and the measures taken to protect it must be disclosed in open court for the plaintiff to demonstrate that its information is valuable and secret and has been subject to reasonable efforts to maintain its secrecy. Clearly, trade secret owners do not want to disclose the nature of their trade secrets or describe their security measures and systems. Courts have fashioned a variety of remedies to protect the secrecy of the information and the nature of the plaintiff's security measures, including closed sessions in chamber with the judge, sealing court files, and ordering parties not to disclose information without prior court approval.

As an alternative to civil litigation, under the Economic Espionage Act of 1996, a trade secret owner may request the assistance of the Department of Justice in investigating the alleged misappropriation. Some experts have predicted that the mere launching of a criminal investigation by the federal government with its significant negative publicity may well induce a misappropriator to settle privately with the trade secret owner.

Disclosure to Government Agencies

Companies doing work with federal and state government agencies often are required to submit detailed bids that might include trade secret information. Under freedom-of-information acts, the information might then be released to others. To prevent the loss of trade secrets, the submitter should designate certain information as trade secrets. The agencies must then block the designated information out before releasing it to others. If the agency wrongfully discloses the information, the trade secret owner may sue on the basis that such conduct was a wrongful taking of its property.

18

Unfair Competition

Unfair competition laws are a type of catch-all provision designed to protect against unfair, unethical, and predatory practices in the marketplace. In many instances, a competitor's conduct may not precisely constitute infringement of trademark, copyright, patent, or trade secret. In those events, general unfair competition statutes, both at the federal and state level, ensure that conduct in the marketplace is based on standards of ethical business conduct.

Governing Law

All states have their own individual state statutes protecting against unfair competition. In addition, Section 43(a) of the Lanham Act (the U.S. Trademark Act) generally is referred to as a federal unfair competition law. Section 43(a) prohibits any false designation of origin or any false or misleading representation of fact in connection with the interstate offering or sale of goods or services that is likely to cause confusion, mistake, or deception in the marketplace. Section 43(a) protects even unregistered trademarks against infringement. A civil action may be brought in federal court for violation of Section 43(a). Finally, Section 5 of the Federal Trade Commission Act prohibits unfair and deceptive acts and practices in or affecting commerce. Thus, parties injured by unfair competition often can depend on a variety of laws, from their state statutes, to the U.S. Trademark Act, to the Federal Trade Commission Act.

Forms of Unfair Competition

The most common forms of unfair competition include false advertising, product disparagement, passing off, and violations of the right of publicity. Other types of unfair competition include trademark dilution (discussed in Chapter 6) and infringement of trade dress (discussed in Chapter 2).

False Advertising

Until passage of Section 43(a) of the Lanham Act, generally only consumers who were induced to buy goods by a false statement could bring an action for false advertising. Manufacturers who were injured by false advertising by their competitors generally could not recover for such acts. However, Section 43(a) makes it clear that any person who uses any word, name, symbol, or device, any false designation of origin, or false or misleading representation of fact that is likely to cause confusion in interstate commerce is liable to any person who believes he or she is likely to be damaged by such act. "Any person" thus includes competitors as well as consumers. In fact, false advertising claims are brought by competitor companies more often than by consumers because consumer claims are likely to involve only minimal damages. Moreover, damage need not have actually occurred. As long as damage is likely to occur, an action can be brought. Proving that the act occurred in interstate commerce is easy because using the U.S. mail, telephone, television, and the Internet all involve interstate commerce.

Under Section 43(a), advertisements that misrepresent the nature, quality, or characteristics of one's own goods or those of another are actionable. Liability arises not only for expressly or literally false statements but for implicitly false statements as well. An implicitly false statement is one that is not false on its face but is misleading or deceptive to consumers. A statement is implicitly false if a substantial number of consumers, typically as shown by survey evidence, receive a misleading or false impression from the statement.

One specific type of statement that is not actionable is puffery, generally defined as vague and highly subjective statements in the nature of bragging or opinion. Thus, a claim that a product represents a "major breakthrough" is nonactionable puffery. Similarly, statements that products are "superior," represent the "current state of the art," or result in "excellent savings" are puffery. For example, in late 2000, a court held that Papa John's advertising slogan, "Better ingredients, better pizza," was puffery.

In contrast, if statements such as "clinical trials show that X product provides greater relief than Y product" or that "nine out of ten doctors recommend Z" are made, the party making such claims must be able to substantiate them to avoid liability in an action brought for false advertising. Typically, substantiation is shown through surveys and studies. Claims for such false advertising can be brought not only against the advertiser but against those responsible for the false statements, such as advertising agencies and research firms that have incorrectly performed surveys and studies.

One area of particular concern is the use of another party's trademark in advertising. Generally, use of another's trademark for comparative purposes is acceptable as long as there is no falsity. Thus, saying "If you like NIKE® shoes, you'll love our new REEBOK® cross-trainers" is permissible. Similarly, stating that one product fits or works with another's is acceptable, thus allowing such statements as "Our children's blocks fit with LEGO® brand blocks" as long as the statement is true. On the other hand, one cannot falsely suggest that another party sponsors its products. In one case, after the consumer magazine *Consumer Reports* (published by Consumers Union) gave a favorable review to a product, the product's maker used the review in an advertisement about the product. Consumers Union attempted to enjoin the advertisement on the basis that it misleadingly conveyed the impression that Consumers Union sponsored or endorsed the product. Although the court held that the ad in question did not misleadingly suggest sponsorship, the court noted that Section 43(a) could be used to prohibit false claims of sponsorship or approval.

Product Disparagement

Until passage of Section 43(a), claims for intentional and untrue statements about another company or its products or services were brought as common law actions for product disparagement or trade libel. Actions for product disparagement became far less common after passage of Section 43(a), primarily because to prevail in an action for product disparagement one had to show actual economic harm, whereas under Section 43(a) relief is available to one who is likely to be harmed. Moreover, most states required that for liability to be imposed for product disparagement, a plaintiff must have shown that the defendant acted intentionally or recklessly, whereas under Section 43(a) a plaintiff need only show that the statement is false, either explicitly or implicitly.

Passing Off

Passing off, also called palming off, is a form of unfair competition in which one party passes off its goods under the pretense that they are the goods of another. Thus, selling inferior clothing under the mark LIZ CLAIBORNE® is a form of passing off, as is a representation that one is an authorized dealer or repairer of GENERAL ELECTRIC® appliances when one is not. In these two instances, injured parties could sue for trademark infringement; however, passing off also occurs when the injured party has no registered mark, perhaps because the mark is descriptive. Affixing another's mark to one's goods and using a mark so similar to that of another that consumers are deceived are both forms of passing off. If statements made are untrue, they also constitute false advertising. Just as actions for product disparagement are seen less frequently now that Section 43(a) provides such broad protection against acts of unfair competition, actions alleging passing off also are seen less frequently because of the broad coverage of Section 43(a), with its protection of unregistered marks and wide range of remedies, including the ability to file action in federal court.

Violations of the Right of Publicity

The right of publicity protects a person's voice, identity, characteristics, and persona from unauthorized use. There is no federal law protecting one's right of publicity, and state laws vary in their coverage. The right is not a privacy right and is directed to ensuring that individuals can control the commercial use of their identities. Although there is no rule that only celebrities have rights that can be infringed, in practice celebrities' images are more likely to be infringed than those of average consumers, and celebrities are more likely to be able to show damages. Thus, in large part, the right of publicity affords the well known the right to sue for unauthorized use of their images, personas, names, and other identifying characteristics. The theory underlying the action is that celebrities have invested time and effort in becoming well known, and it would be unjust for others to reap the reward of using the celebrity's name or likeness. Moreover, overuse of the celebrity's persona tends to dilute the value of that persona, making it more difficult for the celebrity to commercialize his or her identity.

Following are some recent cases recognizing and protecting the right of publicity:

▾ Johnny Carson was able to prohibit a portable toilet company from using the phrase "Here's Johnny" in connection with its services. Although Carson's last name was not used, the court held that the phrase "Here's Johnny" was highly identified with Carson, and using it without his approval violated his right of publicity.

▾ Woody Allen was able to preclude the use of a lookalike in advertisements for video rental stores on the basis that the ads suggested that Allen sponsored or approved of the services.

▾ Bette Midler successfully sued Ford Motor Co. for using a singer imitating her distinctive singing style in its advertisements.

There is significant variation in state laws as to whether the right of publicity survives the celebrity's death. Some states, such as New York, have held that the right dies with the celebrity, but the majority hold that it would be wrong to deprive the heirs of celebrities the right to seek commercial value from the celebrity's identity and equally wrong to allow advertisers to reap a windfall as soon as a celebrity dies. Thus, most states hold that the right of publicity is a property right, and, like other property rights, it can pass to one's heirs. Nevertheless, many states set a maximum time of existence for the right. In California, the right of publicity survives for seventy years after death. In some states, the right survives death only if the celebrity allowed commercial use of his or her identity during life.

In 1999, California, with its large population of celebrities, passed the Astaire Celebrity Image Protection Act to allow the heirs of celebrities to block certain commercial uses (such that the image of Fred Astaire cannot be used to promote vacuum cleaners) while allowing a safe harbor for certain artistic uses, such as the digital image of President Kennedy used in the movie *Forrest Gump*. Uses for purposes of parody, satire, education, or news reporting ordinarily are permissible. Thus, in the main, it is unauthorized commercial use that is prohibited by most state laws.

To promote uniformity on the topic, both the American Bar Association and the International Trademark Association have proposed adding a federal law to protect the right of publicity.

The Federal Trade Commission

The Federal Trade Commission (FTC) enforces a variety of federal antitrust and consumer protection laws. The basic consumer protection statute enforced by the FTC is Section 5(a) of the FTC Act, which provides that unfair or deceptive acts or practices in or affecting commerce are unlawful. The FTC has the authority to investigate alleged unfair or deceptive practices and then to take action by issuing complaints, seeking injunctions, imposing fines, litigating, or ordering refunds. In many instances, parties charged with FTC violations enter into consent agreements or orders by which they agree to refrain from certain acts or practices.

In many instances, consumers file complaints with the FTC alleging unfair consumer practices and advertising. As in the laws relating to false advertising, the FTC has the authority to prevent even misleading ads and requires that claims such as "Tests show that our product . . ." be substantiated. Cases involving obviously exaggerated claims or puffery are not pursued. In recent years the FTC has shown great interest in claims and ads for food, cigarettes, pharmaceuticals, diet products, and other products that affect the health of consumers. The FTC has also directed efforts toward prohibiting unfair or deceptive advertising in infomercials, through telemarketing, and on the Internet. In mid-2000, the FTC shut down an Internet pyramid scheme that claimed that consumers could lease their "dream vehicles" for free while earning $180 to $80,000 per month by paying an annual fee and small monthly payments. The site was permanently shut down, and the principals were ordered to pay $2.9 million and barred permanently from any multilevel marketing business.

The FTC offers a wide array of information about permissible forms of advertising and an online complaint form on its Web site (www.ftc.gov). Alternatively, consumers can call toll free at (877) FTC-HELP to make a complaint. Finally, because Americans filed nearly 18,000 complaints with the FTC in 1999 alleging Internet fraud, the Department of Justice has launched a new online fraud investigative center to tackle problems ranging from online auctions to sales of products and services. The new site is at www.usdoj.gov/criminal/fraud/Internet.htm.

Many states have statutes similar to the FTC Act prohibiting false and deceptive practices. Such state acts often are called "little FTC acts."

19

Owning the Work Product of Your Employees and Independent Contractors

Some of a company's most valuable assets are highly mobile: employees. Companies need to ensure that any work created by employees and independent contractors on the job is owned by the company and can be exploited to its greatest extent. Similarly, companies need to ensure that former employees do not solicit the company's employees to leave the company, that they protect the company's trade secrets, and that they do not compete against the company after leaving. Prohibitions against competition are strictly scrutinized by courts; however, if they are reasonable in scope and duration, they are generally permissible. Finally, companies must protect themselves against unwanted and unsolicited information submitted to the company. Many companies adopt formal policies prohibiting parties from submitting ideas or information unless the information is specifically requested by the company.

Ownership of Work Created by Employees

The general rule is that employers own the work of their employees created while on the job. In fact, as discussed in Chapter 10, under copyright

217

law, if a work is made for hire, the employer, not the employee, is considered the author of the work.

Although it seems that these general principles should be sufficient to protect employers, employees may attempt to defeat the legal presumptions and claim ownership of their work and inventions by alleging that they created the work on their own time or that they are not employees but rather independent contractors and thus own the fruits of their labor.

There is probably no definitive way to prove where an employee created a work product; however, employers can protect their interests by having a written employment agreement that specifies the employee's duties (for example, "to create an original software program to calculate mortgage rates") and states that all work performed in connection with those duties is done on behalf of the employer. Employees will then have a difficult time proving that they created the software program on their own time. For companies too small to use formal employment agreements, inserting similar phrases in mutually signed offer letters helps. Thus, the offer letter can state, "We are offering you employment as a software developer to create an original software program for our company that will calculate mortgage rates. Any work performed by you in connection with the program will be owned by the company."

Employers who require time sheets from employees can use them to support the fact that a work created by the employee was on company time rather than the employee's. Similarly, status reports and notes kept from progress meetings on the project will confirm the timing and progress of the employee's work.

To defeat any contention that the employee is an independent contractor rather than an employee, an employment agreement confirms the nature of the relationship. Smaller companies that use offer letters can state that the company is offering employment and that benefits offered will be consistent with those offered other employees.

Naturally, the best protection arises from formal written agreements that confirm the employee's title, duties, benefits, term of employment, duties of nondisclosure, and postemployment covenants not to compete or solicit employees. However, such agreements may not be appropriate or practicable for smaller companies. Smaller companies can then use their employee manuals to confirm some of the terms and conditions of employment (as long as employees are required to acknowledge in writing that they understand and agree to the terms of the manual). Agreements should provide that if a court later determines the worker to be an independent contractor rather than an employee, the worker thereby assigns all inventions and work products to the company. Some forms for employment agreements can be found on the Internet. For example, a form is available at www.ilrg.com/forms/employmt.html. See Figure 19-1 for a sample clause for ownership of employee inventions.

Even when employers do not own work and inventions created by their employees (usually because the employee created the work on his or her own time), the employer may be entitled to a shop right, which is a nonexclusive, nontransferable, royalty-free right to use the invention or work product. Shop rights exist in favor of employers if the employee used a sufficient amount of the employer's time, facilities, or materials such that it is equitable to allow the employer to benefit from the final product. Thus, the employee may sell and license the invention or product, but the employer is free to do so also, even after the employee leaves the company.

Ownership of Work Created by Independent Contractors

Recall from Chapter 10 that an employer can own work created by independent contractors if the work falls in one of the ten categories of statutorily designated works (a contribution to a collective work, a part of a motion picture or other audiovisual work, a sound recording, a translation, a supplementary work, a compilation, an instructional text, a test, answer material for a test, or an atlas) and there is a written agreement between the parties specifying that the work is made for hire.

If the work is not within one of the ten enumerated categories, the commissioning party can still own the work if the independent contractor

Figure 19-1. Clause to ensure ownership of the work of employees.

The Company shall own and Employee hereby irrevocably assigns to the Company all right, title, and interest in any invention, technique, process, device, discovery, works, products, improvement, or know-how, whether patentable or not, including all trade secrets and copyrights, in and to any works created by or contributed to by Employee during the course of his or her employment that relate in any manner to the actual or anticipated business of the Company. Employee intends that the Company shall have full ownership of the aforementioned items with no rights of ownership in Employee, and Employee shall perform all acts and execute all documents necessary or desirable to protect Company's rights in and title to any such items and shall not contest or dispute the Company's ownership of or rights to the same.

Employee signature: _____   Date: _____

assigns in writing all rights in the work to the commissioning party. In fact, in every case, even those involving one of the designated ten types of works, the parties should agree in writing that the work is original, it is made for hire, that their intent is that the commissioning party will own the work, and that if for some reason the work is deemed not to be made for hire, that the independent contractor thereby immediately and irrevocably transfers and assigns all rights in and to the work to the commissioning party. See Figure 19-2 for a sample clause for assigning ownership of the work of independent contractors.

In determining whether a party performing work is an employee (whose work product is automatically owned by the employer) or an inde-

Figure 19-2. Clause to ensure ownership of the work of independent contractors.

Any software, inventions, discoveries, materials, work, work product, or other intellectual property ("Intellectual Property") developed by Consultant for Company while on assignment for Company or on assignment to any Company client shall become and remain the property of Company, which shall have the right to use such Intellectual Property in any media for any purpose and to create derivative works based thereon. Such Intellectual Property shall be "works made for hire" as that term is defined in the United States Copyright Act, and, consequently, Company shall be the author for copyright purposes of such Intellectual Property and shall own the copyright to all such Intellectual Property. To the extent that any such Intellectual Property may not be works made for hire, Consultant agrees to and hereby does by this Agreement immediately and irrevocably assign and transfer to Company the right, title, interest, and all ownership of all copyright throughout the world in such Intellectual Property, which shall be treated as though works made for hire with regard to all rights, including moral rights, if any. No claims of ownership of such Intellectual Property by Consultant shall be made or honored, and Consultant shall not hereafter dispute or contest the Company's rights in and to such Intellectual Property. As to such Intellectual Property, Consultant agrees to disclose them promptly to Company, to assign them to Company, and to do all things necessary, including executing documents, to assist Company in obtaining patent, copyright, trade secret, or other legal protection for such Intellectual Property, Company to pay the expenses therefor. Consultant agrees that the entire right, title, and interest in and to such Intellectual Property are hereby irrevocably assigned to and shall become the property of Company without further consideration. Consultant agrees that all work developed or provided by Consultant under this Agreement is original to Consultant and does not violate the proprietary, copyright, or other rights of any third party. Consultant will maintain any confidential information relating to the Company or its business or operations strictly in confidence and will not use such information for any purpose other than the Company's business purposes.

Consultant signature: ＿＿＿＿＿＿＿＿＿＿＿＿ Date: ＿＿＿＿＿＿

pendent contractor (whose work product might be owned by the commissioning party if the work is one of the ten designated types and the parties have agreed such in writing), courts consider a variety of factors. Typically, the following factors, none of which is determinative but all of which characterize a regular and salaried relationship, tend to suggest an employment relationship:

- The employer has the right to determine how the work is done.
- The work is done at the employer's location.
- The employer provides equipment or other means to create the work.
- The employer controls the worker's schedule in creating the work.
- The employer has the right to have the worker perform other tasks.
- The employer determines the method of payment.
- The employer has the right to hire the employee's assistants.
- The employer is in business to produce products of the nature created by the worker.
- The employer provides the worker with benefits or withholds tax from the worker's payment.

In sum, although there is a presumption that work created by employees belongs to employers, no such presumption exists for work created by independent contractors. In fact, the presumption is the opposite. Even if a work is one of the ten designated types, if the parties do not agree in writing as to its ownership, the independent contractor retains ownership rights. Therefore, the only safe course for a commissioning party is to provide by written agreement that if for some reason the work is not deemed a work for hire, by that agreement the contractor assigns and transfers all right, title, and interest in and to the work to the party who engaged the contractor's services.

An additional complication of using independent contractors is that independent contractors who stay in the same job for a prolonged period of time may later claim that they were employees and then sue for certain benefits. In the late 1990s, long-term temporary workers successfully sued Microsoft after alleging that they were employees rather than independent contractors and were therefore entitled to the lucrative stock option packages and savings plan Microsoft had offered to its employees. As a result of the suit, in early 2000 Microsoft announced it would limit its temporary workers to one year of employment at a time, with 100-day intervals in between.

Protecting Your Employees through Nonsolicitation Clauses

In today's information-based economy, many companies have one primary asset: their employees. With some high-tech companies offering cash signing bonuses, cars, stock options, and a host of other benefits to attract and retain workers, losing workers through solicitation by others is a significant threat to profitability. Moreover, many employers, such as computer consulting companies, routinely place their employees on client sites. As clients get to know the employee, they may begin to think, "Why are we paying ABC Inc. for Ted Graham's services? Why don't we just hire Ted ourselves?"

Similarly, once an employee such as Ted leaves for another company, the other company may offer him a referral bonus to bring other employees along with him, a financial inducement few employees can resist. Thus, companies need to protect their employees from being poached by clients, suppliers, and even other employees. Similarly, identifying employees on Web sites and in other highly public ways provides opportunities for employees to be solicited by other companies.

The only sure way to protect against such activity is through the use of nonsolicitation clauses. The nonsolicitation clause can appear as part of an employment agreement, within a mutually signed offer letter or employee manual or handbook (assuming that they are signed by the employee), or as part of a nondisclosure agreement. Because nearly all companies should use nondisclosure agreements, the clause probably is best placed in such an agreement.

Nonsolicitation clauses typically read as follows: "During the term of this agreement and for one (1) year thereafter, [employee or client name] will not solicit, offer employment to, or hire, directly or indirectly, any employee of or personnel engaged by ABC, Inc. without the prior written consent of ABC, Inc. If [employee or client name] violates this provision, ABC, Inc. shall be entitled to, in addition to any other damages it may sustain, an amount equal to twenty-five percent (25%) of the annual base salary of any employee or personnel solicited from ABC, Inc. in violation of this provision."

Consider the following when using nonsolicitation clauses:

• If the clause restricts the other party only from hiring your employees, they may be able to solicit your independent contractors. Thus, include language relating to both employees and "other personnel" or similar terms if you use the services of independent contractors.

▾ Make sure that the phrase "directly or indirectly" is used when referring to solicitation activities. If you forbid only direct solicitation, the other party may be able to use an intermediary to poach your employees.

▾ Nonsolicitation clauses work best with clients when they are mutual. Clients are far more likely to agree not to solicit your employees if they know you are promising the same.

▾ Your large clients naturally will have difficulty agreeing not to hire any of your employees and may reasonably say, "How can we know who our Seattle and Houston offices will hire?" In such cases, the nonsolicitation clauses can be restricted to the actual employees working on the client site or can provide that if the employee himself or herself approaches the client for a job or responds to employment ads placed by the client, there will be no violation of the agreement.

▾ The term of the nonsolicitation clause should be reasonable, and is usually either six months or one year. If employees introduced to clients are highly skilled and you have recruited and trained them at great cost, it may be possible to use a longer term; however, because a nonsolicitation clause narrows the employee's options for other employment, courts are reluctant to enforce long nonsolicitation agreements.

▾ When hiring employees, ask whether they are bound by any nonsolicitation agreements. If so, remind them of their obligations not to poach coworkers from their former place of employment.

▾ When an employee leaves your company, remind him or her of the obligation not to encourage other workers to leave your company.

See Figure 19-3 for forms of nonsolicitation clauses.

Protecting Your Information through Nondisclosure Agreements

A thorough employment agreement includes provisions prohibiting employees from disclosing a company's confidential information, but such clauses can also be presented to employees to sign as standalone agreements or can be placed in employee manuals (as long as employees are required to sign the manuals). See Figure 19-4 for a simple nondisclosure clause that employees can be required to sign.

Figure 19-3. Nonsolicitation clauses.

___

Unilateral Provision Precluding Solicitation of Employees

Client agrees that during the term of this Agreement, and for a period of one (1) year after its termination or expiration, it will not directly or indirectly solicit, hire, or otherwise retain as an employee or independent contractor any person employed by ABC, Inc., or engaged by ABC, Inc., as a consultant or independent contractor or otherwise during the term of this Agreement without ABC's prior written consent.

Mutual Provision Related to Specific Project

During the term of this Agreement and for one (1) year after its termination or expiration, neither party will directly or indirectly solicit, hire, or otherwise retain as an employee or independent contractor any person engaged by the other in connection with the work to be performed under this Agreement without the prior written consent of the other party.

Clause Imposing Damages

In the event of a breach of the foregoing provision, the Company will be entitled to twenty-five percent (25%) of the affected employee's billings or annual base salary, whichever is greater, during the time of breach of said provision.

Clause Allowing Employees to Seek Employment

The foregoing prohibition against solicitation of employees shall not apply to cases in which employees or independent contractors independently and without encouragement or solicitation from a party seek employment with the party and shall not apply to cases in which employees or independent contractors respond to advertisements of a general nature placed for the hiring of employees, regardless of the form of media in which such advertisements are placed, including advertisements placed in print, television, Internet, or other media.

___

Covenants Not to Compete

Employees with special skills and knowledge can be precluded from working for an employer's competitors after they leave their original employer. Restrictions prohibiting such postemployment competition generally are called restrictive covenants. Because restrictive covenants can significantly limit an employee's ability to earn a living, they are disfavored, and courts will not enforce them unless they serve a valid business purpose of the employer and are reasonable in scope, geographic area, and duration. In fact, in California covenants not to compete are invalid as restraints against trade and cannot be enforced unless they are given in connection with the sale of a business.

Figure 19-4. Nondisclosure clause for employees.

Employee recognizes that during the course of his or her employment for the Company he or she may have access to proprietary and confidential information relating to the business and operations of the Company including technical, financial, and business information ("Confidential Information") that constitutes valuable, special, and unique assets of the Company or its clients. Employee agrees that he or she will not at any time or in any manner, either directly or indirectly, use any Confidential Information for Employee's own benefit or divulge, communicate, or disclose in any manner any Confidential Information to any third party without the prior written consent of the Company. Employee will protect the Confidential Information and treat it as strictly confidential and use it only for the Company's business purposes. This provision shall remain in full force and effect during and after the termination or expiration of Employee's relationship with the Company. In the event that Employee reveals or threatens to reveal such Confidential Information, and in addition to any other remedies the Company is entitled to pursue, the Company shall be entitled to injunctive relief restraining the Employee from disclosing the same or from rendering services to any entity to whom such Confidential Information has been or is threatened to be disclosed. Upon termination of employment with the Company the Employee shall return to the Company all property of the Company including any materials including Confidential Information, in whatever media it may exist. This Agreement is assignable by the Company to any successor in interest or other transferee.

Employee signature: _____   Date: _____

Because individuals need to practice their professions to earn a living, restrictive covenants must serve a valid business purpose to survive court review. Thus, an employer cannot preclude all its employees from working for competitors. There would be no legal justification for preventing file clerks, support staff, receptionists, and similar workers from performing similar services for other companies (unless those workers had access to proprietary information). On the other hand, if an employer has hired skilled workers, trained them, and invested time and money in teaching them the company's practices and business, it would be inequitable to allow a competitor to reap the rewards of such an investment. Thus, in most states employers can prevent highly skilled workers from working for competitors.

In any event, restrictive covenants must be reasonable in scope, duration, and geographic area. For example, preventing a computer analyst or scientist from working anywhere in the United States in any business related to computers for five years after leaving the employer's business is unreasonable. Companies must structure covenants not to compete so that they are not overbroad, considering both the employee's skill and the industry.

In some instances, companies specifically identify competitors for whom the employee is precluded from working. In other instances, agreements require employees to agree that they will not work in a certain industry within a fifty-mile radius of any company facility for a period of one year. In today's global economy, a geographic restriction may not be sufficient, and an employer may want a worldwide restriction. In such cases, the duration of the restriction probably should be shorter.

Recently, courts have paid greater attention to the types of industries involved in interpreting restrictive covenants. In one case in 1999, the Southern District of New York held that a provision prohibiting a Web site content manager from working in the field for one year was the equivalent of several generations in other fields of endeavor and struck the covenant in its entirety. Thus, what may be an acceptable period of duration in one industry may be overlong in another. Restrictive covenants may be more palatable to courts if employees are given some benefits for agreeing not to practice their professions. Thus, employers should consider providing severance payments, benefits, or stock options during the restricted period.

In some states, if a covenant not to compete is overbroad, courts will rewrite it to comply with the intention of the parties, a practice called bluepenciling. In other states, if the covenant violates standards of commercial reasonableness, it will be struck in its entirety. Thus, drafting covenants not to compete for senior employees should be given serious consideration. Similarly, the second employer will scrutinize the covenant carefully to find loopholes. For example, if the covenant merely restricts the employee from being employed by a competitor, the employee might circumvent the restriction by providing consulting services to the competitor as an independent contractor.

Additionally, as discussed in Chapter 17, a new doctrine, called the doctrine of inevitable disclosure, holds that if it is inevitable that an employee will use proprietary information or trade secrets gained from a previous employer at a new place of employment, the first employer can enjoin the employee from working at the new location. Some experts have predicted that the doctrine of inevitable disclosure will be used in states such as California that prohibit covenants not to compete and that employers in those states will simply rely on the inevitable disclosure doctrine to prevent employees from working for competitors.

Employers can also deter employees from working for competitors by having employees agree in writing that they will return windfall profits earned to the original employer if they go to work for a competitor within a certain period of time after exercising stock options. Such forfeiture provisions generally are valid in most states.

The danger of asking all employees to sign noncompetition agreements was seen in a California case in 1999 in which Aetna Insurance Company required all its California employees to agree not to work for competitors for six months after leaving Aetna. Because such covenants are invalid in California, the court assessed Aetna more than $1 million in damages. On the other hand, when a party sells a business, it is entirely reasonable to require the party not to reenter the market and compete with the buyer of the business, and covenants in connection with the sale of a business in California are therefore valid.

If an employer merges with another company or sells all or substantially all its assets to another company, restrictive covenants given by employees and employment agreements generally are not transferable to the new employer (unless the employee explicitly agreed that the covenant could be assigned).

In brief, drafting covenants not to compete demands careful consideration and should be done only after consultation with an attorney. Generally, the following principles apply:

- ▾ Covenants not to compete are more likely to be upheld if they restrict senior employees with specialized, valuable, hard-to-replace skill sets rather than all employees.
- ▾ Covenants not to compete should be limited in duration because they adversely affect an employee's right to practice his or her profession and earn a livelihood.
- ▾ Covenants not to compete should be limited in geographic area (unless the company's business is truly national in scope).
- ▾ Covenants not to compete should be reasonable given the circumstances, including consideration of the field of endeavor, the skill level of the employee, the potential hardship to the employee if he or she cannot work for another for a certain period of time, and the potential for harm to the first employer.

When screening new candidates for employment, companies should ask whether the candidate is subject to any noncompete agreements that would prevent him or her from working for the company. It is far better to discover a problem before hiring a person than to discover the problem by being named as a defendant in a lawsuit. See Figure 19-5 for sample noncompete provisions.

Figure 19-5. Noncompete agreement clauses.

General Clause

During the term of Employee's relationship with Company and for six (6) months thereafter, Employee agrees that he or she will not, directly or indirectly, in the County of Hennepin, State of Minnesota, whether as an employee, independent contractor, adviser, consultant, owner, or otherwise, engage in, be employed by, become financially interested in, or have any affiliation or connection with any Web site development content or development provider or provide any services that are essentially the same as those provided by Employee to Company or that pertain to the use, development, support, or implementation of Web sites for financial services.

Employee signature: ————————————————— Date: ——————————

Detailed Prohibition against Competition

(a) **Covenant Not to Compete.**

During the Restricted Period (defined below), the Employee shall not, within a fifty (50) mile radius of any Company office location existing at the time the employment of Employee with the Company is terminated by the Company or Employee for any reason, with or without cause, either directly or indirectly:

    (i)   Engage in any business or activity that competes with the Company's business or operations whether conducted now or at any time during Employee's employment with the Company ("Company Business")

    (ii) Solicit business or perform work for any past or present client of the Company for the benefit of anyone other than the Company or participate or assist in any way in the solicitation of business from or performance of work for any such clients as an independent contractor or consultant or in any other capacity to or for any other person or entity

    (iii) Except for employment by the Company, enter the employ of any person or entity engaged in any business that competes with the Company Business

    (iv) Hire any past or present employee of the Company or solicit or encourage any employee to leave the employment of the Company

    (v) Have an interest in any entity engaged in any business that competes with the Company Business, directly or indirectly, in any capacity, including, without limitation, as a member, partner, shareholder, officer, director, principal, agent, or trustee, or any other relationship or capacity; provided, however, the Employee may own, solely as an investment, securities of any entity that are publicly traded if the Employee (A) is not a controlling person of or a member of a group that controls such entity or (B) does not, directly or indirectly, own five percent (5%) or more of any class of securities of such entity

    (vi) Interfere with business relationships (whether formed heretofore or hereafter) between the Company and employees, consultants, or clients of the Company

(b) **Confidential Information; Personal Relationships.**

During the Restricted Period, the Employee shall keep secret and retain in strictest confidence, and shall not use for the benefit of himself or others except in connection with the business and affairs of the Company, all confidential information relating to the Company Business and the Company, including, without limitation, know-how, trade secrets, client lists, details of contracts, pricing policies, marketing plans or strategies, sales information, business opportunities, sales opportunities or prospects, business development techniques or plans, business acquisition plans, personnel information, processes, designs and design projects, inventions, and research projects and other business affairs relating to the Company Business (collectively, "Confidential Information"), learned by the Employee heretofore or hereafter, and shall not disclose them to anyone outside the Company, except with the Company's express written consent. Notwithstanding the foregoing, the obligations of the Employee under this Section shall not apply to Confidential Information (i) that at the date hereof or thereafter becomes a matter of public knowledge without breach by the Employee of this Agreement or (ii) that is obtained by the Employee from a person or entity (other than the Company) under circumstances permitting its disclosure to others.

(c) **Restricted Period.**

For purposes of this Agreement, the term "Restricted Period" shall mean the period commencing on the date of this Agreement and continuing for one (1) year after the employment of Employee with the Company is terminated by the Company or Employee for any reason, with or without cause.

(d) **Restrictive Covenants.**

For purposes of this Agreement, the term "Restrictive Covenants" shall mean the provisions of Sections (a) and (b) of this Agreement.

(e) **Specific Performance.**

If the Employee breaches, or threatens to commit a breach of, any of the Restrictive Covenants, the Company shall have the right to have the Restrictive Covenants specifically enforced by any court having jurisdiction, it being acknowledged and agreed that any such breach or threatened breach will cause irreparable injury to the Company and that money damages will not provide an adequate remedy to the Company. Such rights and remedies shall be in addition to, and not in lieu of, any other rights and remedies available to the Company under law or in equity. If Employee violates any of the restrictions contained in this Agreement, the restrictive period shall not run in Employee's favor until such time as such violation shall by cured by Employee to the satisfaction of the Company.

(f) **Severability of Restrictive Covenants.**

The Employee acknowledges and agrees that the Restrictive Covenants are reasonable in geographic and temporal scope and in all other respects and are reasonably required for the protection of the Company and its legitimate business interests. If any court determines that any of the Restrictive Covenants or any part thereof is invalid or unenforceable, the remainder of the Restrictive Covenants shall not thereby be affected and shall be given full effect, without regard to the invalid portions.

Figure 19-5. (Continued).

(g) **Blue-Penciling.**

If any court determines that any of the Restrictive Covenants, or any part thereof, is unenforceable because of the duration or geographic scope of such provision, such court shall have the power to reduce the duration or scope of such provision, as the case may be, and, in its reduced form, such provision shall then be enforceable and shall be enforced.

(h) **Further Covenants and Assignability.**

Employee represents that his or her performance of all the terms of this Agreement does not and will not breach any agreement entered into by Employee. Employee agrees to advise the Company of the identity of any successor employer, if known, for whom he or she is scheduled to work before he or she terminates employment with the Company and further agrees to disclose to any future employer the existence of this Agreement and his or her obligations hereunder. The parties expressly agree that this Agreement and the covenants made herein are assignable and transferable to any entity with which the Employer merges or that is a successor to Employer or that buys all or substantially all its assets.

Employee signature: _____ Date: _____

Idea Submission

In some cases, individuals may submit ideas to your company for a product or slogan and thereafter expect compensation. Under copyright law, ideas are not protectable; only the expression of those ideas can be copyrighted. Once an idea is set forth in some tangible and fixed form, however, it is subject to copyright protection.

The entertainment, toy, and game industries often litigate idea submissions, whether because an individual claims that the idea for a television sitcom was actually his or hers, that the plot of a movie has been stolen from a letter written to a studio, or that the individual is really the creator of a board game or television game show. Generally, courts have held that an abstract idea is not protectable and that parties who submit ideas without protecting them have only themselves to blame for losses sustained when the idea is used by another. In most cases, courts have held that only concrete and specific information is protectable. Thus, when a woman argued that she was the originator of the idea for *The Cosby Show*, the court held that her vague idea of a wholesome, happy African-American family lacked specificity and novelty and denied recovery. However, if a detailed and concrete proposal is submitted to a company that thereafter implements the proposal, the submitter may be entitled to compensation, as was seen in the late 1990s when writer Art Buchwald successfully argued that the plot for the movie *Coming to America* was based on his specific written proposal rather than the studio's proposal. Similarly, in late 2000, a Florida jury awarded $240 million in damages to two individuals who submitted an idea to the Walt Disney Company for a sports theme park. The submitters had provided plans and a model to Disney executives and documented more than 200 calls with Disney representatives. It is possible that the award may be tripled due to the jury's finding that Disney acted with malicious intent. Disney has stated that it will appeal the verdict.

Courts have developed a variety of doctrines explaining why even unsolicited submissions should be compensated, ranging from the theory that there is an implied contract between the parties that if the idea is used, the submitter will be paid, to the equitable doctrine that a party should not be unjustly enriched by another's efforts.

To avoid such cases, some companies expressly reject any unsolicited submissions and return them without opening them. In sum, companies should be careful in documenting the process by which products, slogans, ads, and other materials are created to help defeat allegations that the product is the work of another.

20

Internal Processes for Greater Protection: Audits and Infringement Policies

The first step in protecting intellectual property is to understand what intellectual property assets your company owns. Once you know what assets exist, you can protect them through trademark registration, copyright registration, patent registration, or trade secret protection. To determine what intellectual property assets exist, most companies conduct audits or inventories, which disclose the valuable and proprietary information owned by the company.

Although most of this book has been devoted to steps that can be taken to protect and preserve your company's or department's intellectual property rights, it is equally important to consider the affirmative steps a company can take to avoid infringement of others' rights.

Intellectual Property Audits

An intellectual property audit or review is conducted to disclose the particular types of intellectual property owned by a company. The results of the audit are evaluated, and the company then determines the appropriate measures it needs to take to obtain the broadest possible protection for its intellectual property assets.

Companies often retain law firms to conduct the audit. Typically, the law firm provides the company with a questionnaire and requires it to assemble the materials requested for review by the firm. Thus, whether the audit is conducted by outside counsel or by the company itself, company involvement is significant.

If outside counsel is engaged to conduct the audit, the company should appoint a liaison to work with counsel on the audit. Generally, once the company assembles the materials requested, attorneys and paralegals from the firm come to the company's offices and review the materials. Some material is photocopied for further review by counsel. The law firm usually provides a written report to the client, providing its conclusions, inventorying the company's intellectual property assets, and suggesting the best means to protect each item.

Companies that want to conduct their own audits can do so easily. A sample questionnaire or intellectual property audit form is provided in Figure 20-1. Figure 20-2 lists actions the company can take to protect the property identified through the audit. Before conducting the audit, the company should prepare its employees by informing them that the company will be conducting the audit and stating what the purpose of the audit is, what intellectual property is, and why the company needs to protect its intellectual capital. Employees will be more responsive if they understand the reason for conducting the audit. As employees complete their work and assemble materials in response to the audit, they should inform their department mangers, who should then report to an audit compliance officer or team appointed by the company to oversee the project. Any audit team should include employees of the company who create intellectual property as well as those who manage the company's intellectual property.

The intellectual property audit form provided in Figure 20-1 can also be used by a company that intends to purchase another company or assets of another company. Such an audit reveals what intellectual property the seller will bring to the buyer. Similarly, the buyer must determine whether any claims have been made against the seller within the past several years that the seller infringed the intellectual property rights of another. Typically, such transactions are handled by outside legal counsel, who will use their own questionnaires and audit forms as part of their due diligence process to ensure that the transaction is prudent for the buyer.

Many companies appoint an intellectual property compliance officer

Figure 20-1. Intellectual property audit form.

The Company has determined that it is in the best interests of the Company to identify and protect all its intellectual property. Therefore, the Company is conducting an inventory or audit of its intellectual property assets. Please review the following audit form carefully and assemble any materials you have that are responsive to the audit. If you have any doubts whether material qualifies as intellectual property, err on the side of doubt and include the material for review.

Although the audit form is categorized by department, review all of the form because your department may have materials that are responsive to the requests.

Once you have assembled the materials asked for in the audit form, inform your manager.

ABC, Inc. Intellectual Property Audit

Introductory Information

1. Employee's name _____

2. Employee's department _____

3. Date audit completed _____

Sales and Marketing

1. Assemble all sales and marketing brochures, videos, CD-ROMs, Power Point® presentations, scripts for radio or television ads, copies of advertisements or notices placed in any medium (whether print media, television, radio, or Internet), written presentations, and any other materials used in your department within the past three years to promote the Company's business.
2. Assemble any Company give-aways, including promotional materials such as clothing, pens, coffee mugs, thermoses, hats, accessories, or any other material that displays any Company name, logo, slogan, or matter relating to the Company.
3. Assemble any materials relating to the way by which the Company conducts its sales processes as well as pricing lists and lists of customers and sales commission plans.
4. Assemble any materials relating to any proposed or planned advertising campaigns, brochures, or marketing matter.
5. Assemble any contracts or agreements by which your department retained or engaged the services of others to prepare or design materials for use in your department.

Human Resources

1. Provide a copy of any materials sent or given to new employees.
2. Assemble all employee manuals, handbooks, or notices relating to employment at the Company.

Figure 20-1. (Continued).

---

3. Assemble all materials (whether in written form or Power Point® or other presentation media) relating to Company programs such as mentoring programs, orientation events, training programs, and so forth.
4. Assemble all forms and written materials relating to interviews of prospective employees, offer letters, employee reviews and performance appraisals, termination procedures, and exit interviews for employees separating from the Company.
5. Assemble written copies of Company newsletters, policies, or other written communications to Company employees. If material was distributed electronically, provide written copies of such materials.

Contracts and Administrative

1. Assemble all standard forms and templates used in the Company's business, including forms for providing services, purchase orders, statements of work, invoices, nondisclosure agreements, agreements by which the Company has partnered with other parties for any purpose, agreements by which the Company has retained the services of independent contractors, letterhead, form of business cards issued to employees, and any other forms or agreements used on a routine basis.
2. Assemble any methodology materials used by the Company, whether in written form or other media.
3. Identify any journals or other trade publications to which the Company subscribes and describe how they are distributed or routed within the Company.
4. Determine whether music is played on Company telephone lines while callers are placed on hold or whether any music is piped in at any Company offices.
5. Describe the process by which the Company provides software programs for its employees. What programs are installed on employees' computers (whether desktop or laptop)? Provide copies of all license agreements with others by which the Company has the right to use software or other products owned by others.
6. Has the Company acquired another company or any of its assets such that the Company might have the right to use that company's trademarks, copyrights, or patents? If so, describe and provide all available documentation.
7. Has the Company licensed the right to use the products or inventions owned by another company? If so, provide all license agreements.

Graphics, Production, and Information Services

1. Assemble all materials relating to any logos, slogans, designs, or other material used by the Company.
2. Provide printouts of each screen displayed on the Company's Web site (and any previous screens used by the Company on its Web site) and describe the process by which the Company created or developed its Web site (namely, was the site created in house, or was another company retained to develop the site?).
3. Identify any Web sites owned by others on which the Company, its products, logos, slogans, or trademarks are identified.
4. Conduct Internet searches as needed to determine whether any other companies use or post the Company's trademarks on their sites, whether other companies link

to the Company's site, and whether there are any other similar domain names to that used by the Company.

5. Assemble any materials relating to registration of the Company's domain name.

Research, Engineering, and Development

1. Assemble all materials developed or designed for the Company within the past five years, including inventions, discoveries, and software programs and any revised or customized versions of software programs, whether they are the Company's software or those owned by another party.
2. Assemble any useful products, inventions, or discoveries produced for the Company and describe in detail any processes or methods by which the Company conducts its business.
3. Provide any notes, notebooks, or other materials describing the process by which work, inventions, and discoveries have been created for the Company.

All Departments

1. Describe, identify, or provide all slogans, logos, designs, or other trademarks used by the Company in the past five years.
2. Provide copies of all written materials in your possession that promote or offer the Company's services and products to others.
3. Identify and describe any unique items, inventions, discoveries, methods of doing business, or processes by which the Company conducts its business operations.
4. Identify any articles, case studies, or other matter you have written in the past three years, whether for the Company or published independently, that might relate to the Company's business. Similarly, describe any oral presentations you have given in the past three years relating to the Company, its business, or operations and provide copies of any written materials distributed in connection with those presentations.
5. Do you maintain the Company's confidential materials in locked drawers or cabinets? Is your office door capable of being locked?
6. Describe any claims you know of that have been made by others within the past five years that the Company's intellectual property (specifically, its trademarks, copyrights, patents, or trade secrets) violates the rights of others.
7. Identify or describe any methods of doing business or any Company information that if known by a competitor you believe would damage the Company.

---

who maintains the list of the company's intellectual capital and updates it annually or semiannually through periodic audit updates. Other companies assemble intellectual property committees made up of representatives from their marketing, sales, research, and development teams to periodically review the company's products and services to ensure that the company recognizes its intellectual capital. In many cases, companies send committee members to workshops and seminars to enhance their knowledge of intellectual property.

Figure 20-2. Action plan to protect intellectual property.

Trademarks, Service Marks, Slogans, and Logos

▼ The Company must identify the trademarks, service marks, slogans, domain names, and logos ("Marks") it uses and has used to conduct its business.

▼ The Company must ensure that the Marks do not infringe those of others by conducting routinely scheduled trademark availability searches.

▼ For Marks used in interstate commerce, consideration should be given to applying for federal registration with the U.S. Patent and Trademark Office (PTO). Marks that are significant to the Company should be registered with the PTO, but Marks that will be in use only for a short period of time may not warrant registration. For Marks in use only in intrastate commerce, the Company should consider applying for state trademark registrations.

▼ For all Marks, whether registered or not, place the appropriate notice when a Mark is displayed on written materials, the Web site, or on products (use ® only for marks registered with the PTO and ™ or ℠ for unregistered Marks).

▼ Review all materials that display Marks to ensure that Marks are used consistently.

▼ If others are allowed to use the Company's Marks, ensure that those Marks are used properly by conducting periodic reviews of their materials.

Copyrights

▼ The Company should consider applying for copyright registration for its written materials (including marketing materials and presentations) and any other forms or agreements that are more than mere "blank forms," software programs, and Web site content.

▼ Whether or not material is registered with the U.S. Copyright Office, a copyright notice should be displayed on all written materials, software sold by the Company, and the Company's Web site (example: © 2000 ABC, Inc.).

▼ The Company's Web site should include a screen outlining the terms and conditions for its use.

▼ If music is played on hold or piped into Company offices, the Company should make arrangements with the American Society of Composers, Authors, and Publishers, Broadcast Music, Inc., or SESAC to obtain permission to play such music.

▼ If the Company copies articles from magazines and trade journals and distributes them throughout the office, the Company should make arrangements with Copyright Clearance Center to obtain permission to do so. Notices should be placed near the Company's photocopy machines to remind users of copyright obligations.

Patents

▼ If the Company has invented patentable items or developed novel and useful processes and methods of doing business, it should consider applying for patent protection with the PTO (assuming that the Company is not barred by the one-year "on sale bar" that precludes one from seeking patent protection more than one year after a product is described, offered, or sold).

- ▾ The Company should ensure that it does not use any notice of patent unless a patent has been granted by the PTO.
- ▾ The Company should adopt a process for authorizing publication of materials related to the Company's methods and inventions to ensure that inadvertent publication does not later bar the Company from applying for a patent for an invention disclosed in a publication.

Trade Secrets

- ▾ The Company must implement and enforce policies to protect its confidential trade secrets. Specifically, the Company must do the following:
  - ▾ Ensure that employees and independent contractors agree that the work they perform for the Company is original, does not infringe the rights of others, and belongs to the Company, and that they will not solicit the Company's employees.
  - ▾ Ensure that its senior employees and key personnel are subject to appropriate restrictive covenants.
  - ▾ Ensure that employees with access to confidential information have signed written nondisclosure agreements and understand their duties to keep confidential information secure.
  - ▾ Ensure that employees understand their obligations not to copy materials belonging to others, including software programs and material posted on others' Web sites.
  - ▾ Develop hire and exit procedures to remind employees of their obligations to protect confidential information.
- ▾ Stamp trade secret material as "Confidential" or "Proprietary."
- ▾ Control access to trade secret material and ensure that it is disclosed only to those who have a need to know and who have signed nondisclosure agreements.
- ▾ Maintain trade secret materials in locked drawers, cabinets, or locked offices.
- ▾ Review contracts with others to ensure that clients and third parties are prohibited from soliciting or hiring the Company's employees.
- ▾ Develop a procedure for clearing the publication of professional papers and for presentations at industry or trade shows and professional seminars.

Contracts and Miscellaneous

- ▾ The Company should carefully review all contracts and agreements with its clients to ensure that each party has agreed to protect the other's valuable confidential information and agreed not to solicit the other's employees.
- ▾ The Company should investigate the costs of obtaining insurance coverage to protect it against claims that the Company has infringed the intellectual property rights of others.
- ▾ The Company should carefully review any agreements by which it licenses intellectual property from others to ensure that the owner of the intellectual property will defend against any claim that the intellectual property infringes the rights of another.
- ▾ The Company should appoint an intellectual property compliance officer to conduct annual intellectual property audits and to ensure that Company policies designed to protect intellectual property are updated as necessary.

Figure 20-2. (Continued).

▾ Department managers and employees should be asked to be alert to possible infringements of the Company's intellectual property assets. For example, the Information Services Department should conduct routine Internet searches to determine whether other companies are using the Company's trademarks on their sites or linking to the Company's site. Sales staff can be tasked with reviewing trade journals and business press releases to locate infringing uses. The Company can also subscribe to clipping services to locate other uses of the Company's valuable intellectual property assets.

▾ The Company's intellectual property compliance officer should implement and maintain a docketing system to ensure that appropriate documents are filed with the PTO to maintain registered trademarks and to ensure that maintenance fees are paid for utility patents.

▾ The Company should conduct an online search of the records of the PTO and Copyright Office to determine whether the Company owns any registered trademarks, copyrights, or patents.

▾ If the Company has acquired another company or some of its assets or if the Company has changed its name or address, appropriate documents should be filed with the PTO and Copyright Office to ensure that records reflect the current owner of trademarks, patents, and copyrights.

Conducting the audit not only discloses the assets the company owns but is useful if the company is engaged in selling any of its divisions or assets because the buyer will always demand to know what intellectual property it is buying and whether there are any outstanding claims of infringement relating to the intellectual property. Moreover, companies that have identified their intellectual property assets can use those assets as collateral to secure loans from banks and other lenders. Lenders may be willing to lend the company money if certain assets, such as trademarks, copyrights, and patents, are pledged as collateral to secure repayment of the obligation. Companies that conduct intellectual property audits and update them routinely are thus positioned for such transactions or loans. In one of the newest uses of intellectual property, a number of corporations have donated patents to universities and research institutions. In 1999, Du Pont Corporation donated $64 million in patents to three universities. The donations usually are tax deductible, generally are made with patents that are no longer strategic to the company's core business objectives but are of value to the donee, and enhance the donor's reputation and image. Finally, some experts have predicted that companies that fail to protect their intellectual capital will face lawsuits from their shareholders. Thus, auditing and protecting your company's intellectual capital is critical in today's information-based economy.

Employees should be alert to possible infringements of the company's intellectual property. Ask employees to watch for possible misuses of the company's trademarks or copyrighted materials in trade journals, at trade shows, and by competitors. Similarly, competitors' Web sites should be routinely monitored and periodic reviews should be conducted of domain name registrations to contest conflicting domain names. Registered Internet domain names can be checked at no cost through www.nsi.com and www.domainit.com.

At online intellectual property bazaars, companies can value, sell, license, or trade intellectual property; they include www.yet2.com, www.IPNetwork.com, http://valuationcorp.com, and www.pl-x.com.

Avoiding Infringement of Others' Intellectual Property

Tips to Avoid Infringement

Companies must avoid infringing intellectual property owned by others because claims involving intellectual property are contentious and expensive. At a minimum, such matters are distracting to a company and require the time and involvement of senior managers and others, who are then focused on the claim rather than the company's business. Matters that proceed to litigation can be particularly expensive. Claims made against a company must be disclosed to insurers, lenders, and others and may seriously affect the company's ability to obtain needed capital. If the company is involved in a sale of its assets, the buyer may require that the claim be satisfied before the sale, may require the company's owners to indemnify the buyer for any adverse judgment in connection with the claim, or may set aside certain funds in an escrow account pending resolution of the claim.

The following are some tips to avoid infringement of others' intellectual property:

- Ensure that you own the work product created by your employees and independent contractors by requiring them to verify in writing that the work they create is original, does not infringe the rights of others, and will be owned by you (see Figures 19-1 and 19-2 for clauses to ensure ownership of work created by employees and independent contractors).
- Insist that all marketing materials be reviewed to ensure that copy

is original and that slogans, designs, and logos are designed for the company and not taken from others.

▾ Maintain logs or lists of companies with which your company has entered into nondisclosure agreements to ensure that your company does not inadvertently disclose the confidential information of those companies.

▾ Implement policies for employees to ensure that they are fully informed that they must keep confidential the company's information and receive written permission to use the information or materials of others, whether those materials are in conventional form or posted on the Internet (see Figure 19-4 for an employee nondisclosure agreement and Figure 12-2 for a sample Internet usage policy).

▾ Review software to ensure that all software used by the company is properly authorized or licensed (see Figure 12-1 for a sample software usage policy).

▾ Interview prospective employees to verify that they are not subject to any agreements that would prohibit them from working for your company (see Figure 19-5 for a sample clause confirming that an employee is not subject to restrictive covenants imposed by others).

▾ Maintain detailed records (whether in paper or electronic form) as to the development and creation of trademarks, slogans, marketing materials, and inventions

▾ Remind employees of their obligations through the use of periodic columns in company newsletters, e-mail messages, and reminders at company meetings.

▾ Investigate the costs of obtaining insurance coverage for intellectual property infringement claims.

What to Do if a Claim of Infringement Is Made against Your Company

If a claim for intellectual property infringement is made, the company should conduct an immediate internal investigation to determine whether there is a valid basis for the claim. If so (for example, the company may have innocently used a trademark similar to that of another), some companies contact the owner of the mark or the attorney who wrote the letter setting forth the claim and ask whether there might be a way to resolve the matter amicably. In some instances, the owner of the mark is satisfied if the company agrees to cease use of the infringing matter. If a company has a significant amount of marketing materials that display the infringing matter, the company may be able to obtain an agreement that it can continue to use the offending materials until they are depleted, at which time new noninfringing materials will be prepared. In other cases, the company may be required to agree to destroy any infringing materials on hand.

If a claim is made for patent infringement or any infringement for which there may be a basis in fact, seek the immediate advice of experienced intellectual property counsel. You do not want to jeopardize any defense you may have by making an innocent remark to the adverse party or its counsel. In some instances, infringement that continues after notice gives rise to claims for punitive damages. Thus, a letter informing the company that it is infringing another's patent must be given immediate attention. Simultaneously, review the company's insurance policies to determine whether coverage exists for the claim and whether the company is required to notify the insurer of any such claims within a certain period of time. Similarly, agreements with bankers, lenders, and strategic partners must be reviewed to determine whether the claim must be disclosed to them. Finally, the company must consider whether the claim has any effect on the company's contracts with its suppliers, customers, or licensees. For example, if the company must cease use of a patented item, will this affect any company customers who are using the invention?

Experienced counsel will be able to assist the company in considering the many issues that arise once a claim has been made against the company. In the event of any claim, whether well founded or not, maintain all correspondence, notes, and other materials. If the company is approached by a buyer, even years later, it is customary for the buyer to ask, "Has a claim been made against the company within the past five years that it infringed the intellectual property or proprietary rights of another?" Maintaining accurate records gives the company the opportunity to resolve any issues relating to such claims and assure the buyer that it will not be subject to liability.

In sum, claims relating to infringement are serious, distracting, and expensive and often have far-reaching effects on a company. Companies that implement and enforce vigorous intellectual property policies are in the best position to avoid claims by third parties.

Appendix
Information Resources

Government Agencies

U.S. Patent and Trademark Office
Commissioner of Patents and Trademarks
Washington, DC 20231
www.uspto.gov

The PTO Web site offers basic information about trademarks and patents, fee schedules, forms, links to related sites, links to pertinent statutes, and information about pending legislation and rule changes; allows searching of the PTO's database of trademarks and patents; and provides information about the status of pending and registered trademarks and issued patents.

Register of Copyrights
Copyright Office
Library of Congress
101 Independence Avenue S.E.
Washington, DC 20559-6000
www.lcweb.gov/copyright

This Web site offers basic information about copyright, fee schedules, application forms, circulars explaining copyright principles, and links to copyright statutes.

Federal Trade Commission
600 Pennsylvania Avenue N.W.
Washington, DC 20580
www.ftc.gov

The Federal Trade Commission Web site provides information about FTC rules and regulations, complaint forms, text of speeches and announcements, articles related to consumer protection or unfair and deceptive practices, and links to sites of interest.

Educational Sites

www4.law.cornell.edu/uscode

The Web site of Cornell Law School provides easy access to the text of federal statutes relating to trademarks (see 15 U.S.C. Section 1051 et seq.), copyrights (see 17 U.S.C. Section 101 et seq.), and patents (see 35 U.S.C. Section 100, et seq.). Searching can be done by citation of statute, key word, or topic.

www.ll.georgetown.edu

This Web site of the law library of Georgetown University Law Center provides easy access to federal and state statutes as well as a host of other legal information relating to intellectual property law. Searching can be done by topic.

www.ipmall.fplc.com

This Web site of Franklin Pierce Law Center is commonly known as the Intellectual Property Mall and provides access to hundreds of journals and articles related to intellectual property law as well as numerous links to other valuable intellectual property sites.

www.lib.utexas.edu

This site, offered by the University of Texas at Austin, offers free patent searching for patents issued since 1969. Locate the "search box" and type in the word "patents." You will be directed to the specific site (www.libs/ENG/PTUT/comp.html) for patent searching. Searching can be done by topic name, inventor name, or patent number.

www.law.duke.edu/copyright/index.htm

This site, titled "Friends of Active Copyright Education," is maintained by Duke University School of Law and provides understandable information about copyright law.

Commercial Sites

www.findlaw.com

FindLaw is one of the best legal sites and allows easy access to general information about nearly any legal topic, including trademarks, copyrights, patents, and trade secrets. Searching can be started by selecting "Intellectual Property."

www.lectlaw.com

The site of the 'Lectric Law Library allows access to forms relating to intellectual property including forms for assignments and licenses. Access "Rotunda," then "Forms Room," then "Business and General Forms."

www.lexisone.com/html/legal_guide/
general_practice_areas_intellectual_property.htm

This site offers links to more than thirty intellectual property sites, including direct links to statutes, treaties, journals, foreign intellectual property offices, and cases relating to intellectual property.

www.nsi.com

This Web site of Network Solutions, Inc., allows you to check the availability of domain names at no cost.

www.domainit.com

On this site you can check the availability of domain names at no cost.

www.thomson-thomson.com

The site of Thomson & Thomson allows online ordering of trademark and copyright search reports.

www.corsearch.com

The site of CCH Corsearch, Inc., allows online ordering of trademark and copyright search reports.

www.ascap.com

The site of the American Society of Composers, Authors, and Publishers provides information about obtaining licenses to play background music and music on hold.

www.bmi.com

The site of Broadcast Music, Inc. provides information about obtaining licenses to play background music and music on hold as well as basic information about such topics.

www.copyright.com

The site of the Copyright Clearance Center provides information about copyright compliance issues and information about obtaining permission to distribute copyrighted materials.

www.delphion.com

The site allows access to patents issued since 1976. Searching can be done by patent registration number, description of invention, or inventor name.

www.yet2.com; www.pl-x.com; http://valuationcorp.com
www.Ipnetwork.com

These sites offer information about valuation, selling, and licensing of intellectual property.

Organizations

www.inta.org

The site of the International Trademark Association offers invaluable information about trademarks and links to numerous other intellectual property–related sites.

www.aipla.org

The site of the American Intellectual Property Association provides valuable information on recent and pending legislation affecting intellectual property issues, publications and articles related to intellectual property, and links to other valuable intellectual property sources.

www.wipo.org

The site of the World Intellectual Property Organization offers the text of various treaties and other international agreements relating to intellectual property, including the Paris Convention and the Berne Convention.

www.icann.org

The site of the Internet Corporation for Assigned Names and Numbers provides information about disputes over domain names.

www.siia.net

This site of the Software and Information Industry Association offers white papers and articles about intellectual property and software-related issues.

www.bsa.org

The site of Business Software Alliance offers a free software audit tool to determine whether software is properly licensed. The audit tool can also be found at www.nopiracy.com.

Law Firm Sites

The following sites are provided by law firms and attorneys specializing in intellectual property law. Nearly all the sites offer excellent basic information, tips, and strategies, and most publish periodic newsletters relating to new and emerging intellectual property trends.

www.oblon.com
www.patents.com
www.ipcounselors.com
www.iwaynet.net/~jkwak/
www.kuesterlaw.com
www.ladas.com

Index

251

LaVergne, TN USA
12 November 2009
163822LV00003B/13/A

9 780814 473818